Clock Wise Cuisine

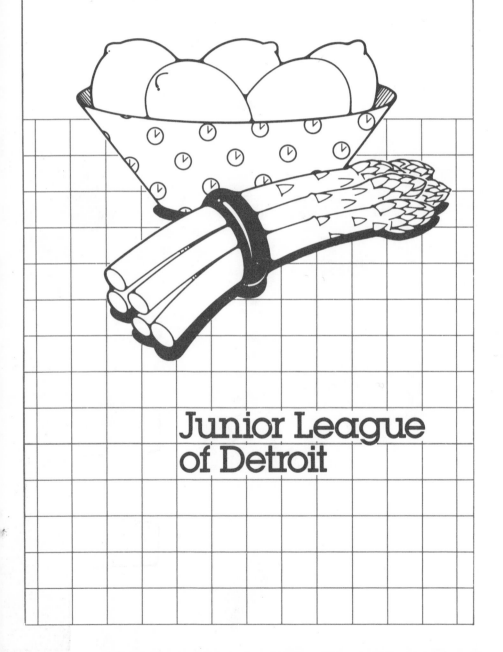

Junior League of Detroit

The purpose of the
Junior League of Detroit, Inc.
shall be exclusively
educational and charitable,
to promote voluntarism,
to develop the potential
of its members for
voluntary participation
in community affairs,
and to demonstrate the
effectiveness of trained volunteers.

The Junior League of Detroit, Inc. reaches out to all young women who demonstrate an interest in and a commitment to voluntarism.

The proceeds realized from the sale of Clock Wise Cuisine
will be returned to the community through projects of
the Junior League of Detroit, Inc.

Additional copies may be obtained by addressing:
Clock Wise Cuisine
The Junior League of Detroit, Inc.
32 Lake Shore Road
Grosse Pointe Farms, MI. 48236
(313) 881-0040
For your convenience, order forms are included in the back of the book.

Design: Cato Johnson Detroit, Karen Tarapata
Title: Karen Schaupeter
Clock Concept: Lois Bryant

To make the best use of this book, first select the food category you desire. Turn the section Tab over. There you will find all the recipes for that section arranged according to preparation time required. Check your own clock. Identify the total amount of time you have available, remembering that these recipes are accurately timed for prep time to final preparation. Then, simply make your selection from the clock category which best meets your time schedule. The clocks and a description of their meanings are pictured below. Remember, check your clock, match it to one of those below and then select a recipe that's both delicious as well as perfectly timed for your individual lifestyle.

 QUALITY QUICKIES: When the day has produced the unexpected
Max Prep Time = ½ hour
Total Kitchen Time: not more than 1 hour

 TERRIFICALLY TIMED: When you have a limited schedule and want to prepare something special
Max Prep Time = ½ hour
Total Kitchen Time: (+ lapse time) exceeds 1 hour

 DELECTABLE DELIGHTS: When you have both breathing time and pride in presentation
Max Prep Time exceeds ½ hour
Total Kitchen Time: not more than 2 hours

 FANTASTIC FEASTS: When you throw away the clock and create your own special ambiance
Max Prep Time exceeds ½ hour
Total Kitchen Time: exceeds 2 hours

Appetizers & Beverages

Appetizers & Beverages

ASPARAGUS ROLL-UPS

keep in freezer for lunch or cocktails

3 oz. bleu cheese, crumbled
1 pkg. (8 oz.) cream cheese, softened
1 egg
20 slices Pepperidge Farm thin-sliced bread
1 pkg. (10 oz.) frozen asparagus spears, cooked
½ lb. butter, melted
Toothpicks

Preheat oven to 400°. Blend cheeses with egg. Remove crusts from bread. Flatten bread with a rolling pin. Spread each slice with cheese mixture. Place one cooked asparagus spear on each slice, and roll bread around it. Secure with toothpick if necessary. Dip each roll into melted butter, slice into thirds and place on cookie sheet. Bake at 350° for 15 minutes.

May be frozen whole before baking. When ready to use, thaw, slice into thirds and bake.
Yields 60 pieces

Variations: Parmesan cheese instead of bleu cheese. Can be left whole and used on luncheon plate.

STUFFED BRUSSELS SPROUTS

30 small brussels sprouts
1 pkg. (3 oz.) cream cheese, softened
1 Tbsp. whipping cream
1½ tsp. horseradish
Salt to taste

Blanch brussels sprouts three minutes in boiling, salted water, just long enough to obtain a brilliant green color. Be sure to remove from the fire before they lose their color. Drain and set aside. Mix the cream cheese with the whipping cream, and add horseradish. Cut each sprout three-fourths of the way through the center and stuff with cream cheese mixture. Sprinkle with salt. Refrigerate. Let stand at room temperature for 30 minutes before serving. Make ahead.
Serves 15

CHICKEN DRUMETTES

18-20 drumettes (chicken
  wings cut in half, tip
  removed)
¼ cup soy sauce
1 clove garlic, pressed (or ½
  tsp. garlic powder)
1 tsp. salt
½ tsp. M.S.G. (or Accent)
1 tsp. powdered ginger
½ tsp. cayenne pepper

Place drumettes on cookie sheet. Brush with soy sauce. With mortar and pestle (or in small bowl) mix garlic with salt, M.S.G., ginger and pepper. Brush mixture on drumettes. Refrigerate for 6 hours or overnight.

Preheat oven to 400°. Bake drumettes at 400° for 50 minutes, turning twice while baking until browned.   Serves 8

CRAB PUFFS SUPREME

1 can (6½ oz.) crab meat,
  drained and flaked
½ cup grated sharp cheddar
  cheese
3 green onions, chopped
1 tsp. Worcestershire sauce
1 tsp. dry mustard
1 cup water
½ cup butter
¼ tsp. salt
1 cup flour
4 eggs

Preheat oven to 400°. Combine crab meat, cheddar cheese, onions, Worcestershire sauce and dry mustard in medium bowl and mix well. Set aside.

Combine water, butter and salt in large saucepan and bring to a boil. Remove from heat and immediately add flour, beating until mixture leaves sides of pan and forms a ball. Add eggs, one at a time, beating thoroughly after each addition. Stir in crab mixture. Drop by ½ teaspoonsful onto ungreased baking sheet. Bake 15 minutes at 400°, then reduce heat to 350° and bake 10 minutes more. Unbaked puffs can be frozen on baking sheet and transferred to plastic bags. Heat without thawing at 375° until crisp. Yields 60-80 puffs

CHICKEN NUGGETS

men really like these

2½–3 lbs. boneless chicken breasts cut in bite-sized pieces (about 20–24 pieces per lb. of chicken)
Salt
Paprika
1 cup flour
3 eggs
3 Tbsp. water
3 cups crushed Pepperidge Farm Herb-Seasoned Stuffing crumbs
Oil for deep fat frying

Generously sprinkle chicken pieces with salt and paprika. Put flour, 3 eggs beaten with 3 Tbsp. water, and stuffing crumbs in 3 separate bowls. Dip each piece into flour, then eggs, then crumbs. Deep fry nuggets in hot oil until golden brown, about 3–4 minutes. Drain on brown paper grocery bags. Can be made ahead.   Yields 60 pieces

Variation: Can serve with sauces for dipping.

GRAVLOX WITH GREEN MAYONNAISE

terrific Danish marinated salmon

Gravlox
Fresh salmon (20–24 oz.)
Fresh dill
¼ cup kosher salt
¼ cup sugar
2 Tbsp. white peppercorns, crushed
½ onion, sliced thinly
½ lemon, sliced thinly

Green Mayonnaise
2 cups Hellmann's mayonnaise
1 pkg. (10 oz.) frozen spinach, thawed and squeezed dry
¼ cup coarsely chopped parsley
2 tsp. chopped chives
½–1 tsp. dill
½ tsp. dry tarragon
1 tsp. lemon juice

Gravlox
Clean, halve and bone salmon, or have it prepared at fish market. Place ½ of salmon skin-side down in a 9x13 baking dish. Sprinkle with dill, salt, sugar, pepper, lemon and onion. Top with other ½ of salmon skin-side up. Cover dish with foil and weight down with heavy object. Refrigerate. Turn every 12 hours to baste. After 3 days, shave and serve with green mayonnaise and party rye bread.

Green Mayonnaise
Combine all ingredients, in blender and refrigerate.
          Serves 20

SWEDISH MEATBALLS

Meatballs
2 lbs. ground beef
1 lb. bulk sausage
2 eggs
⅓–½ cup bread crumbs
2 med. onions, finely
  chopped
1 tsp. salt
¼ tsp. pepper
Dash ground cloves
Dash nutmeg
Dash allspice
2 Tbsp. chopped parsley

Gravy
1 med. onion, finely chopped
½ lb. fresh sm. mushrooms,
  cleaned
2 Tbsp. flour
2 tsp. Worcestershire sauce
½ tsp. paprika
1 cup beef stock
1 cup sour cream, room
  temperature

Meatballs
Combine all ingredients. Shape into 1-inch balls. Brown meatballs in skillet. Transfer meatballs with slotted spoon to baking dish. Set aside skillet with drippings. Bake meatballs at 350° for 20 minutes.

Gravy
Saute onions and mushrooms in skillet with drippings. Stir in flour to thicken. Add Worcestershire, paprika and beef stock. Simmer until it begins to thicken. Stir in sour cream. Simmer to heat. Add meatballs. Continue simmering to heat. Can be made ahead and frozen.
Yields 80 meatballs

Variation: Can be served with egg noodles or spaghetti for a main course.

MINI BACON AND TOMATO APPETIZER

½ cup Hellmann's
  mayonnaise
¼ cup chopped onion
1 cup grated cheddar cheese
½ lb. bacon, cooked and
  crumbled
1 pt. cherry tomatoes, sliced
1 pkg. round crackers or
  bread rounds

Mix mayonnaise, onion, cheese and crumbled bacon. Place sliced tomatoes on crackers or bread. Dot cheese mixture on top of tomato. Broil for 2 minutes. Yields 20

STUFFED MUSHROOMS

1-2 lbs. fresh mushrooms,
  cleaned and stemmed
  (save stems)
¼ cup butter, melted

Swiss Cheese Stuffing
1 cup fine, dry bread crumbs
1 cup grated Swiss cheese
2 eggs, well beaten
2 tsp. parsley
2 tsp. dill weed
1 tsp. lemon peel
¼ cup lemon juice

Spinach Stuffing
3 Tbsp. Hellmann's
  mayonnaise
Dash of Tabasco
½ tsp. Worcestershire sauce
Juice of 1 lemon
1 pkg. (10 oz.) frozen,
  chopped spinach, cooked
  and drained
1 tsp. seasoned salt
3 Tbsp. grated Parmesan
  cheese
Mushroom stems, chopped
Dash nutmeg (optional)

Oyster Stuffing
½ cup grated Swiss cheese
1 can (3¾ oz.) smoked
  oysters
1 cup Pepperidge Farm
  stuffing
1 egg

Preheat oven to 350°. Dip
mushrooms in melted butter.
Place on baking sheet. Combine
ingredients in choice of stuffing.
Spoon into mushroom caps.
Bake at 350° for 15 minutes.
Bake sausage stuffing at 400°,
15-20 minutes; run under
broiler until browned.

Serves 8-16

Bacon Stuffing
1 pkg. (8 oz.) whipped cream
  cheese with chives
10 slices bacon, cooked crisp
  and crumbled

Sausage Stuffing
½ lb. sausage meat
1½ lg. apples, peeled and
  grated

Helpful Hint: May be stuffed ahead and refrigerated until
        baking time.

MUSHROOM PUFFS

or use your favorite filling

Puffs
½ cup flour
Pinch pepper
Dash cayenne pepper
Dash nutmeg
½ cup water
3 Tbsp. butter
¼ tsp. salt
4 drops Tabasco
2 eggs
¼ cup grated Parmesan
   cheese

Filling
1 lb. mushrooms, cleaned,
   dried, chopped
3 Tbsp. butter
¼ cup minced shallots
Pinch of nutmeg
Salt and pepper to taste
1 pkg. (8 oz.) cream cheese,
   softened

Puffs
Preheat oven to 425°. Combine flour, peppers and nutmeg in a small bowl. Set aside. Mix water, butter and salt in heavy saucepan. Bring to a boil, stirring occasionally until butter is melted. Reduce heat, add flour mixture all at once, and stir vigorously until smooth and batter pulls away from pan. Cool 5 minutes.

Using a food processor, beat Tabasco into batter. Add eggs one at a time, beating after each addition until mixture is smooth and shiny. Beat in cheese. Drop in ½-inch mounds on greased cookie sheet. Bake at 425° for 20 minutes. Slit tops, turn off oven, and cool in open oven for 10 minutes. Remove from oven and finish cooling on rack.

Filling
Melt butter in heavy saucepan over medium-high heat. Add shallots and mushrooms and cook until pieces begin to dry and separate (10–15 minutes). Avoid burning. Reduce heat and cook until brown. Season with salt, pepper and nutmeg. Blend in cream cheese. Cool.

Preheat oven to 300°. Fill puffs with mushroom mixture. To serve, heat at 300° for 5 minutes or until hot. Can be made ahead.   Yields 2 dozen

REBEL YELLS

a Southern favorite

1¼ lbs. butter, room
temperature
6 cups grated sharp cheddar
cheese, room
temperature—DO NOT
use processed cheese
7 cups flour
Flour for dusting
1 scant Tbsp. salt
1½ scant tsp. cayenne
pepper

In large mixing bowl, work butter and cheese with hands, adding flour a little at a time. Add salt and pepper halfway through adding of flour. Work until completely mixed and all flour is absorbed.

Preheat oven to 450°. Spread pastry cloth on large cutting board. Sprinkle with flour. Put sock on rolling pin and sprinkle with flour. Divide dough into large balls and roll ⅟₁₆- to ⅛-inch thick. Cut dough with twin curl cutter into strips 2½ x ½ inches or use miniature cookie cutter. Transfer to cookie sheets and bake at 450° for approximately 8 minutes. Note: They will not brown. Can be made ahead. Freezes well.   Yields 11 dozen

Variation: Recipe can be doubled or divided
Helpful Hint: Grate cheese in food processor.

ARLENE'S SPICED PECANS

1 egg white
1 Tbsp. rum
½ cup sugar
¼ tsp. salt
½ Tbsp. cinnamon
1 lb. pecan halves

Preheat oven in 225°. Beat egg white with rum until frothy. Combine sugar, salt and cinnamon. Add to egg mixture, stirring to blend. Add pecans and toss to coat. Spread on cookie sheet and bake 1 hour at 225°.

Yields 1 pound nuts

TERRIFIC SPICY COCKTAIL NUTS

1½ cups sugar
1 tsp. cinnamon
1 tsp. curry powder
1 tsp. ground cloves
1 tsp. nutmeg
2 egg whites
2 lbs. pecan halves

Preheat oven to 200°. Combine first five ingredients. Beat egg whites until foamy. Dip nuts into egg whites, then into spice mixture. Make sure the nuts are well coated. Place nuts in single layer on a teflon baking sheet. Bake at 200° for 3 hours, turning once every hour. Make ahead.

Yields 2 pounds nuts

Helpful Hint: Bake on parchment paper if teflon pan not available.

ROQUEFORT QUICHE

9" pie crust, prebaked
6 oz. cream cheese, softened
3 oz. Roquefort cheese, crumbled
2 Tbsp. butter, softened
3 eggs, beaten
½ pt. coffee cream
1 Tbsp. butter, melted
1 Tbsp. finely chopped parsley
2 tsp. finely chopped chives
Freshly ground pepper
Salt

Preheat oven to 375°. In a bowl, blend cream cheese, Roquefort cheese and softened butter until smooth. Add beaten eggs, cream and melted butter. Blend thoroughly. Stir in herbs. Season to taste with ground pepper and salt. Fill pie shell evenly with cheese mixture and bake 30 minutes or until filling is puffed and a light golden color. Cut into wedges. Serve hot, lukewarm or cold.   Serves 6

Timely Tip:
If you have leftover bleu or Roquefort cheese, combine it with an equal amount (by weight) of sweet butter, add a teaspoon or so of cognac and store in a covered jar in the refrigerator. It will last and last. This is great on crackers too.

SAUSAGE ROLL-UPS

10 slices white sandwich
  bread
Dijon hot mustard
¾ cup sauerkraut, drained
  and squeezed
10 Smokey links
Butter, melted
Toothpicks

Preheat oven to 350°. Remove crusts from bread and roll flat with a rolling pin. Spread mustard and then drained sauerkraut on bread slices. Roll around Smokey links. Cut into 5 bite-sized pieces. Fasten with toothpick. Brush with melted butter. Bake at 350° for 20 minutes. Can be frozen and then defrosted before baking.

Yields 50 pieces

BETTY ANNE'S PICKLED SHRIMP

2 lbs. fresh shrimp, cooked
  and cleaned
1 med. onion, thinly sliced

Sauce
½ cup ketchup
½ cup cider vinegar
2 Tbsp. Worcestershire sauce
½ tsp. Tabasco
1 Tbsp. lemon juice
¼ cup salad or olive oil
½ tsp. crushed bay leaf
½ tsp. marjoram
½ tsp. black pepper
½ tsp. thyme

Layer shrimp and sliced onion in a wide-mouth quart jar. Prepare sauce and pour over shrimp and onion. Shake well and store in refrigerator for 2 days, turning occasionally to insure even marination. Can be made ahead up to 10 days.   Serves 6–8

SUNDAY AFTERNOON FOOTBALL FAVORITE

1 pkg. all beef hot dogs, cut in bite-sized pieces
¾ cup Jack Daniels Black Label
½ cup brown sugar, packed
½ cup ketchup
1 tsp. grated onion
Toothpicks

Combine all ingredients. Simmer for 1 hour on stove. (Do not use microwave.) Serve hot in chafing dish with toothpicks. Can be made ahead several days. Freezes.   Serves 6–8

Variation: Use sliced kielbasa instead of hot dogs.

QUICHE TARTS

Pastry for 2-crust pie
1 Tbsp. poppy seeds
4 eggs, slightly beaten
1⅓ cups sour cream
1 tsp. salt
1 tsp. Worcestershire sauce
1½ cups grated Swiss cheese
⅔ cup chopped salami
⅓ cup sliced green onions

Preheat oven to 375°. Prepare pastry for 2-crust pie, stirring in the poppy seeds. Roll pastry ¹⁄₁₆-inch thick. If using already prepared pastry, press in seeds. Use a glass or cutter to cut circles and fit in muffin tins. Stir eggs, sour cream, salt and Worcestershire sauce together. Add cheese, salami and onion. Pour 1 Tbsp. of mixture into each muffin cup. Bake at 375° for 20–25 minutes. Can bake 5 minutes less and freeze. Before serving, partially thaw and then bake at 375° until heated through.   Yields 24 tarts

ZUCCHINI APPETIZER

4 eggs, beaten
3 cups shredded zucchini
1 cup Bisquick
½ cup finely chopped onion
½ cup grated Parmesan
   cheese
2 Tbsp. chopped parsley
½ tsp. salt
Pepper to taste
½ tsp. seasoned salt
½ tsp. oregano
1 sm. garlic clove, chopped
½ cup vegetable oil

Preheat oven to 350°. Grease a 9x13 pan. Mix all ingredients together. Spread in pan. Bake uncovered at 350° for 25 minutes or until golden brown. Cut into 1x2-inch squares. Serve warm Can be made ahead.

Yields 4 dozen

Helpful Hint: Use a food processor.

SUE PITTMAN'S BACON BLEU CHEESE DIP

4 oz. bleu cheese
1 pkg. (8 oz.) cream cheese,
   softened
1 Tbsp. dry white wine
¼ cup sour cream
1 tsp. minced onion
4 strips bacon, cooked and
   crumbled
Milk to thin dip consistency
1-2 lg. green peppers

Combine bleu cheese, cream cheese, wine, sour cream, onion and bacon. Add milk to get desired consistency. Cut tops off green peppers and clean out seeds and membranes. Fill peppers with mixture. Serve with crackers or chips. For better flavor, mixture can be made 1 day ahead.   Yields 1½-2 cups

To cook bacon for garnish, cut bacon into 1-inch pieces. Place pieces between layers of paper towels. Cook 6-8 minutes on High or until crisp. Remove from paper toweling to cool. Crumble.

CHEESE DIP

Very, Very Hot!!

1 jar (12 oz.) Cheese Whiz
1 can (10¾ oz.) cream of
mushroom soup,
undiluted
1 pkg. (10 oz.) frozen
chopped broccoli, cooked
and drained
2–3 tsp. Tabasco to taste
2 tsp. garlic powder

Melt cheese in double boiler. Add remaining ingredients. Serve from chafing dish with Doritos or Fritos. Make ahead. Freezes.   Serves 8

Helpful Hint: Freezes well, but stir when re-heating.

 Place broccoli in paper package in microwave. Cook on High for 5 minutes. Drain. In large glass bowl combine cheese, soup, Tabasco and garlic powder. Cover and microwave on Medium–High 5–7 minutes, stirring several times during cooking, until bubbly. Fold in broccoli. Transfer to chafing dish and serve.

CRAB CHEESE FONDUE

½ cup butter
½ lb. Velveeta cheese
1 tsp. Worcestershire sauce
1 egg yolk
1 can (6½ oz.) crab meat
Crusty pcs. of French bread

Melt butter and cheese in a 2-quart heavy saucepan. Stir in remaining ingredients one at a time. Keep warm in fondue pot. Serve with crusty French bread pieces.   Serves 8

Helpful Hints: Can thin mixture with small amount of milk. Can double with only one can of crab meat. Egg yolk helps to bind butter and cheese.

 Cut cheese into cubes and melt 2–3 minutes on High, covered. Add butter and melt 30–45 seconds on High. Blend in Worcestershire and egg yolk. Add crab meat and heat 1 minute on High or until thoroughly heated.

CURRY DIP I

3 Tbsp. chili sauce
2 tsp. Worcestershire sauce
½ tsp. onion salt
½ tsp. Lawry's seasoned salt
2 tsp. curry powder
2 cups Hellmann's
    mayonnaise

Combine first five ingredients. Add to mayonnaise and blend. Refrigerate overnight or at least 4 hours. Serve with shrimp or raw vegetables.   Yields 1 pint

Helpful Hint: Will last 3 weeks, but stir before serving. May be doubled.
Variations: Serve a dollop of curry dip with consomme to which flaked crab meat or chopped shrimp has been added before jelling.

CURRY DIP II

1 Tbsp. sugar
1 tsp. garlic salt
1 tsp. curry powder
1 tsp. horseradish
1 tsp. grated onion
1 Tbsp. vinegar
½ cup sour cream
½ cup mayonnaise

Mix ingredients in the order listed. Chill and serve with raw vegetables.   Make   ahead. Freezes.   Yields 1 cup

DILL DIP

¾ cup Hellmann's
    mayonnaise
¾ cup sour cream
1 Tbsp. parsley flakes
1 Tbsp. minced onion
1 Tbsp. dill
1 tsp. beau monde

Combine first two ingredients. Add remaining ingredients. Chill. Serve with colorful variety of fresh raw vegetables. Can be prepared 1 day ahead.
    Yields 1½–2 cups

LAYERED GUACAMOLE

2 avocados, mashed
1 can (3 oz.) green chilies,
 chopped
1-2 drops Tabasco
1 tsp. lemon juice
½ cup sour cream
⅛ cup hot or mild taco
 sauce, according to taste
2-4 spring onions, thinly
 sliced
1 med. tomato, finely
 chopped
24 black olives, sliced
 (optional)
4 oz. Colby or cheddar
 cheese, grated
4 oz. Monterey Jack, grated
Doritios or Tostitos

Mash avocados until smooth. Add green chilies, Tabasco, and lemon juice; mix well. Spread avocado mixture on the bottom of a 9x9x2 baking dish or 9 inch pie plate. Spread sour cream on top of avocado mixture. Spread taco sauce on top of sour cream. Layer onion, tomato and black olives on top of taco sauce. Sprinkle grated cheeses over top until thoroughly covered. Chill at least 30 minutes before serving with Doritos or Tostitos. Can be made the day ahead.

Serves 12

Timely Tip:
Wipe cheese with vinegar before storing to help prevent mold.

SLIM'S GUACAMOLE

2 med. ripe avocados
½ tsp. garlic powder
½ tsp. onion powder
1 Tbsp. lemon juice
¼ tsp. chili powder
1 can (4 oz.) green chilies,
 diced
½ tsp. salt
½ cup Hellmann's
 mayonnaise
Tortilla chips

Mash avocados. Cream with remaining ingredients. Serve with tortilla chips.   Serves 6

Variations: Add chopped tomatoes and/or more chili
 powder.
Helpful Hints: Use a food processor. Put avocado pit in the dip
 to keep green.

MEXICAN APPETIZER

1 pkg. (8 oz.) cream cheese, softened
1 can (10½ oz.) chili (no beans)
1 med. onion, finely chopped
1 sm. green pepper, finely chopped
1 can (4 oz.) green chilies, chopped
1 pkg. (8 oz.) Monterey Jack cheese, grated
Doritos or Tostidos

Preheat oven to 350°. Spread cream cheese along sides and bottom of a 10-inch pie plate. Layer chili, onion, green pepper and green chilies in order given on top of cream cheese. Top with cheese. Bake at 350° for 5 minutes or until bubbly. Serve with Doritos or Tostidos. Can be assembled 1 day ahead.

Serves 10

MEXICAN DELIGHT

1 can (16 oz.) refried beans
1 lb. hamburger, cooked and drained
2 cans (4 oz. each) green chilies, chopped
1 jar (8 oz.) mild taco sauce
1 pkg. (8 oz.) Colby cheese, grated
2 cups sour cream
Tostidos

Preheat oven to 350°. Spread refried beans in 9x13 baking dish. Spread cooked hamburger, chilies, taco sauce and cheese in order given on top of refried beans. Bake uncovered at 350° for 25–30 minutes or until bubbly. Let stand 10 minutes before serving. Place dollops of sour cream on top of bean mixture. Serve with Tostidos. Serves 12

Variation: Top with chopped green olives.

MARINATED STEAK AND DIP

1 pkg. meat marinade (your
   choice)
1 lg. round steak

Dip
1 cup Hellmann's mayonnaise
2 Tbsp. chopped parsley
2 Tbsp. lemon juice
2 Tbsp. chili sauce
2 Tbsp. prepared mustard
¼ tsp. garlic salt

Use any packaged marinade, and marinate steak a minimum of 3 days, turning every now and then. Keep in covered dish in refrigerator. On day of party, barbecue steak. Cut beef into small bite-sized pieces, refrigerate.

Combine all ingredients for dip in blender, scrape sides, blend 30 more seconds. Refrigerate at least 2 hours. When ready to serve, put pieces of steak around dip. Add celery and carrot sticks for color.   Serves 8–12

SPINACH DIP

1 round loaf French bread,
   (or pumpernickel or dark
   rye)
1 pkg. (10 oz.) frozen
   chopped spinach,
   well-drained
1 cup Hellmann's mayonnaise
1 cup sour cream
1 Tbsp. grated Parmesan
   cheese
1 pkg. Knorr's vegetable
   soup mix
Water chestnuts (optional)
Chopped green onion
   (optional)

Cut out the inside of round loaf. Save pieces of the inside, and cube them to be used as dippers. Combine the remaining ingredients. Chill at least 4 hours or overnight. Place dip in hollowed-out bread. Serve with fresh vegetables and bread cubes.   Serves 12–16

BAKED BRIE

1 pkg. (4½ oz.) Baby Brie
1 Tbsp. butter
1½ Tbsp. brown sugar
2 Tbsp. slivered toasted
   almonds

Cut off rind of Brie. Place in a small souffle dish, approximately same size as cheese. Combine butter and brown sugar and spread on top of cheese. Sprinkle almonds on top, and bake for 15–20 minutes at 325°. Serve with thinly sliced French bread.   Serves 4

Variations: Omit brown sugar.
Helpful Hint: Do not use fully ripened Brie.

EGG SALAD CAVIAR

elegant picnic starter

1 pkg. (8 oz.) cream cheese,
   softened
1 cup sour cream
1 bunch of green onions,
   chopped
3 Tbsp. mayonnaise or salad
   dressing
6 eggs, hard-boiled and
   chopped
1 jar (3 oz.) caviar
Lemon wedges
Parsley

Combine softened cream cheese and sour cream. Spread in a 9x12 baking dish. Sprinkle chopped green onions on mixture. Sieve eggs and blend with mayonnaise until moist. Spread egg mixture on chopped green onions. Refrigerate for 3 hours.

To serve, spread caviar on egg mixture. Decorate with lemon wedges and parsley. Serve with plain crackers. Can be made the day ahead.   Serves 12

LAYERED CAVIAR MOLD

also excellent without caviar

1 env. unflavored gelatin
¼ cup cold water

Sour Cream Layer
1 cup sour cream
¼ cup minced onion

Avocado Layer
1 med. avocado, puréed
1 med. avocado, diced
1 lg. shallot, minced
2 Tbsp. lemon juice
2 Tbsp. Hellmann's
    mayonnaise
½ tsp. salt
Dash Tabasco

Egg Layer
4 eggs, hard-boiled,
    chopped
½ cup Hellman's mayonnaise
¼ cup minced parsley
1 lg. green onion, minced
1 tsp. salt
Dash Tabasco

Caviar Layer
4 oz. black or red caviar
Lemon juice

Grease a 9-inch pie pan or 9-inch spring form pan with mayonnaise. Soften gelatin in ¼ cup cold water, and liquefy by placing in small heat-resistant container in a pan of hot water. Portions of this mixture will be used in each layer. Keep remaining portions in hot water as you make each layer.

Sour Cream Layer
Mix sour cream, onion and 2 Tbsp. of gelatin mixture and spread in the bottom of pan. Chill until set.

Avocado Layer
Combine ingredients with 1 Tbsp. of gelatin mixture. Blend well and spread on top of sour cream layer. Chill until set.

Egg Layer
Combine ingredients and remaining 1 Tbsp. of gelatin mixture. Spread on top of avocado layer. Cover with plastic wrap. Refrigerate overnight.

Caviar Layer
When ready to serve, unmold carefully onto serving plate. Rinse caviar with cold water, drain well. Spread caviar on top of mold and sprinkle with lemon juice. Serve with crackers or thinly sliced pumpernickel bread.   Serves 12–16

CAMEMBERT CHEESE PASTRY BALL

Cheese Pastry Ball
1 pkg. (3 oz.) cream cheese, softened
¼ cup butter
½ cup flour
Dash salt
8 oz. Camembert cheese

Glaze
1 egg yolk
1 Tbsp. water

Preheat oven to 425°. Cut cream cheese and butter into flour, seasoned with dash of salt. Roll into ball and refrigerate for 1 hour. Divide pastry so that one portion is twice the size of the other. Roll larger section into circle ⅛-inch thick and use it to cover top and sides of Camembert cheese. Roll smaller section ⅛-inch thick and cover bottom of cheese. Seal edges together using a little water if needed. Use left over pastry for design on top. Mix glaze ingredients and brush lightly on pastry ball. Refrigerate 1 hour. Bake on cookie sheet for 20 minutes. Cool 30 minutes before serving.   Serves 6

EAST INDIAN CHEESE BALL

2 pkgs. (8 oz. each) cream cheese, softened
½ cup chopped chutney
½ cup almonds, toasted
½ tsp. dry mustard
1½ Tbsp. curry powder
Shredded coconut

Combine first five ingredients. Roll into ball. Roll ball in shredded coconut. Serve with crackers. Will keep in refrigerator for several weeks.
              Serves 6-8

Variation: For a spread, thin with 2½ Tbsp. sherry and top with coconut.

SHERRIED EDAM

1 baby Edam cheese
½ cup butter, softened
½ cup chopped walnuts
3 Tbsp. dry sherry
Assorted crackers

Bring Edam to room temperature. Slice off top half of cheese. Peel red wax from top and grate cheese. Hollow out remaining half of cheese, leaving wax on and a ¼-inch shell. Grate cheese. Combine grated cheese, butter, walnuts and sherry. Repack into cheese shell. Refrigerate for several days to allow cheese to mellow. Allow cheese to come to room temperature before serving with crackers.   Serves 4-6

LAGER CHEESE SPREAD

1 can (12 oz.) beer
1½ lbs. cheddar cheese,
    grated
5 oz. bleu cheese, crumbled
3 Tbsp. butter
1 tsp. dry mustard
1 tsp. Worcestershire sauce
Dash onion powder (or 1
    Tbsp. grated onion)
Several dashes Tabasco
Chopped nuts, if desired

Put half the beer and cheeses in blender or food processor and blend until smooth. Add half remaining ingredients, except nuts, and blend again. Transfer to a large bowl. Repeat with remaining ingredients, again except nuts. Chill until firm. Pack into crocks or roll into balls or logs and cover with nuts.
                    Yields 5 cups

Timely Tip:
Use a pair of pliers to hold food to be grated.

CRAB BALL

1 pkg. (6 oz.) frozen snow
  crab meat
1 pkg. (8 oz.) cream cheese,
  softened
2 tsp. finely chopped chives
¼ tsp. garlic powder
¼ tsp. salt
½ cup chopped pecans

Thaw and drain crab meat. Blend cream cheese, chives, garlic powder, and salt. Fold in crab meat. Shape into ball or log. Roll in pecans. Serve with crackers or raw vegetables. Make ahead.   Serves 6-8

BRAUNSCHWEIGER PATÉ

12 oz. braunschweiger,
  mashed
1 sm. onion, grated
Juice of ½ lemon
1 tsp. lemon pepper
  marinade
1 pkg. (8 oz.) cream cheese,
  softened
Dash of milk
Caviar
3 cooked egg yolks,
  crumbled
Parsley, chopped

Mash braunschweiger and add onion, lemon juice and lemon pepper marinade. Form into a flat-topped cake shape. Cover and refrigerate overnight or longer.

The day of serving, place paté on serving platter. Blend cream cheese and milk to spreading consistency. Decorate paté with cream cheese mixture, using a pastry tube to make a rosette border around top and bottom edges. Within top rosette spread a 1-inch ring of caviar. Place another rosette border along inner edge of caviar ring. Put crumbled egg yolk in center of paté. Put chopped parsley around outside of dish. Serve with crackers or party rye bread. Must be made ahead, up to 3 days. Freezes.   Serves 6-8

CHICKEN LIVER PATÉ

½ lb. chicken livers
2 Tbsp. butter, melted
2 eggs, hard-boiled
1 pkg. (8 oz.) cream cheese,
  softened
¾ tsp. salt
2 or 3 twists of the pepper
  mill
2 Tbsp. dry sherry
Sunflower seeds to sprinkle

In heavy skillet, sauté chicken livers in butter. Work hard-boiled eggs and sautéed chicken livers through meat grinder on finest grind. Cream the cream cheese and add ground livers and eggs. Add salt, pepper and sherry to mixture. Mix well.

Line 1 lb. loaf pan with aluminum foil. Spoon paté into pan and press down evenly. Close foil over paté and refrigerate several hours (or overnight) until firm. Gently lift paté out of pan by foil and turn out on serving plate. Cover paté with sunflower seeds. Serve with unseasoned crackers.   Serves 6–8

Variations: Cover paté with finely chopped parsley. Leftovers good in sandwiches.
Helpful Hints: Recipe may be doubled; unused portion may be returned to foil wrappings and refrigerated up to 1 week.

HOLIDAY CHEESE BALLS

2 pkgs. (8 oz. each) cream
  cheese
3 pkgs. (4 oz. each) dried
  beef, chopped
4 Tbsp. Hellmann's
  mayonnaise
10 green onions, chopped
½ tsp. horseradish
¾ cup chopped walnuts

Combine first five ingredients. Roll into bite-sized balls. Roll balls in chopped walnuts. Refrigerate 3 hours. Can be made up to 3 days ahead.
                          Serves 8

ROQUEFORT SOUFFLÉ

2 eggs, separated
1 lb. Roquefort cheese,
  cumbled
1 pkg. (8 oz.) cream cheese
½ cup unsalted butter
2 envs. gelatin
2 Tbsp. cold water
1 tsp. prepared mustard
½ pt. whipping cream

Whip egg yolks in blender until lemon colored. Add Roquefort cheese and blend until smooth. Blend in cream cheese and butter. Soften gelatin in cold water and place in pan of hot water to liquefy. Add gelatin and mustard to cheese mixture. Beat egg whites until stiff and fold into mixture. Whip cream and fold into mixture. Pour into greased mold and refrigerate. Serve with crackers. Can be made ahead. Freezes for up to 2 months.

Serves 25

SALMON CUCUMBER MOUSSE

1 can (16 oz.) salmon (pink
  is O.K.)
1 cup sour cream
2 pkgs. unflavored gelatin
1 cup Hellmann's
  mayonnaise
2 Tbsp. lemon juice
1 tsp. horseradish
¼ tsp. salt
1 Tbsp. finely grated onion
2-3 cucumbers, peeled,
  seeded, finely ground,
  drained
Parsley to garnish

Variations: Use a fish mold, and garnish with capers and tip of hard-boiled egg or slice of stuffed olive for eyes.

Drain salmon, reserving liquid in small pan. Remove skin and bones. Flake. Beat sour cream until almost double in volume (it will thin, then thicken; allow time). Add cold water to salmon liquid to make ½ cup, spinkle in gelatin, let stand 5 minutes, boil to dissolve. Mix dissolved gelatin into mayonnaise. One at a time, blend lemon juice, horseradish, salt, onion and cucumber into mayonnaise - gelatin mixture. Fold in salmon and sour cream.

Turn into a 5-6 cup mold (spray mold with Pam) or individual molds. Chill thoroughly. Flavor improves the second day. Unmold and garnish with parsley. Serve with crackers. Serves 12

GRASSHOPPER

2⅔ cups vanilla ice cream
2 oz. green Creme de
   Menthe
1 oz. white Creme de Cacao

Variation: Substitute brandy for Creme de
   Cacao.

Blend ingredients in mixer at high speed until just blended. Serve in large wine glass or old fashioned glass. Can make ahead and store in freezer. Remove from freezer shortly before serving.   Serves 2

HUMMER

popular at Bayview Yacht Club

1 qt. vanilla ice cream
   (Breyer's, Hagen Dazs, or
   other natural flavored ice
   cream)
1 oz. Kahlua
3 oz. white rum

Place all ingredients in a blender and run until smooth. May be made well in advance and stored in the freezer until needed. Stir well before serving.
     Serves 4

Variation: May use butter pecan ice cream.

IRISH CREAM

¾ oz. Jameson Irish Whiskey
   (do not substitute)
2 oz. whipping cream or half
   and half
¾ oz. Creme de Cacao

Blend all ingredients and pour over ice.   Serves 1

JAMAICAN YELLOW BIRD

1½ oz. rum
½ oz. Kahlua or Tia Maria
½ oz. Creme de Banana
4 oz. orange juice, or to taste

Pour liqueurs over ice cubes in appropriate glass. Fill with orange juice to taste.
     Serves 1

LOVE COCKTAIL PUNCH

nice for brunch

2 cups vodka
1 cup bourbon
4 bottles (16 oz. each) 7-Up
2 cans (12 oz. each) frozen
   concentrated orange juice
2 cans (12 oz. each) frozen
   concentrated lemonade
Lemon slices (optional)
Strawberries (optional)

Mix all ingredients in a punch bowl. Serve with ice ring and float lemon slices and strawberries on top if desired.

Yields 16 cups

BURGUNDY PUNCH

4 cups Gallo Burgundy
1 can (6 oz.) frozen
   concentrated lemonade
¼ cup Grenadine
1 lemon
1 orange
2 cups club soda
Ice

Combine Burgundy, lemonade and Grenadine in a bowl. Slice lemon and orange in round slices, and place in punch. Let punch stand overnight unrefrigerated. Just before serving, add club soda and ice.

Yields 7 cups

RUSSELL'S PUNCH

a Grosse Pointe Hunt Club favorite

46 oz. pineapple juice
4 cans (6 oz. each) frozen
   concentrated lemonade
46 oz. orange juice
1 qt. 7-Up
1 qt. club soda
1 bottle champagne

Mix all ingredients together. Serve chilled. Can combine the fruit juices ahead of time.

Yields 25 cups

Variations: You can float an ice mold in a punch bowl with sliced oranges and lemons. Equally good without the champagne.

HOT BUTTERED RUM

wonderful on cold snowy nights

1 lb. brown sugar
1 cup butter
1 tsp. cinnamon
1 tsp. nutmeg
½ tsp. ground cloves
Dash salt
Light rum
Boiling water
Cinnamon sticks

Cream butter and sugar. Add spices and continue creaming. Place in refrigerator for ½–1 hour. Roll into balls about the size of small walnuts. The balls may be stored in a covered container in refrigerator for months.

To serve, place one cinnamon ball in each mug with 1½ oz. light rum. Add boiling water. Stir with a cinnamon stick.

Yields 20 balls

CAFÉ BRULOT

wonderful holiday beverage

1 stick cinnamon
12 whole cloves
Peel of 1 orange (keep in
    one circular piece, if
    possible)
Peel of 1 lemon (one circular
    piece)
2 Tbsp. sugar
8 oz. brandy, heated
8 oz. Curacao
1 qt. freshly brewed, strong,
    hot, black coffee
Whipped cream
Chocolate shavings

In a chafing dish, put cinnamon, cloves, orange and lemon peels and sugar. Add brandy and Curacao and stir. Ignite the brandy and gradually add coffee to extinguish the flame. Garnish with whipped cream and chocolate shavings on each serving. Yields 6 cups

Timely Tip:
The appropriate liquor may be served in a decanter next to punch so that guests may spike to taste. The children can enjoy the same drink as their parents.

CAFÉ COLOMBIAN ROYAL

½ cup whipping cream
1 Tbsp. powdered sugar
1 oz. semi-sweet chocolate,
   coarsely chopped
2 Tbsp. sugar
¾ tsp. ground cinnamon
¼ tsp. ground nutmeg
3 cups water
1 Tbsp. instant coffee
2 cups milk
¼ cup Kahlua
½ tsp. vanilla extract
Ground cinnamon

Beat whipping cream, gradually adding powdered sugar, until soft peaks form. Chill. Combine chocolate, cinnamon, nutmeg and water in a heavy saucepan, stirring constantly until mixture comes to a boil. Add coffee, stir until dissolved. Add milk and heat thoroughly. Stir in Kahlua and vanilla. Pour into mugs. Top with whipped cream and sprinkle with cinnamon.

Beat whipping cream, gradually adding powdered sugar until soft peaks form. Chill. Combine chocolate, sugar, cinnamon, nutmeg and water in a deep 3-quart casserole or bowl. Microwave on High 5–8 minutes, stirring twice, or until chocolate melts and water is boiling. Add coffee granules, stirring until dissolved. Gradually stir in milk and cover with heavy duty plastic wrap. Microwave on High for 2–4 minutes or until thoroughly heated. Stir in Kahlua and vanilla. Pour into mugs. Top with whipped cream and sprinkle with cinnamon.

Yields 6 cups

Variation: Other coffee flavored liqueurs may be substituted for Kahlua.

CAFÉ PRADO

24 oz. brewed coffee
3 Tbsp. sugar
¾ cup chocolate chips
⅜ tsp. cinnamon
6 cups hot milk
6 oz. rum

Add sugar to coffee and heat. Add chocolate chips and cinnamon. Stir over low heat until chocolate is melted. Mix with hot milk and whip until frothy. Add rum. Serve immediately.

Yields 10 demitasse cups

MOCHA MIX

a great gift

1½ cups sugar
1 cup instant coffee granules
1 cup powdered non-dairy
   coffee cream
¼ cup cocoa
½ tsp. salt
½ tsp. cinnamon (optional)

Mix ingredients thoroughly. Store in airtight container. When ready to serve, mix 2 Tbsp. mocha mix with 1 cup boiling water.   Yields 30 servings

AFTER SKI BOWL

2 sm. apples, sliced
3-4 Tbsp. white corn syrup
¼ cup sugar
½ tsp. cinnamon
3 cups Chablis
1½ cups unsweetened apple
   cider
¼ tsp. nutmeg
1 twist lemon peel per
   serving

Preheat oven to 400°. Roll apples in corn syrup to coat. Sprinkle sugar and cinnamon over apples. Bake in 400° oven for 15 minutes. Meanwhile, combine remaining ingredients and heat 15-20 minutes over medium-low heat until hot. Pour in preheated wide mugs. Float an apple slice in each mug. Use a lemon peel twist for second round.   Yields 4½ cups

TEA BRACER

great after a long day on the slopes

2 qts. cold water
2 tsp. grated lemon rind
8 whole cloves
8 tea bags
4 Tbsp. brown sugar
1 pt. dark or light rum
1 thin lemon slice, studded
   with cloves per person
1 cinnamon stick per person

Combine water, lemon rind and cloves in a saucepan. Bring to a full rolling boil and immediately add tea bags. Brew 4 minutes. Stir and strain into a preheated serving pitcher. Add brown sugar and stir until dissolved. Add rum. Serve in mugs and garnish with clove studded lemon slices and cinnamon sticks. Can be made ahead and reheated.   Yields 10 cups

RUSSIAN TEA

a great gift

18 oz. powdered orange
   breakfast drink
1 cup sugar
½ cup instant tea or ¾ cup
   instant tea with lemon
1 tsp. cinnamon
½ tsp. ground cloves
½ tsp. allspice

Combine all ingredients in a bowl. Blend small amounts at a time in blender, until a fine powder. Store in jar and use as needed. Use 2 tsp. per 8 oz. serving. Serve hot or cold.
            Yields 98 servings

WHISKY SOUR

1 can (6 oz.) frozen
   concentrated lemonade
6 oz. whisky or bourbon
6 oz. beer
Orange slices and cherries
   for garnish

Mix concentrated lemonade, whisky or bourbon and beer in blender. Serve with garnish over ice.   Yields 4 servings

Timely Tip:
Party ice cubes if put in brown paper bag will not stick together.

HOT CRANBERRY PUNCH

*great holiday punch for those who don't drink
alcoholic beverages*

1 lb. fresh cranberries
3-4 sticks cinnamon
10-12 cloves
3 pts. water
1 cup sugar
¼ can (6 oz.) frozen
   concentrated lemonade,
   or 1-2 Tbsp. fresh lemon
   juice
¼ cup orange juice

Put cranberries and spices in water and heat until the berries pop. Strain liquid and add sugar. Heat to a boil. Add lemon and orange juices. Stir and serve. Can be made ahead.

Yields 6 cups

LEMON LIME SPRITE PUNCH

good on a hot summer day

1 pkg. (6 oz.) lime gelatin
2 cups hot water
2 cans (12 oz. each) frozen
   concentrated limeade (or
   lemonade)
½-1 cup bottled lime juice,
   to taste.
1 tsp. almond extract
1½ qts. cracked ice
10 bottles (10 oz. each)
   Sprite
1 fifth vodka
Lemon slices and mint sprigs
   to garnish

Dissolve gelatin in hot water. Stir in concentrated limeade. Add lime juice and almond extract.

To serve, pour into punch bowl over 1½ quarts cracked ice. Add Sprite and vodka. Float slices of lemon and green mint sprigs on top. Yields 22 cups

Timely Tip:
To keep punches cold, freeze water in heavy plastic bags. Place a bag in the bottom of punch bowl and pour over ingredients. Change bag if necessary. This saves refrigerator space, as punch cools on counter without getting diluted.

Soup & Sandwiches

AVOCADO SOUP

rich and delicious

2 avocados, peeled and
chopped
1 can (13 oz.) evaporated
milk
1 cup half and half
1 cup chicken broth
½ tsp. celery salt
½ tsp. garlic salt
Pepper to taste
Watercress to garnish

Combine all ingredients except
watercress in a blender. Blend
until satin smooth. Serve well
chilled. Garnish with watercress.

Yields 4–6 cups

SCOTCH BARLEY AND BEEF SOUP

1 lg. onion, diced
4 Tbsp. oil
1 (2 lb.) arm roast
5 cups water, divided
4 cans (10½ oz. each) beef
broth
1 cup diced carrots
½ cup diced celery
2 tsp. salt
¼ tsp. pepper
1 bay leaf
½ cup quick Scotch barley
¼ cup flour

In a large dutch oven, brown
onion in 4 Tbsp. oil. Remove
onion and set aside. Brown roast,
adding more oil if needed. Put
browned onion in with roast, and
add 4 cups water and the
canned beef broth. Simmer,
covered, for 2½ hours. Add carrots, celery, salt, pepper, bay
leaf and barley. Simmer for 1
hour.

Remove roast and shred half the
meat. Can freeze other half.
Thicken soup with a paste made
by whisking ¼ cup flour into
1 cup water. Bring soup to a
medium boil and pour the paste
slowly into soup, stirring constantly. Put shredded meat into
soup and simmer for 5–10
minutes. Can be made ahead.

Yields 12 cups

GREEN BEAN AND POTATO SOUP

1½ lbs. green beans
Water to cover beans
2 med. potatoes
2 beef bouillon cubes
4 slices bacon, thick cut and
　　minced
2 Tbsp. butter
1 lg. onion, chopped
3 Tbsp. flour
¼ cup sour cream
¼ tsp. dried dill
Salt and pepper to taste
Milk (optional)

Clean and cut green beans into 1½-inch pieces. Place in 4-quart saucepan and cover with water to 1 inch above beans. Bring to a boil. Simmer for 10 minutes. Peel and cube potatoes. Add potatoes and bouillon cubes to beans. Cook until potatoes are tender, about 10–15 minutes. Set aside.

In frying pan, brown minced bacon. Remove bacon and add to soup. Add butter to remaining bacon drippings. Saute' onions in drippings. Add onion to soup. Add flour to drippings, stirring to keep smooth. Cook on low heat for 3–4 minutes. Remove 1 cup of liquid from soup and gradually add to flour mixture, stirring well. Add sour cream to flour mixture. Cook 2 minutes. Add to soup, stirring well. Add dill, salt and pepper to soup. Cook on low until thoroughly heated. Soup is thick; if desired add milk to thin. Can be made ahead.　　　　Yields 4–6 cups

NAVY BEAN SOUP

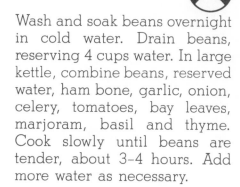

2 lbs. dried navy beans
10 cups water
1 ham bone
1 clove garlic, minced
1 sm. onion, minced
½ cup chopped celery
1 can (28 oz.) tomatoes,
    chopped or 3½-4 cups
    fresh chopped
2 bay leaves
1 tsp. dried marjoram
¼ tsp. dried basil
¼ tsp. dried thyme
Dash of Tabasco sauce
Salt and pepper to taste
Croutons

Wash and soak beans overnight in cold water. Drain beans, reserving 4 cups water. In large kettle, combine beans, reserved water, ham bone, garlic, onion, celery, tomatoes, bay leaves, marjoram, basil and thyme. Cook slowly until beans are tender, about 3-4 hours. Add more water as necessary.

Remove ham bone. Cut meat into small pieces and return to kettle. Mash half of beans with back of wooden spoon. Season with salt, pepper and Tabasco to taste. Serve with croutons. May be made ahead. Yields 12 cups

Timely Tip:
If soup is too salty, add a few slices of raw potato. Boil a few minutes and remove.

BROCCOLI SOUP

2 pkgs. (10 oz. each) frozen,
    chopped broccoli
2 cans (10¾ oz. each) cream
    of mushroom soup,
    undiluted
2⅔ cups milk
½ cup dry white wine
4 Tbsp. butter
½ tsp. dried tarragon or dill,
    crushed
Dash white pepper
Salt to taste

In large saucepan, cook broccoli as directed on package and drain. Return broccoli to pan and add remaining ingredients. Heat and serve. Can be made ahead. Yields 8 cups

CHEF SCHNEIDER'S CHEESE SOUP

8 Tbsp. butter
2½ Tbsp. minced onion
¾ cup flour
2½ cups chicken stock
1 tsp. Dijon mustard
4½ cups milk, heated
1 lb. American cheese,
  sliced
1¼ cups water
¾ cup finely diced celery
¾ cup finely diced carrots
Salt and pepper to taste
½ cup flat beer (optional)
2 cups popped popcorn
Chopped parsley

Melt butter in 2½-quart saucepan and saute onions until transparent (about 3 minutes). Add flour and cook 3 minutes on low. Do not brown. Stir in chicken stock slowly until completely added. Add mustard and hot milk and bring to a boil. (Do not boil more than 2 minutes.) Shut off heat and add sliced cheese. Set aside.

Combine water, celery and carrots in a saucepan and bring to a boil. Simmer until tender. Add all this mixture to cheese mixture. Season with salt and pepper. The ½ cup flat beer may be added. Serve in a bowl; garnish with popcorn and chopped parsley.   Serves 10-12

BISQUE OF HAMPTON CRAB

1 cup crab meat
½ cup sliced mushrooms
1 Tbsp. butter
1 can (10½ oz.) cream of
  asparagus soup, undiluted
2 cups coffee cream
1½ cups milk
½ tsp. Worcestershire sauce
¼ – ⅓ cup dry sherry, to taste

Pick over crab meat to clean. Set aside. Saute mushrooms in 1 Tbsp. butter, set aside. Place remaining ingredients in a medium-sized saucepan, cooking slowly until smooth. Remove and discard asparagus pieces. Add flaked crab meat and mushrooms to soup. Heat thoroughly. Do not boil. Can be made ahead.   Yields 6 cups

MANHATTAN CLAM CHOWDER

¼ lb. salt pork, diced
1 doz. chowder clams or 1
   lb. steamers
1 can (1 lb.) tomatoes,
   chopped
1 onion, diced
1 carrot, diced
1½ cups diced potatoes
3 cups water
1 Tbsp. diced celery
Pepper to taste
Dash thyme or to taste

Brown salt pork and set aside. Steam clams until open. Reserve broth. If using steamers, remove the necks. Chowder clams can be used whole. Set aside to cool until touchable.

Combine all ingredients in soup pot, including reserved broth. Cook, covered, over low heat 3–4 hours. After cooking, chowder can be refrigerated for use later.

To steam clams: Scrub clams. Soak in cold brine ½ hour. Rinse in several changes of water. Place 4 Tbsp. water in a pot, add the clams and boil gently over low heat until they open.

Serves 4–6

NEW ENGLAND CLAM CHOWDER

2 slices bacon
1 cup finely chopped onion
2 cups cubed potatoes
1 tsp. salt
Dash pepper
1 cup water
1 pt. shucked fresh clams,
   chopped coarsely or 3
   cans (6½ oz. each)
   minced clams including
   liquid
2 cups half and half
2 Tbsp. butter

Chop bacon coarsely. Sauté bacon in large kettle until crisp. Add onion and cook until soft. Add cubed potatoes, salt, pepper and water. Cook uncovered 15 minutes or until potatoes are fork tender. Drain clams, reserving liquid. Chop clams coarsely if using fresh clams. Add clams, clam liquid and half and half to kettle, mixing well. Heat until boiling. Add butter and serve. Can be made ahead.

Yields 6 cups

QUICK CRAB MEAT SOUP

½ cup chopped onion
1 cup chopped celery
½ cup chopped green
  pepper
3 Tbsp. butter
1 lb. crab meat, fresh flaked
  or frozen
1 can (10¾ oz.) tomato soup,
  undiluted
1 can (10¾ oz.) cream of
  potato soup, undiluted
1 tsp. dried oregano, crushed
1½ soup cans milk
1 jar (2 oz.) pimento, drained
  and chopped
2 bay leaves
Salt and cayenne pepper to
  taste

Sauté onion, celery and green pepper in butter. Combine sautéed vegetables with the remaining ingredients in a large saucepan. Simmer for 20–30 minutes before serving. Can be made ahead.   Yields 6 cups

SPICE ISLANDS FISH CHOWDER

from Lochmoor Club Chef George Lackey

½ cup butter
½ cup diced onion
½ cup diced carrots
½ cup diced green pepper
3 Tbsp. curry powder
4 Tbsp. flour
1 qt. fish stock
1 cup firm fish, such as
  scallops, shrimp, sole,
  sword fish, tuna or halibut
1 cup whipping cream
2 Tbsp. coconut cream
Salt and pepper to taste
2 Tbsp. dark rum

Melt butter in saucepan. Sauté carrots, onions and green pepper lightly. Add curry and flour and stir to make a roux. Slowly stir in stock. Bring to a boil and continue to stir. Add fish and simmer 15 minutes. Add whipping cream and coconut cream. Season with salt and pepper. Add rum before serving. Can be made ahead. Freezes.
            Yields 8 cups

Helpful Hint: Make fish stock by boiling shrimp or other firm
            fish in 1 quart chicken stock.

CORN CHOWDER

good basis for clam or fish chowder

1 cup butter, divided
4 Tbsp. flour
Pinch of salt
2½ qts. half and half
½ cup chopped parsley
1–2 tsp. honey
1 bay leaf
¼ tsp. black pepper
Nutmeg to taste
3–4 med. potatoes, peeled
  and diced
1 lg. Spanish onion, minced
3 cloves garlic, minced
1 leek, white only, sliced
3 scallions, chopped
¾ tsp. dry mustard
Dash cayenne pepper
Salt to taste
6 celery stalks, diced
6–7 ears corn or 1 pkg. (20
  oz.) frozen corn
3 vegetable or chicken
  bouillon cubes

In a large heavy saucepan, melt ¼ cup butter. Add flour and pinch of salt. Cook over low heat 10 minutes. Add half and half to flour mixture, and cook stirring constantly for 15 minutes. Add parsley, honey, bay leaf, pepper and nutmeg.

In a separate saucepan, parboil or steam potatoes in water to cover for 7–8 minutes. Drain and reserve potatoes.

In medium saucepan, melt ¾ cup butter. Sauté the onions, garlic, leeks and scallions for 20–25 minutes. Season with mustard, cayenne pepper and salt to taste. Raise heat and add celery. Cook 3–4 minutes.

Slice corn from cobs. Add corn and bouillon cubes to vegetable mixture and cook 3–4 minutes. Scrape cobs with a knife to remove the milk. Add the corn milk and the sautéed vegetables to the half and half mixture. Add potatoes and heat thoroughly before serving. Can be made ahead.   Yields 6 quarts

Helpful Hints: Better second day. Recipe can be halved.

ENGLISH CUCUMBER SOUP

1¾–2 lbs. English
   cucumbers
3 cups chicken stock
3 cups sour cream
3 Tbsp. white wine vinegar
1 clove garlic
2 tsp. salt
Dash white pepper

Wash and seed cucumbers. Do not peel. Cut cucumbers into 1 inch cubes. Combine all the soup ingredients in a blender and purée. Refrigerate for 2–3 hours. Serve in chilled bowls, passing the condiments. May be made day ahead. Yields 8 cups

Condiments
1 hard-boiled egg, chopped
1 lg. tomato, seeded and
   diced
1 avocado, peeled and diced
1 bunch green onions,
   chopped
1 cup croutons

Variation: Regular cucumbers may be used, but they must be peeled and seeded.

SWEDISH FRUIT SOUP

serve hot or cold for breakfast or brunch

½ lb. dried prunes, seeded
½ lb. dried apricots, seeded
1 cup raisins
4 Tbsp. pearl tapioca
2 qts. water
1½ cups sugar
1 stick cinnamon
3 apples, cored and diced
1 lemon, quartered and
   thinly sliced
1 orange, quartered and
   thinly sliced
¼ tsp. salt
½ cup maraschino cherries

Soak dried fruits and tapioca in water to cover overnight. In morning, combine all ingredients except cherries. Add 2 quarts more water and cook on medium heat, uncovered, until soft, approximately 1 hour. Add cherries. Heat thoroughly. Serve hot, cold or at room temperature. Yields 10–12 cups

Variation: May be topped with a dollop of sour cream.

CHILLED GARDEN SOUP

1 med. potato
1 med. onion
1 cucumber
1 lg. stalk celery with leaves
1 tart apple
1 tsp. salt
1 pt. chicken broth
1 Tbsp. butter
1 cup coffee cream
1 tsp. curry powder
Few grains pepper
Chives, cut

Peel and chop vegetables and apple. Add vegetables, apple, salt and butter to chicken broth, and simmer until vegetables are tender. Purée in a blender until smooth. Stir in cream, curry powder and pepper. Chill thoroughly. Serve with sprinkle of chives. May be made several days ahead.   Yields 6 cups

SEMI-MINESTRONE

¼ lb. lean salt pork, diced
2 qts. hot water
2 cups tomato juice
1 can (10¾ oz.) black bean
    soup, undiluted
6 beef bouillon cubes
1 cup sliced carrots
1 cup diced celery
½ cabbage, shredded
1 cup chopped green onions
2 cups chopped spinach
1 tsp. dried basil
1 tsp. M.S.G.
½ tsp. salt
¼ tsp. pepper
¾ cup broken spaghetti
½ cup grated Parmesan
    cheese
Parmesan cheese to pass

Sauté salt pork in a deep kettle until crisp. Add water, tomato juice, soup and bouillon cubes, stirring well. Add vegetables. Add seasonings to taste. Bring to a boil, cover and simmer for 1 hour, stirring occasionally. Add spaghetti and cook for an additional ½ hour. Before serving, stir in ½ cup Parmesan cheese. Pass Parmesan cheese to garnish. Can be made ahead. Freezes well.
     Yields 3½–4 quarts

Variation: Add 1 lb. cubed stew beef to salt pork.

SHRIMP GUMBO

dinner in a dish

1 lb. okra, cleaned, fresh or frozen
2 Tbsp. olive oil
1 lg. onion, chopped
2 green peppers, cut into ½" squares
2 cloves garlic, minced
¼ cup flour
1 can (1 lb. 12 oz.) tomatoes
2 cans (14½ oz. each) chicken broth
2 cups water
2 bay leaves
¼ tsp. thyme
¼ tsp. Tabasco
½ tsp. Worcestershire sauce
1–2 tsp. salt to taste
1 lb. shrimp, shelled and deveined
4 Tbsp. hot cooked rice

Heat oil in a large saucepan over medium heat. Sauté fresh okra, onion, green pepper and garlic in hot oil. If using frozen okra, add after other vegetables have been sautéed. Sprinkle with flour and stir until the flour becomes golden brown. Add tomatoes, chicken broth, water, bay leaves, thyme, Tabasco, Worcestershire and salt. Cover and bring to a boil. Reduce heat and simmer for 45 minutes. Add shrimp and cook 7 minutes. Put a spoonful of rice in each soup bowl and ladle Gumbo over rice. Can be made ahead. Serves 4

Variations: Vary spices to suit your own taste. Substitute green beans for okra.

SOPA DE LIMA FROM YUCATAN

¼ corn tortilla per person, fried and broken into 2–3 pieces
1 thin slice onion per person
2 limes
¼ cup coarsely shredded chicken, cooked
2 thin strips pimento per person (optional)
2 cans (14½ oz. each) chicken broth (**not** bouillon cubes)
1½ tsp. coriander
2 Tbsp. sherry
Salt and pepper to taste

In the bottom of each soup bowl, place broken ¼ tortilla, onion slice, 1 thin slice of lime, a few pieces of chicken and pimento. You may cover and keep at room temperature up to 2 hours. Combine broth, coriander, sherry, salt and pepper. Simmer for 10 minutes. Pour into bowls and serve immediately.

Yields 4 cups

COMPANY TOMATO SOUP

2 cups sliced onions
½ tsp. dried thyme
½ tsp. dried basil
¾ cup butter, divided
2 Tbsp. olive oil
2 cans (1 lb. 15 oz. each)
 Italian tomatoes
4 Tbsp. tomato paste
3¾ cups chicken broth,
 divided
¼ cup flour
1 cup whipping cream
1 tsp. sugar
Salt and fresh ground pepper
 to taste

Croutons
8 bread slices
2 cloves garlic, crushed
½ cup olive oil

In a large kettle, sauté onion, thyme and basil in ½ cup butter and 2 Tbsp. olive oil until onion wilts. Add tomatoes and tomato paste. Simmer 10 minutes. Slowly add 5 Tbsp. chicken broth to ¼ cup flour mixing until smooth. Remove tomatoes from heat and stir in flour mixture. Add remaining broth and return to heat. Simmer 30 minutes, stirring frequently. Put soup through a blender or food processor. Can be prepared ahead to this point. Just before serving, add cream and sugar and bring to a simmer. Add ¼ cup butter and season to taste with salt and pepper. Serve with croutons.

Yields 8–10 cups

Croutons
Preheat oven to 400°. Crush garlic and sauté in ½ cup olive oil until golden. Remove garlic. Brush bread slices with seasoned oil. Bake bread until golden on both sides. Slice into croutons.

TOMATO MUSHROOM SOUP

2 cans (10¾ oz. each) tomato
  soup, undiluted
2 cans (10¾ oz. each) beef
  bouillon, undiluted
1 cup water
1 sm. onion, thinly sliced
4 black peppercorns
¼ tsp. salt
1 Tbsp. lemon juice
¼ tsp. nutmeg
¼ lb. mushrooms, finely
  chopped
1 shallot, finely chopped
1 Tbsp. butter
½ cup sherry
Chopped parsley (optional)

In a large saucepan, stir together first eight ingredients. Bring mixture to a boil, then reduce heat and simmer, covered, for 30–40 minutes. Strain soup, discarding onions and peppercorns. Sauté mushrooms and shallot in butter until liquid evaporates. May be made ahead to this point.

Just before serving, add sherry, mushrooms and shallot to soup. Heat thoroughly. Do not boil. If desired, top each serving with finely chopped parsley.

Yields 6 cups

VICHYSOISSE

4 leeks, sliced (white part
  only)
1 med. onion, sliced
2 Tbsp. butter
5 med. potatoes, peeled and
  sliced
1 qt. chicken broth or ½
  broth and ½ water
1 Tbsp. salt
2 cups milk
2 cups coffee cream
1 cup whipping cream
Chives, chopped

In a large saucepan, sauté leeks and onions in butter until golden. Add potatoes, broth and salt. Simmer for 35–40 minutes. Put mixture in blender and purée until smooth. Return to saucepan and add milk and coffee cream. Heat soup thoroughly. Cool and return to blender. Refrigerate. Before serving, blend in whipping cream. Garnish with chives. Can be made day ahead.   Yields 8–10 cups

WATERCRESS SOUP

equally delicious hot or cold

2 bunches of watercress
3 Tbsp. butter
1 med. onion, chopped
1 tsp. curry powder
4 lg. potatoes, peeled and
    chopped
4 cups chicken stock
1 cup mushroom broth
Salt and white pepper to
    taste
1 cup coffee cream

Mushroom Broth
½ lb. mushrooms
1 Tbsp. butter
2 cups water

Cut off bottom ½ inch of watercress stems and discard. Carefully wash remaining watercress. Cut off the leafy tips of sprigs and set aside on absorbent towels. Coarsely chop stems. Heat butter in large saucepan. Cook onion in butter until lightly browned. Add watercress stems and cook 5 minutes longer. Stir in potatoes; then pour in chicken stock and mushroom broth. Simmer over low heat until potatoes are completely soft.

Pureé mixture in batches in food processor. If necessary, put mixture through a coarse sieve to remove any remaining stems. Return to heat and add remaining watercress leaves. Simmer for 1 minute. Pureé in food processor once more. Season with salt and white pepper to taste.

To serve hot, stir in cream and heat through. Do not boil. To serve cold, refrigerate and add cream just before serving.

Yields 8 cups

Mushroom Broth
Wash and slice mushrooms. Sauté in butter. Add water and simmer for 3 minutes. Strain; reserving liquid.

Variation: Garnish with crumbled bacon.
Helpful Hint: Mushroom broth may be prepared ahead and frozen.

PUMPKIN SOUP

1 can (16 oz.) unseasoned
    pumpkin
2 cans (13 oz. each)
    evaporated milk
1 env. Lipton's onion soup
    mix
Celery salt to taste
Ground ginger to taste
Green onions, chopped as
    garnish

Combine all ingredients together in blender. Chill for 2–3 hours.   Yields 4 cups

ZUCCHINI SOUP

6 cups chicken stock
4 med. zucchini
1 sm. onion
1-2 shallots or scallions
4 Tbsp. butter
3 Tbsp. cream of wheat
½ tsp. chervil or tarragon
Ground white pepper to taste
2 egg yolks, beaten
½ cup coffee cream
Parsley to garnish

Heat stock in a 3-quart kettle. Cut zucchini, onion and shallots into chunks using the steel blade of a food processor. Melt butter in a skillet. Add cut vegetables and cook over medium heat 5–10 minutes. Do not allow vegetables to brown. Sprinkle cream of wheat over vegetables. Cook 1–2 minutes more. Add vegetables to hot broth and boil 20 minutes. Pureé and reheat to boiling.

Mix eggs with cream to make an enrichment. Whisk enrichment into soup and immediately remove from heat. Do not allow to boil. Add pepper. Serve with parsley as a garnish. May be made a day ahead.

Yields 6–8 cups

Variations: Serve cold with dollop of sour cream and
    sprinkle of dried dill.

COLD SQUASH SOUP

3 med. onions, chopped
2 Tbsp. butter
3 med. yellow summer
    squash, seeded and
    chopped
4 cups chicken broth
1 pt. half and half
1 tsp. salt
1 Tbsp. sugar
Nutmeg to taste

In a large saucepan, sauté onions in butter until translucent. Add chicken broth and squash. Simmer until squash is tender. Purée squash mixture in a blender until very smooth. Stir in half and half, salt, sugar and nutmeg, blending well. Chill before serving. Yields 6–8 cups

ENGLISH MUFFIN TOPPINGS OR PITA BREAD FILLINGS

English Muffin
1 English muffin split per
    serving

English Muffin
Split necessary number of muffins. If desired, spread each half with butter or mayonnaise. Top with favorite filling and broil on second rack from top until bubbling and brown.

Pita Bread
1 round pita per serving

Pita Bread (Pocket Sandwich)
Preheat oven to 325°. Cut pita bread round in half, and open each half to make a pocket. Fill with favorite filling. Wrap tightly in foil. Stand upright in a baking pan and heat 30 minutes at 325°. If wrapped sandwiches are put into a styrofoam cooler, they will hold their heat for several hours. Perfect for tailgating. For a cold sandwich, wrap in foil and stand in refrigerator. Transport for tailgate in a cooler.

Chicken Salad
2 English muffins split, or 2
   pita bread
1⅔ cups chopped cooked
   chicken
½ cup chopped celery
⅓ cup Hellmann's
   mayonnaise
1½ Tbsp. lemon juice
Salt and pepper to taste
3 egg whites
¾ cup grated cheddar

Chicken Salad
Combine chicken, celery,
mayonnaise, lemon juice, salt
and pepper. Spread on English
muffins. Beat egg whites with a
pinch of salt. Fold in cheese and
spread over chicken mixture.
Broil. For pita bread, combine
all ingredients except egg whites
and stuff.

Swiss Sandwich
2 English muffins split, or 2
   pita bread
1½ cups grated Swiss cheese
⅓ cup chopped tomatoes
¼ cup chopped green onion
⅓ cup Hellmann's
   mayonnaise
Pinch basil
Seasoned salt to taste

Swiss Sandwich
Combine all ingredients, mound
on English muffins and broil. Or,
stuff pita bread and heat.

Hot Tuna Sandwich
2 English muffins split, or 2
   pita bread
1 can (7 oz.) tuna, drained
12 stuffed green olives,
   sliced
4 oz. cheddar or Swiss
   cheese, grated
3 hard-boiled eggs, chopped
⅓ cup Hellmann's
   mayonnaise
2 Tbsp. chopped onion
¼ tsp. salt

Hot Tuna Sandwich
Combine all ingredients, mound
on English muffins and broil. Or,
stuff pita bread and heat.

ENGLISH MUFFIN TOPPINGS OR
PITA BREAD FILLINGS (continued)

Cheddar Sandwich
2 English muffins split, or 2
   pita bread
½ cup Hellmann's
   mayonnaise
½ cup chopped onion
1½ cups grated cheddar
1 cup chopped black olives
½ tsp. salt
1 tsp. curry powder
   (optional)
½ cup julienned pepperoni

Cheddar Sandwich
Combine ingredients, mound on
English muffins and broil. Or
stuff pita bread and heat.

Pimento Cheese
2 English muffins split, or 2
   pita bread
1 lb. cheddar cheese, grated
1 jar (4 oz.) pimento,
   chopped
1 cup Hellmann's mayonnaise
   (do not substitute)
1 Tbsp. Durkee's mustard
   (do not substitute)

Pimento Cheese
Combine ingredients, mound on
English muffins or bread and
broil or stuff pita bread and
heat.

Crab Sandwich
2 English muffins split, or 2
   pita bread
½ can (7½ oz.) crab meat
3 oz. cream cheese, softened
1 tsp. lemon juice
⅛ tsp. salt
⅙ cup finely chopped celery
1 hard-boiled egg, chopped
4 tomato slices
¼ cup mayonnaise
¼ cup grated cheddar
   cheese

Crab Sandwich
Combine crab, cream cheese,
lemon juice, salt, celery and
egg. Place a tomato slice on
each prepared muffin, top with
crab mixture. Blend cheese into
mayonnaise, spread on top of
crab and broil. For pita bread,
combine all ingredients except
tomato, stuff pita and heat.

Helpful Hint: Serve the Pimento Cheese Sandwich with watermelon rind pickles and fresh tomatoes.

BARBECUED BEEF SANDWICHES

flavor improves if prepared at least a day in advance

6–7 lb. whole beef brisket
Salt and pepper to taste
3 med. onions, diced
6 Tbsp. butter
2½ cups water
¼ cup lemon juice
3 Tbsp. vinegar
4½ tsp. dry mustard
3 cups ketchup
6 Tbsp. brown sugar
9 Tbsp. Worcestershire
Sandwich buns, toasted

Preheat oven to 300°. Place beef brisket in shallow baking pan. Add salt and pepper. Cover with aluminum foil. Bake 3–4 hours or until meat falls apart. Cool. When beef is cool enough to handle, cut into small pieces.

In a large saucepan, saute onions in butter until transparent. Add remaining ingredients except meat and buns. Bring to a boil. Immediately turn down heat and simmer for 30 minutes. Add beef to sauce, cover and heat for 20 minutes. Serve on toasted buns.

Yields 15–20 sandwiches

LEMON PEPPER SANDWICH LOAF

after game fare

Lemon Butter
1 cup butter, softened
2 Tbsp. snipped chives
1 tsp. grated lemon peel
1 Tbsp. lemon juice
Fresh pepper to taste

1 Tbsp. prepared mustard
2 tsp. poppy seeds

1 loaf unsliced bread
8 slices Swiss cheese
8 slices bacon, cooked and
  crumbled

Preheat oven to 350°. Mix ingredients for Lemon Butter and reserve 3 Tbsp. Mix mustard and poppy seeds with remaining butter. Slice bread horizontally. Spread both halves with butter-mustard mixture. Place cheese slices on bottom half of bread. Sprinkle bacon over cheese. Cover with top half of bread. Spread reserved butter on top crust. Bake on ungreased cookie sheet for 15–20 minutes. Slice to serve.

Yields 4 sandwiches

SKIERS' PICNIC

1 pkg. Pillsbury crescent
    rolls, separated

Reuben Filling
1 cup shredded corned beef
¾ cup shredded Swiss
    cheese
1 cup drained sauerkraut
1½ tsp. mustard

Ham Filling
1 cup chopped ham
¾ cup shredded Swiss
    cheese
2 green onions, chopped
1½ tsp. mustard

Crab Filling
1 pkg. (6 oz.) frozen crab,
    thawed, drained and
    chopped
½ cup mayonnaise
½ cup shredded cheddar
    cheese
1 Tbsp. minced green onion

Preheat oven to 375°. Combine the filling mixture of your choice. Spread mixture on the wide end of each triangle. Roll up each triangle, sealing ends. Bake on cookie sheet for 12–15 minutes. Can be frozen after baking. Thaw to room temperature and reheat 5–10 minutes at 350°.   Yields 8 rolls

Variations: You may brush tops of rolls with 1 beaten egg and 1 Tbsp. water; sprinkle with poppy seeds. You may slice triangles in half and wrap around a small amount of filling; bake as above and serve as an hors d'oeuvre. You may use 4 patty shells rolled out into 6-inch circles; place filling in each shell and fold in boat shape and bake 450° for 20 minutes.

ICED SANDWICHES

2 loaves Pepperidge Farm
  sandwich bread
2 cups ground ham
½ cup finely chopped olives
4 hard-boiled eggs, finely
  chopped
½ cup mayonnaise
¼ cup chopped onions
  (optional)
½ cup grated Swiss cheese
  (optional)
¼ cup finely chopped green
  pepper (optional)
8 Tbsp. butter, softened
Tomato slices (optional)

Icing
2 jars (4 oz. each) Kraft
  Olde English cheese
  spread
2 eggs
4 Tbsp. butter, melted

Cut each slice of bread into a round — three rounds per sandwich. Mix ham, olives, hard-boiled eggs and mayonnaise using, if desired, any of the optional ingredients. Lightly butter the tops of two rounds. Spread the buttered rounds with the ham mixture. For each sandwich, stack two ham rounds, placing a plain round on top.

Mix ingredients for icing. It is best to start with a whisk and finish with an electric mixer until smooth. Ice each sandwich, top and sides, with the cheese icing. Place on a cookie sheet. At this point, the sandwiches **must** be refrigerated 24 hours, or can be frozen until ready to use. Preheat oven to 350°. Bake sandwiches 20 minutes at 350°. If frozen, thaw before baking.   Serves 8

Variations: Can substitute chicken or crab for ham.

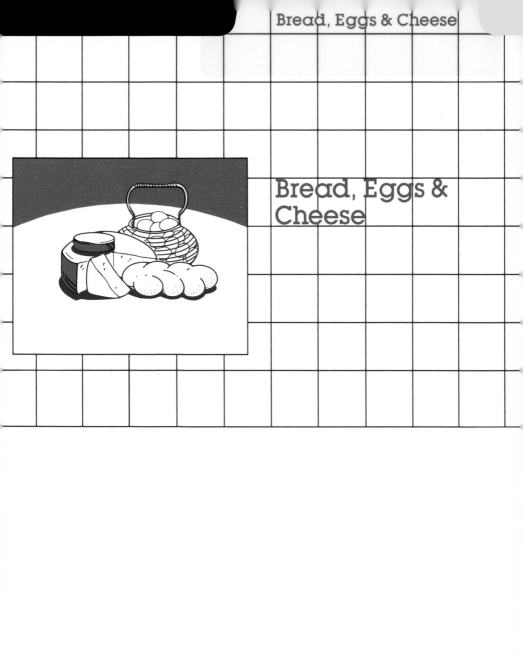

Bread, Eggs & Cheese

Bread, Eggs & Cheese

CHEESE BREAD

1 cup milk
1 Tbsp. butter
2 tsp. salt
2 cakes or pkgs. yeast
2 Tbsp. sugar
1¼ cups lukewarm water
6 cups flour
3 cups grated natural **extra**
    sharp cheddar cheese
Vegetable oil

Scald milk and stir in butter and salt. Pour into large bowl and cool to lukewarm. Sprinkle yeast and sugar into water. Stir until dissolved. Beat 2 cups flour into the milk mixture until smooth. Add cheese and yeast mixture and blend well. Add the remaining flour and beat until smooth.

Knead dough on lightly floured surface until smooth and elastic. Place in greased bowl, brush with vegetable oil and cover with a cloth. Let rise in warm place until doubled in size, about 1 hour.

Punch down and fold edges under. Cut in half and let stand 10 minutes. Shape into 2 loaves, and place in 2 greased loaf pans. Cover with a cloth and let rise for 1 hour.

Preheat oven to 400°. Bake 40 minutes or until browned and sides have pulled back from sides of pan.   Yields 2 loaves

 To scald milk or cream in microwave, place it in a glass measuring cup and cook on Medium 3–5 minutes.

Timely Tip:
To determine when dough has doubled in bulk, lightly press tips of two fingers ½-inch into dough; if the dents remain, the dough has doubled.

ENGLISH MUFFIN LOAVES

makes great toast

2 cups milk
½ cup water
5½–6 cups flour, divided
2 pkgs. active dry yeast
1 Tbsp. sugar
2 tsp. salt
¼ tsp. baking soda
Cornmeal

In medium saucepan, combine milk and water and heat until very warm (120°–130°). In large bowl combine 3 cups of flour, yeast, sugar, salt and baking soda. Add liquid to flour mixture gradually, beating constantly until batter is smooth. Gradually add enough of remaining flour to make a moderately stiff batter.

Preheat oven to 400°. Prepare 2 8½x4½ loaf pans by greasing lightly and sprinkling with cornmeal. Divide batter in half and place equal amounts in each pan. Sprinkle tops with additional cornmeal. Let stand in warm place until almost doubled in size, 1–2 hours. Bake at 400° for 25 minutes, until tops are lightly brown and loaves sound hollow when tapped. Remove from pans at once and let cool on wire rack. Freezes.

Yields 2 loaves

HERB BUTTER FOR FRENCH BREAD

1 loaf French or Italian
  bread (sourdough is
  great)
½ cup butter, softened
1 tsp. parsley
¼ tsp. oregano
¼ tsp. dill
1 clove garlic, minced
Parmesan cheese

Preheat oven to 400°. Mix together softened butter, parsley, oregano, dill and garlic. Cut bread into 1½-inch slices. Do not cut all the way through. Spread butter mixture on slices of bread. Sprinkle Parmesan cheese on top of loaf. Bake for 10 minutes at 400°.

Yields 1 loaf

OATMEAL BREAD

makes excellent toast, bread and rolls

2 cups oatmeal
4 cups boiling water
2 cakes yeast
1 cup lukewarm water
1 cup dark molasses
2 tsp. salt
6 Tbsp. butter, melted
11-12 cups white flour

Grease **very large** bowl. In it put oatmeal and cover with 4 cups boiling water. Let stand 20 minutes. Dissolve yeast cakes in 1 cup lukewarm water and let stand 20 minutes. Add yeast mixture plus molasses, salt, melted butter and flour to oatmeal.

Cover bowl and allow to rise until doubled, about 1½ hours. Stir down and let rise again, about an hour. Turn onto floured board and punch down (do not knead bread). Allow to rest for 10 minutes. Make into 3 loaves. Place in pans. Let rise to about double, approximately 1 hour. Bake at 350° for 50 minutes. Make ahead. Freezes.

Yields 3 large loaves

VIENNA STUFFED BREAD

1 loaf French or Italian bread
8 oz. Swiss or mozzarella
   cheese, or 4 oz. of each,
   grated
½ cup butter, melted
1 Tbsp. dry mustard
1 Tbsp. poppy seed
2 Tbsp. diced onion
½ tsp. Lawry's seasoned salt,
   or to taste
½ tsp. lemon juice

Preheat oven to 350°. Slice loaf horizontally almost all the way through. Layer cheese inside loaf. Melt butter and mix with the remaining ingredients. Slice bread on the diagonal almost through and place on aluminum foil. Pour butter mixture over bread. Wrap loaf in foil and bake for 30-40 minutes. Can reheat if made ahead.

Serves 8

 Melt ½ cup butter in microwave on High for 45 seconds.

WHOLE WHEAT BREAD

3 Tbsp. yeast (4 packets)
½ cup warm water
4 cups boiling water
1 Tbsp. salt
1 cup crushed or very fine
  bulgar
1 cup brown sugar
½ cup butter, sliced, or ½
  cup oil
6 cups whole wheat flour
4 eggs, beaten
8-10 cups white flour
Additional pats of butter for
  tops

Dissolve yeast in warm water. In **very large** mixing bowl, combine boiling water, salt, bulgar, brown sugar and butter. Let cool. Add whole wheat flour and mix well. Add eggs and yeast. Add white flour and mix until elastic. Knead until dough comes up from board without sticking. Lightly oil dough by oiling hands and smoothing over dough. Let rise in bowl with damp towel over top until doubled in size, 45-60 minutes. Punch down. Shape into 4 loaves and put in greased and floured pans. Let rise again until dough peeks over pans, 45-60 minutes.

Preheat oven to 350°. Slit tops of loaves and top with pats of butter. Bake at 350° for 1 hour. Let cool before slicing. Recipe can be cut in half. Freezes.

Yields 4 loaves

ATLANTA BANANA BREAD

flavor improves with time

1¼ cups sugar
¼ cup butter, softened
2 eggs
1 tsp. baking soda
4 Tbsp. sour cream
1¼ cups flour
1 cup mashed bananas
1 tsp. vanilla
1 tsp. salt

Preheat oven to 350°. Cream sugar and butter. Add eggs. In separate bowl, mix baking soda and sour cream. To sugar, butter and egg mixture add flour, bananas, vanilla and salt. Fold in baking soda and sour cream mixture. Pour into greased loaf pan. Bake at 350° for 1 hour. Make ahead. Freezes.

Yields 1 loaf

APRICOT BREAD

1¼ cups finely chopped
   dried apricots
1 cup apricot nectar
½ cup butter, softened
1 cup sugar
2 eggs
2¼ cups flour
1 tsp. baking soda
1 tsp. baking powder
½ tsp. salt
¾ cup chopped walnuts

Bring the apricots and nectar to a boil. Remove from heat and let stand 1 hour.

Preheat oven to 350°. Cream butter and sugar until smooth. Add eggs and blend. Add apricot mixture alternately with sifted dry ingredients. Add nuts. Bake in greased loaf pan at 350° for 40 minutes, then 325° for 20 minutes or until toothpick comes out clean. Cool on rack and refrigerate overnight before slicing. Store in the refrigerator. Make ahead. Freezes.

Yields 1 loaf

Variation: For mini-muffins, bake in greased tins at 350° 15-20 minutes. Makes 3-4 dozen.

IRISH BREAD

delicious warm

1 cup raisins
1 cup hot water
3 cups flour
3 tsp. baking powder
¼ tsp. salt
½ cup sugar
2 Tbsp. butter
1 egg
1¼ cups milk
Mixture of cinnamon and
   sugar to sprinkle

Preheat oven to 375°. Soak raisins in hot water until plumped, drain. Mix together flour, baking powder, salt and sugar. Cut butter into mixture. Add raisins, egg and milk. Mix well. Pour into greased loaf or cake pan. Sprinkle with cinnamon and sugar mixture. Bake 50-60 minutes at 375°. Cool, slice and serve.

Yields 1 loaf

Timely Tip:
If using glass loaf pans, reduce oven temperature by 25°F.

CROCODILE BREAD

a monster bread sculpture

1 loaf (16 oz.) frozen bread
  dough
2 raisins
Flour
Butter

Place dough on a lightly floured board and let sit at room temperature until it thaws and begins to rise, about 3 hours. Cut 1½ inches off each end of dough with scissors. Put dough on greased cookie sheet. Squeeze one end of dough to make a neck and pull to form a nose. Pull other end to shape a tail. Roll extra pieces of dough to form legs and put under body. Let dough rise until double, about 1 hour.

Heat oven to 350°. Cut mouth and fill with foil to keep it apart. Pinch some dough up to form an eye and press raisins into the dough. Snip dough with scissors to make crocodile skin. Kids like to do this. Bake 25–30 minutes. Freezes.   Yields 1 loaf

LEMON BREAD

½ cup shortening, softened
1 cup sugar
2 eggs, beaten
½ cup milk
1½ cups flour
1 tsp. baking powder
Dash salt
Grated rind of 1 lemon
Juice of 1 lemon
¼ cup sugar

Preheat oven to 325°. Combine shortening, 1 cup sugar, eggs, milk, flour, baking powder, salt and grated lemon rind. Pour into a greased loaf pan. Bake at 325° for 45 minutes. While bread is hot combine juice of lemon and ¼ cup of sugar and pour on top of bread. Serve warm or cool. Make ahead. Freezes.

Yields 1 loaf

STRAWBERRY NUT BREAD

great for gift giving

1 cup butter, softened
1½ cups sugar
1 tsp. vanilla
¼ tsp. lemon extract
4 eggs
3 cups flour, sifted
1 tsp. salt
1 tsp. cream of tartar
½ tsp. baking soda
1 cup strawberry jam
½ cup sour cream
1 cup chopped walnuts

Preheat oven to 350°. In mixing bowl, cream butter, sugar, vanilla and lemon extract until fluffy. Add eggs, one at a time, beating well after each addition. Sift together flour, salt, cream of tartar and baking soda. Combine jam and sour cream. Add jam mixture alternately with dry ingredients to creamed mixture, beating until well combined. Stir in nuts. Divide among five greased and floured 4½x 2¾x2¼ loaf pans. Bake in 350° oven for 50–55 minutes. Cool 10 minutes in pans. Remove from pans and cool completely on wire racks. Can be made ahead. Freezes.   Yields 5 mini loaves

RHUBARB BREAD

Bread
1½ cups brown sugar
⅔ cup oil
1 egg
1 tsp. salt
1 tsp. baking soda
1 tsp. vanilla
½ cup milk
½ tsp. lemon juice
2½ cups flour
2 cups finely diced rhubarb
1½ cups chopped nuts

Topping
½ cup sugar
½ tsp. cinnamon
1 Tbsp. butter, melted

Preheat oven to 350°. Combine brown sugar and oil. Stir in egg, salt and baking soda. Add vanilla, milk and lemon juice. Mix well. Add flour. Stir in rhubarb and nuts. Pour into 2 well-greased loaf pans. Combine topping ingredients and sprinkle on loaves. Bake at 350° for about 40 minutes. Do not overbake. Remove from pans after 3 minutes. Make ahead. Freezes.   Yields 2 loaves

PINEAPPLE ZUCCHINI LOAF

a very unusual zucchini bread

3 eggs
2 cups sugar
1 cup oil
3 Tbsp. vanilla
2 cups peeled, grated
   zucchini
3 cups all-purpose flour
1 tsp. baking powder
1 tsp. baking soda
1 tsp. salt
1 can (8 oz.) crushed
   pineapple, undrained
1 cup chopped pecans or
   walnuts
1 cup raisins, plumped in
   rum (optional)

Preheat oven to 350°. Grease and flour 2 9x5 loaf pans. Beat eggs until fluffy. Add sugar, oil and vanilla and blend well. Add zucchini. Sift together flour, baking powder, baking soda and salt, and add to batter. Stir in undrained pineapple and nuts. Mix well and turn into pans. Bake until toothpick inserted in center comes out clean, about 1 hour. Cool on wire rack before removing from pans. Wrap and store overnight to develop flavors before serving. Must be made ahead. Freezes.   Yields 2 loaves

EASY MONKEY BREAD

serve with brunch

2 loaves frozen Rhodes or
   Rich's bread dough,
   partially thawed
½ cup butter, melted
1 pkg. (3⅝ oz.) butterscotch
   pudding (**not** instant)
1 cup brown sugar
¾ tsp. cinnamon
½ cup chopped nuts (pecans
   are good)

Cut and shape frozen bread into ping-pong sized balls. Dip balls into melted butter, then into combined remaining ingredients. Place balls in greased bundt pan. Put pan in cold oven and let rise overnight. Remove dough from oven.

Preheat oven to 350°. Bake for 30–35 minutes. Let cool 10–15 minutes and turn out on a plate. Make ahead.   Serves 8

Variations: Add candied cherries and/or raisins for color.

APPLE COFFEE CAKE

perfect Christmas gift for neighbors

1 cup oil
2 cups sugar
3 eggs
3 cups flour
1 tsp. baking soda
1 cup chopped nuts
3 cups peeled, diced apples
1 cup raisins (optional)
½ tsp. salt
1 tsp. vanilla
1 tsp. cinnamon

Topping
Mixture of sugar and
    cinnamon for sprinkling

Preheat oven to 350°. Grease 2 8-inch cake pans. Mix together oil, sugar and eggs; set aside. Mix together flour, soda, nuts, apples, raisins, salt, vanilla and cinnamon. Combine the two mixtures. Divide the batter between the two cake pans and sprinkle top with mixture of sugar and cinnamon. Bake at 350° for 45 minutes. Make ahead. Freezes.   Serves 6-8

BLUEBERRY BUCKLE

a different coffee cake

½ cup unsalted butter,
    softened
¾ cup sugar
1 egg, room temperature
2 cups flour
2 tsp. baking powder
½ tsp. salt
½ cup whole milk, room
    temperature
1 pt. fresh blueberries or 2
    cups frozen
1 tsp. vanilla (optional)

Topping
½ cup sugar
⅓ cup flour
½ tsp. cinnamon
¼ cup unsalted butter, room
    temperature

Preheat oven to 375°. Grease and flour a 9-inch square pan. Mix butter and sugar together until creamy. Add egg and mix well. Sift together flour, baking powder and salt. Add dry ingredients to butter mixture alternating, ⅓ at a time, with the milk. Mix until well blended. Fold in blueberries. Spread batter in pan.

Topping
Combine all ingredients and sprinkle on top of cake. Bake at 375° for 45 minutes or until toothpick comes out clean when center is tested. Freezes.
                    Serves 8–10

SWEDISH TEA LOGS

1 pkg. active dry yeast
¼ cup warm water
2¼ cups all-purpose flour
2 Tbsp. sugar
1 tsp. salt
½ cup butter, melted
1 egg, beaten
¼ cup evaporated milk
¼ cup dark raisins

Filling
½ cup dark brown sugar
¼ cup butter, softened
½ cup flaked coconut
½ cup chopped pecans

Topping
2 Tbsp. butter, melted
¾ cup powdered sugar
3 Tbsp. evaporated milk

Dissolve yeast in warm water. Sift together flour, sugar and salt. Blend butter, egg and milk, and add to flour mixture. Stir well. Add raisins. Add yeast and stir. Cover dough with plastic wrap and refrigerate overnight.

Next day divide dough into 2 equal parts. Roll each out on floured board to a 9x12 inch rectangle. For filling, combine sugar and butter until smooth. Add coconut and pecans. Spread each rectangle with ½ filling. Roll from 12-inch side as a jelly roll. Place seam side down on a greased cookie sheet. Cover. Let rise for 1–1½ hours, or until double in size.

Preheat oven to 350°. Bake in 350° oven 25–30 minutes. Combine topping ingredients and spread over logs after taking out of oven. Must be made partially ahead. Freezes.   Yields 2 logs

Timely Tips:

For a different garlic bread, use any ½ package salad dressing mix mixed with ½ cup butter.

If bread sticks to whatever you are cooking or heating it in, wrap the bread and pan in a dry towel while hot, and let cool outside the oven for 5 minutes. Unwrap.

BAGELS MIT EGG

¾ cup warm water, divided
(105°–115°F)
1 tsp. sugar
1 pkg. dry yeast
2½ cups flour
1 Tbsp. vegetable oil
1 tsp. salt (optional)
2 eggs, divided
2 qts. water
2 Tbsp. sugar
2 Tbsp. cold water

Heat ¼ cup water to correct temperature. Add 1 tsp. sugar and yeast. Let stand until bubbly and spongy. Process flour, oil and salt 5 seconds with steel blade of food processor. Add yeast mixture and 1 egg. Process for 10 seconds. With the processor running, dribble ¼–½ cup warm water over dough to make it soft, but not sticky. Dough should ball. Turn around bowl 15 times.

Turn out on lightly greased surface, shape into ball, cover with plastic wrap and let stand 15 minutes. Divide dough into 12 equal parts. Roll each ball into 6-inch lengths, and form into doughnut shape by moistening the ends. (This dough likes to be handled.) Place bagels on greased cookie sheet and let them stand approximately 15 minutes at room temperature.

Heat oven to 425°. Bring 2 quarts water and 2 Tbsp. sugar to a boil in a wide pot. Slip 3 or 4 bagels slowly into boiling water, but do not break boil. When they rise to the surface, turn over gently and cook about 2 minutes longer or until puffy. Remove with slotted spoon to greased cookie sheet.

Cool on rack. Make ahead. Can be frozen.
Yields 12 bagels

Beat 1 egg and 2 Tbsp. cold water until mixed. Brush onto bagels. Bake until crisp and golden, about 20–25 minutes.

BLEU CHEESE BISCUITS

1 pkg. of 10 refrigerator
   biscuits.
⅓ cup unsalted butter,
   melted
4 oz. bleu cheese (or to
   taste), finely crumbled
Poppy or caraway seeds

Preheat oven according to biscuit instructions. Cut biscuits into quarters. Whisk together bleu cheese and melted butter. Dip biscuit quarters into mixture, shaking to remove excess. Put 3 or 4 quarters into each cup of a muffin tin. Sprinkle with poppy or caraway seeds. Bake according to biscuit instructions. Serve without butter.

Yields 10–12 rolls

BEST-EVER BLUEBERRY MUFFINS

6 Tbsp butter, softened
1¼ cups sugar
2 lg. eggs
2 cups flour, unsifted
½ tsp. salt
2 tsp. baking powder
½ cup milk
1 pt. blueberries, washed
   and divided
2 tsp. sugar

Preheat oven to 375°. Cream butter and 1¼ cups sugar. Add eggs, one at a time, and beat well. Sift flour, salt and baking powder together, and add to egg mixture alternately with the milk. Reserve ½ cup blueberries; dry remaining berries very well with paper towels. Crush the ½ cup blueberries with a fork and mix them into the batter by hand. Fold in remaining blueberries.

Grease the flat top of muffin pan and place paper cups in each well. Fill cups ⅞ full. Sprinkle with 2 tsp. sugar. Bake at 375° for 30 minutes or until nicely browned. Cool for 30 minutes before removing from pan. Store uncovered or they will be too moist the second day. Make ahead. Freezes.

Yields 16 muffins

REFRIGERATOR BRAN MUFFINS

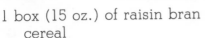

fresh-baked muffins in minutes

1 box (15 oz.) of raisin bran cereal
2 cups sugar
5 cups flour
5 tsp. baking soda
2 tsp. salt
1 cup raisins (optional)
4 eggs, beaten
1 cup oil
1 qt. buttermilk

Preheat oven to 400°. Grease muffin tins (do not use paper liners). Mix the raisin bran, sugar, flour, soda, salt and extra raisins (if desired) in a large bowl. Combine the beaten eggs, oil and buttermilk, and mix thoroughly with dry ingredients. Spoon batter into muffin tins. Bake at 400° for 15–20 minutes.

Batter will keep in air-tight container in refrigerator for up to six weeks for fresh baked muffins in minutes. Do not stir batter after it has been refrigerated — just scoop from the top.

Yields 4 dozen

For best flavor, bake on High at serving time. To bake muffins in microwave use the following time chart.

1 muffin 20–40 seconds
2 muffins ½–1½ minutes
4 muffins 1–2½ minutes
6 muffins 2–4 minutes

Bake muffins in muffin papers, in custard cups or microwave muffin dish. If cooking a single muffin, place in center of oven. If cooking more than one muffin, arrange in a circle spacing at least an inch apart. Do not cook more than 6 muffins at once. Remove from oven immediately.

Timely Tip:
If you discover you are out of baking powder, you may substitute the following: for every cup of flour, mix 2 teaspoons cream of tartar, 2 teaspoons baking soda, and ½ teaspoon salt. This mixture does not keep; use immediately.

NO BEAT POPOVERS

3 eggs
1½ cups milk
1½ cups flour, sifted
¾ tsp. salt
2 Tbsp. melted shortening
  (to grease pans)

Break eggs into bowl. Add milk, flour, and salt, mixing well with spoon. May have lumps. Fill well-greased muffin pans ¾ full. Put in center of cold oven and turn heat to 450°. Bake 45 minutes.   Yields 12 popovers

Helpful Hint: Start with cold pan, cold oven and don't peek for a full 30 minutes or more! Serve at once while piping hot. Can freeze leftovers.

Timely Tip:
If muffins stick to the baking tins, put tin on a wet towel; the muffins should come free in a few minutes.

LITTLE PUFFS

use your imagination

½ cup butter
1 cup boiling water
1 cup flour, sifted
4 eggs

Preheat oven to 425°. Combine butter and water in large saucepan and bring to a boil. Reduce heat and add flour all at once, stirring rapidly. Remove from heat, stirring until mixture thickens and leaves sides of pan. Add eggs one at a time, beating thoroughly after each addition. Beat whole mixture until it looks satiny and breaks off when spoon is raised.

Drop by scant teaspoonsful onto ungreased cookie sheet about 1 inch apart. Bake at 425° for 15 minutes or until golden brown. Cool. Slit and fill with mixture of your choice. Make ahead. Freezes.   Yields 4-6 dozen

ZUCCHINI GEMS

great for breakfast

¾ cup flour
¼ tsp. baking powder
¼ tsp. baking soda
¼ tsp. salt
¼ tsp. cinnamon
1 egg
½ cup sugar
¼ cup oil
1 cup unpeeled, grated
   zucchini
¼ cup raisins
¼ cup chopped walnuts

Preheat oven to 350°. Stir together flour, baking powder, baking soda, salt and cinnamon. Beat together egg, sugar and oil until blended. Add flour mixture to egg mixture. Add zucchini, raisins and walnuts. Stir only until dry ingredients are moistened. Fill greased muffin tins ⅔ full. Bake at 350° for 25 minutes. Loosen edges and remove from tins. Make ahead. Freezes.

Yields 8 muffins

INDIVIDUAL YORKSHIRE PUDDINGS

marvelous roast beef accompaniment

2 eggs
1 large clove garlic
   (optional)
½ tsp. salt
1 cup milk
2 tsp. butter, melted
1 cup flour
Beef drippings

Preheat oven to 425°. Beat eggs until frothy. Mash and add garlic. Stir in salt, milk, melted butter and flour. Beat until just smooth, but be sure mixture is smooth before stopping. Heat 1 pan of 12 muffin wells (or 2 pans of 6) in oven until very hot. Pour in beef drippings from roast pan to ¼ inch deep. Return pans to oven until very hot again. Remove from oven and pour in batter until ⅔ full. Return to oven. Bake 15 minutes at 425°. Reduce heat to 300° and continue baking 15 more minutes. Remove. This cannot be done in the same oven with roast. It works best to remove roast 30 minutes before serving in order to cook the puddings, if only one oven is available.

Yields 12 puddings

STICKY BUNS

Basic Roll Dough
1 cup warm milk (110°–115°)
1 pkg. active dry yeast
¼ cup warm water
   (110°–115°)
¼ cup butter, softened
¼ cup sugar
1 tsp. salt
3½ cups sifted flour
1 egg, well-beaten

Cinnamon Mixture
5 Tbsp. butter, softened
½–¾ cup brown sugar
2 tsp. cinnamon

Caramel Topping
1 cup brown sugar
½ cup butter, melted
2 Tbsp. light corn syrup
½ cup chopped pecans or
   walnuts
¼ cup butter, melted

Dough
Warm milk. Soften yeast in ¼ cup warm water and let stand 10–15 minutes. Put butter, sugar, and salt in a medium bowl. Pour warm milk over the ingredients, stirring to melt butter and dissolve sugar. Allow to cool.

Stir in 1 cup flour. Add yeast mixture and egg. Mix thoroughly. Add remaining 2½ cups flour to make a soft dough. Turn dough out on lightly floured surface, cover and allow to rest 5–10 minutes. Knead until smooth and elastic, 2–3 minutes. Shape into a ball and place in a greased bowl. Roll ball over to coat it with grease. Cover with wax paper and a towel and allow to stand in a warm place until double in bulk, about 1½ hours.

Assembly
Punch dough down. Roll out to 8x24 rectangle, or 2 8x12 rectangles. Spread dough with 5 Tbsp. softened butter. Mix brown sugar and cinnamon and sprinkle over butter. Beginning with long side, roll dough tightly. Press edges to seal.

Mix caramel topping ingredients together. Spread evenly on bottom of 2 8-inch square greased baking pans or divide evenly into 32 muffin tins. Cut rolled dough into about 32 slices. Place cut side down on caramel topping. Brush tops with melted butter. Cover with wax paper and a towel and allow to stand in a warm place until double in size, about 45 minutes.

Preheat oven to 375°. Bake for 20–25 minutes. Turn hot pan upside down at once on a platter and leave it alone for a minute to allow topping to dribble down. Can make ahead. Freezes.   Yields 32 buns

COTTAGE CHEESE PANCAKES

1 tsp. baking powder
1 cup flour
¼ tsp. salt
¼ cup sugar
4 eggs, beaten
1 lb. container small curd
    cottage cheese
⅓ cup milk

Sift together baking powder, flour, salt and sugar. Add eggs, Combine cottage cheese and milk. Add to flour mixture and mix until blended. Fry ¼-cup dollops in a greased electric skillet at 325° until bubbles appear. Flip and cook until done.
Yields 12–15 pancakes
Serves 4

OVEN FRENCH TOAST

terrific way to serve a group French toast

2 eggs, beaten
1 cup milk
¼ tsp. nutmeg or cinnamon
Dash salt
8 slices French bread

In shallow bowl combine eggs, milk, nutmeg or cinnamon and salt. Dip bread slices in mixture, coating both sides. Place on buttered baking sheet. Broil 4–5 minutes on each side or until golden brown.   Serves 4

CALORIE COUNTER'S CHEESE BLINTZES

from La Costa Spa

Filling

1 egg, beaten
1½ cups pot or farmer cheese
1 tsp. vanilla
¼ tsp. cinnamon

Crèpes

2 eggs
1½ cups skim milk
1 cup flour
Melted diet margarine

Filling

Mix filling ingredients in small bowl. Chill.

Crèpes

Combine eggs and milk in small mixing bowl. Beat or whip until smooth. Add flour and salt. Beat until smooth. Preheat a 7-inch nonstick skillet over medium-high. Coat surface with vegetable food spray. Pour 2 Tbsp. batter into pan, tipping and rolling pan to quickly spread the batter evenly. Pour off any excess batter. Cook until lightly browned on bottom and dry on top. Remove from pan. Repeat to make 12 crèpes.

Assembly

Preheat oven to 400°. Spoon 2 Tbsp. filling mixture on browned side of each crèpe. Fold two opposite edges over filling. Fold in remaining ends, envelope style, to enclose filling completely. Arrange blintzes, fold side down, in a shallow baking dish. Brush lightly with diet margarine, if desired. Bake in a 400° oven for 25-30 minutes. Serve hot.

175 calories each.   Serves 6

GERMAN PANCAKE

3 eggs, room temperature
½ cup sifted flour
½ tsp. salt
½ cup milk, room
  temperature
2 Tbsp. butter, melted
Lemon wedges
100% pure maple syrup,
  heated

Preheat oven to 450°. Beat eggs in large bowl. Sift flour and salt into eggs in 4 batches, blending after each addition until smooth. Add milk in 2 batches, blending after each. Stir in butter. Generously butter 9 or 10-inch glass pie plate. Pour in batter. Bake at 450° for 20 minutes. Reduce temperature to 350° and continue cooking 10 minutes. Do not open oven between temperature changes. Slice and serve immediately. Pass hot syrup and lemon wedges. Be sure to try both flavors together. Great!   Serves 4

GIANT POPOVER

dramatic when removing from oven

4 Tbsp. butter
½ cup flour
½ cup whole milk
2 eggs, beaten
Dash of cinnamon or nutmeg
1 Tbsp. powdered sugar
1½ tsp. lemon juice

Preheat oven to 425°. Melt butter in 11-inch ovenproof skillet (cast iron is best) in hot oven. (Do not let butter get brown.) Combine flour and milk in bowl. Add eggs and cinnamon or nutmeg. Stir flour, milk and egg mixture — batter should be lumpy. Add batter to hot skillet. Bake at 425° for 15-20 minutes until popover is puffed up high and light golden brown. Immediately remove from oven and spinkle with lemon juice and powdered sugar. (Popover will fall when taken from oven.)
                    Serves 2-3

LEMON PANCAKES

2 cups flour
2½ Tbsp. sugar
1½ Tbsp. baking powder
½ tsp. salt
2 egg yolks
2½ cups milk
2 Tbsp. butter, melted
1 lemon rind, grated
2 Tbsp. lemon juice
2 egg whites, beaten stiff
Dash of nutmeg (optional)

Sift together flour, sugar, baking powder and salt. Beat egg yolks until creamy. To egg yolks add milk, butter, lemon rind and lemon juice. Stir egg yolk mixture into dry ingredients using few strokes. Fold in egg whites. Prepare as normal pancakes (on hot griddle). Serve with melted butter and honey.   Serves 4

ANN MARIE'S EGGS FLORENTINE

2 pkgs. (10 oz. each) frozen
    chopped spinach, cooked
    and well-drained
½ tsp. salt
2 Tbsp. coffee cream
3 Tbsp. butter, divided
⅓ cup grated Parmesan
    cheese, divided
1½ Tbsp. flour
Dash pepper
⅛ tsp. nutmeg
1 cup milk
6 eggs

Preheat oven to 350°. Butter an 8x8x2 baking dish. Combine salt, cream, 1 Tbsp. butter and spinach, and mix well. Turn into baking dish, making an even layer. Make 6 small depressions in spinach spacing evenly; sprinkle each with 2 Tbsp. grated cheese.

Melt remaining butter in small saucepan; remove from heat. Add flour, dash of salt, pepper and nutmeg, stirring until smooth. Gradually stir in milk; bring to a boil, stirring. Reduce heat and simmer one minute. Carefully break an egg into each depression in spinach. Spoon sauce completely over top. Sprinkle with rest of cheese. Bake, uncovered, 15 minutes or until eggs are set and top is golden.   Serves 6

SPINACH CREPES
great for brunch

Crêpe Batter
4 eggs
1 cup milk
1 cup water
2 cups flour
2 Tbsp. butter, melted
Pinch nutmeg
1 pkg. (10 oz.) frozen
   chopped spinach,
   thawed, drained and
   dried
Salt and pepper to taste
1 cup grated Swiss cheese

Sauce
2 Tbsp. butter
½ cup flour
1 cup milk
Pinch salt
Pinch nutmeg
1 cup grated Swiss cheese

Crêpe Batter
Put eggs, milk and water in food processor and blend. Gradually add flour while machine is running. Add butter, nutmeg, spinach, salt and pepper. Blend thoroughly. Batter should be consistency of thick cream. If too thick, add a small amount of water. Let batter stand 1 hour. Make crêpes. They may be frozen or refrigerated between wax paper.

Assembly
Sprinkle 1 Tbsp. grated cheese in center of each crêpe. Fold in half, then in half again to form triangle. Arrange crêpes in shallow casserole and sprinkle with remaining cheese. Cover with foil and reheat in low oven for 15 minutes or until hot and bubbling. Uncover. Dribble sauce over crêpes and bake 5 more minutes.

Sauce
Melt butter in saucepan, add flour and stir 1-2 minutes. Remove from heat and add milk, salt, and nutmeg. Whisk until smooth. Return to heat and add cheese. Heat until cheese melts.

May be made ahead. Freezes.
Serves 8-10

BASIC OMELET FOR ONE

3 eggs
1 Tbsp. water
¼ tsp. salt
Dash pepper
1 Tbsp. butter
¼ tsp. favorite herb
   (optional)

Beat together ingredients with a fork until the mixture is blended but not frothy. Heat butter in an 8-inch skillet over medium until sizzling and brown. Lift and tilt the pan to coat the sides. Pour in egg mixture. Continue to cook over medium heat, stirring the top of uncooked eggs with a fork. Shake skillet to keep mixture moving. When the eggs are set on the bottom, but still shiny and soft on top, remove the skillet from the heat. Spoon ½ cup desired filling on one side of eggs. With a spatula, lift the uncovered side and fold over filling. Turn onto plate and garnish.

OVEN OMELET FOR TWO

6 eggs, separated
6 Tbsp. water
Salt and pepper to taste
2½ Tbsp. butter

Preheat oven to 325°. Beat egg yolks with water and seasoning. Beat egg whites until stiff and fold into egg yolks. Heat butter in oven proof 10-inch skillet. Brown slightly. Pour egg mixture into skillet and bake at 325° for 15 minutes. Top with filling and bake 5 more minutes. Fold omelet and serve. Filling can be folded into egg mixture before baking.

FILLINGS FOR BASIC OMELETS

fillings are for 2 basic omelets or 1 oven omelet

Vegetable
2 Tbsp. butter
1 tsp. lemon juice
⅛ tsp. tarragon
1 cup cooked vegetables
 (broccoli and mushrooms,
 cauliflower and carrots,
 zucchini and tomatoes)

Vegetable
Melt butter, stir in remaining ingredients. Heat to warm vegetables. Spoon mixture onto omelet.

Benedict
2 oz. Canadian bacon, cut
 into strips
2 Tbsp. sliced green onion
1 Tbsp. butter
½ cup hollandaise sauce

Benedict
Saute bacon and onion in butter. Before filling omelet, stir half hollandaise into mixture. Spoon mixture onto omelet. After turning omelet out onto plates, top with remaining sauce.

Jarlsberg
½ cup grated Jarlsberg
 cheese
½ cup quartered cherry
 tomatoes
¼ cup sliced green onion

Jarlsberg
Combine ingredients and spoon onto omelet.

Fruit and Cheese
1 tsp. cornstarch
2 tsp. honey
3 Tbsp. orange juice
1 tsp. lemon juice
¾ cup fresh fruit (sliced
 strawberries, orange
 sections, halved grapes)
¼ cup grated cheese

Fruit and Cheese
Combine cornstarch and honey in a saucepan. Stir in juices and cook until thickened. Stir in fruit. Spoon fruit onto omelet and fold over. Top with cheese.

Spinach
2 Tbsp. finely chopped onion
2 Tbsp. butter
1 pkg. (10 oz.) frozen
 chopped spinach, cooked,
 drained dry
⅛ tsp. nutmeg
½ cup grated cheddar, Swiss
 or Parmesan

Spinach
Saute onion in butter until tender. Stir in spinach to heat. Stir in nutmeg. Spoon onto omelet and sprinkle with cheese. Fold omelet over and turn onto plate.

PROVISIONAL EGG CASSEROLE

2 cups soft white bread
   crumbs
1¾ cups milk
8 eggs, slightly beaten
Salt and pepper to taste
6 Tbsp. butter, divided
½ tsp. Lawry's seasoned salt
1 pkg. (8 oz.) sliced Swiss
   cheese
½ cup dry bread crumbs
8 slices bacon, cooked and
   crumbled

Preheat oven to 450°. Soak soft bread crumbs in milk. Drain the milk and save. Add drained milk to eggs, and add salt and pepper to taste — be conservative.

In large frying pan, melt 4 Tbsp. butter. Add the eggs. To cook, hold skillet over high heat. Do not scramble, just cook until slightly thick. Add the soaked bread to eggs and stir to blend. Pour the mixture into a greased 12x7 baking dish. Sprinkle Lawry's seasoned salt over surface. Cover with cheese slices. Melt 2 Tbsp. butter and add dry bread crumbs and crumbled bacon. Spead mixture over cheese slices. Bake 15 minutes at 450° . Allow to set a few minutes before serving.

To freeze, assemble casserole ahead of time, but do not bake. Wrap well and freeze. Thaw before baking.   Serves 8–10

Variation: An additional 8 slices bacon can be cooked, crumbled and added to egg mixture.

LEEK PIE

good for brunch

Pastry
2 cups unsifted flour
½ tsp. salt
¾ cup unsalted butter, cold
2 Tbsp. sour cream
¼ cup ice water

Filling
5 leeks, white part only,
   trimmed and washed —
   divided
¼ cup butter
5 eggs
2 cups half and half
Dash nutmeg
½ tsp. salt
¼ tsp. white pepper

Pastry
Combine all ingredients in food processor and process until a ball of dough forms. Wrap dough in wax paper and chill for 2 hours.

Preheat oven to 375°. Roll out the pastry on a floured surface to a round that is large enough to cover the bottom and sides of an ungreased 10-inch pie pan. Line pan with the dough and make a high, fluted edge. Line pie shell with cheesecloth and fill with uncooked rice, or use pie weights. Bake for 15 minutes. Remove weights and cool.

Filling
Thinly slice 4 leeks and sauté in butter for 10 minutes. Spread the leeks and their juices over the bottom of the pie shell. Beat next 6 ingredients until well-blended and pour over leeks. Bake uncovered at 375° for 40–45 minutes, until puffed, brown and firm in the center.

Cook remaining leek in enough salted water to cover, 10–15 minutes or until tender. Drain. Slice in rounds, to garnish top of pie. Cool 5–10 minutes before cutting.   Serves 6–8

PEELABLE HARD-BOILED EGGS

Eggs
Enough water to cover eggs

Place eggs and cool water in saucepan on a hot burner. Bring to a boil; cover and turn off heat immediately. Allow pan to stand on burner for 30 minutes. Drain. Cool eggs. Peel eggs.

Timely Tips:
Pierce the round end of an egg with a pin to prevent cracking when boiling.
Add 1 tsp. vinegar to the water when poaching eggs. This will keep the egg whites from disintegrating.

MUSHROOM SAUSAGE QUICHE

1 10" unbaked pastry shell
1 med. onion, chopped
1 Tbsp. butter
¾ lb. bulk Italian sausage
6 eggs
1 cup cream
4 oz. cream cheese, softened
½ tsp. salt
¼ tsp. cracked pepper
¼ tsp. nutmeg
½ lb. fresh mushrooms, chopped
Paprika
½ cup grated Swiss cheese

Preheat oven to 375°. Cook onion in melted butter until soft. Add sausage and brown until crisp and finely crumbled. Pour off excess grease and set aside. Beat eggs and add cream, cream cheese, Swiss cheese, salt, pepper and nutmeg. Stir in mushrooms and sausage. Pour into unbaked 10-inch pastry shell. Sprinkle with paprika. Bake at 375° for 40–45 minutes or until toothpick comes out clean.

Yields 1 10-inch quiche

QUICHE BY A "REAL" MAN

1 9" Pet Ritz deep dish pie
  shell, unbaked
½ lb. diced ham, or cooked
  bacon, sausage, chicken or
  tuna
1 green pepper, diced or 1
  pkg. (10 oz.) frozen
  spinach or broccoli,
  cooked and drained
1 can (4 oz.) of mushrooms,
  drained
¼-½ cup diced onion
  (optional)
4 eggs
1 Tbsp. flour
½ tsp. salt
Dash of pepper
1 cup cottage cheese
1 cup grated Swiss cheese
1 cup grated colby or
  cheddar cheese
¼ cup butter, melted
¼ cup Parmesan cheese for
  sprinkling (optional)

Preheat oven to 450°. Bake pie shell for 5 minutes. Spread meat and vegetables in bottom of shell. Add mushrooms and onion. Beat eggs, flour, salt, pepper and cottage cheese together. Add grated cheeses. Pour egg mixture over ingredients in shell. Drizzle butter on top. Bake at 375° for 45 minutes-1 hour. Sprinkle Parmesan cheese on top during last 10 minutes of baking. Freezes.

Yields 1 9-inch quiche

SPINACH QUICHE

1 9" pie shell, unbaked
1 pkg. Stouffer's spinach
  soufflé, thawed
2 eggs, beaten
3 Tbsp. milk
2 tsp. chopped onion
½ cup sliced fresh
  mushrooms
¾ cup cooked, crumbled
  and drained Italian
  sausage
¾ cup grated Swiss cheese

Preheat oven to 400°. Mix all ingredients together in order given. Pour into 9-inch pie shell or quiche dish lined with pastry. Bake at 400° for 25-30 minutes. Cool 10 minutes before serving.

Yields 1 9-inch quiche

JERRE'S VEGETABLE PIE

Crust
1¼ cups flour
2 tsp. baking powder
½ tsp. salt
½ tsp. sweet basil
½ cup shortening
½ cup sour cream

Filling
1 pkg. 10 oz. frozen
  chopped broccoli, cooked
  and drained (or equal
  amount of cooked fresh
  broccoli)
1 Tbsp. chopped onion
1 cup grated cheddar cheese
2 med. tomatoes, sliced
¾ cup mayonnaise

Crust
Combine flour, baking powder, salt and basil. Cut in shortening until mixture is crumbly. Add sour cream and mix well. Chill. Pat dough into greased 9-inch pie pan or quiche dish.

Filling
Preheat oven to 450°. Place filling ingredients in pastry crust in the order given, ending with tomato slices. Spread with mayonnaise. Bake at 450° for 10 minutes, then 350° for 30 minutes or until lightly brown and bubbly. Yields 1 9-inch quiche

ITALIAN ZUCCHINI PIE

this recipe won the Miami Pillsbury Bake-Off

1 can (8 oz.) Pillsbury
  crescent rolls
2 tsp. Dijon mustard
4 Tbsp. butter
4 cups thinly sliced zucchini,
  unpeeled
1 cup finely chopped onion
½ cup chopped fresh
  parsley, or 2 Tbsp. flakes
½ tsp. salt
½ tsp. black pepper
¼ tsp. garlic powder
¼ tsp. dried basil
¼ tsp. oregano
1 egg, well-beaten
8 oz. muenster, mozzarella or
  Swiss cheese, grated, or
  combination of any

Preheat oven to 350°. Press crescent rolls into 10-inch glass pie plate to make a pie crust. Spread Dijon mustard on crust. Bake 10 minutes, checking after 5 minutes to see if it is laying smoothly. If not, prick with fork. Sauté filling ingredients in butter, folding in cheese and egg last. Pour mixture into crust. Bake uncovered at 350° until center tests firm, approximately 30–40 minutes. Freezes.   Serves 6

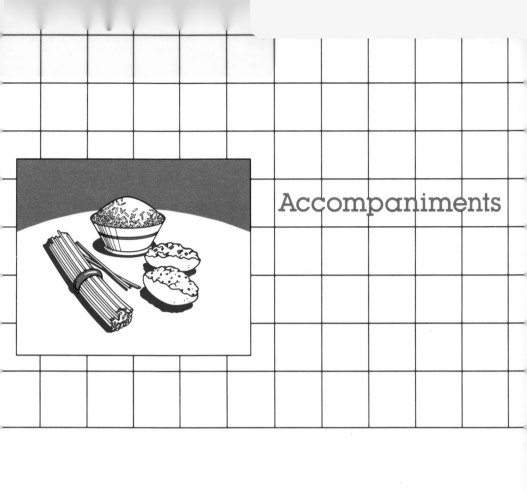

Accompaniments

FETTUCCINE ALFREDO

1 lb. green noodles, cooked
   and drained
½ cup butter
1 Tbsp. flour
1 cup whipping cream
⅔ cup grated Parmesan
   cheese
Pepper, freshly ground

In a medium saucepan, melt butter. Stir in flour and cook 1 minute. Add cream and cook, stirring until slightly thickened, about 4 minutes. Add cheese and stir until melted. Place hot noodles in a heated bowl or deep platter. Pour cheese sauce over and toss lightly. Grate pepper over the top.   Serves 8

 To microwave sauce, place butter in a glass dish. Microwave on High 30–45 seconds. Stir in flour, cook 1 minute. Add cream and stir. Cook 1 minute, stirring after 30 seconds. Add cheese and cook 1–2 minutes, stirring after 1 minute. Pour sauce over hot noodles and toss lightly.

LINGUINE

¼ cup butter
2 Tbsp. olive oil
4 shallots, minced
2 cloves garlic, minced
½ cup clam juice
1 can (6½ oz.) minced
   clams, including liquid
1 green onion, minced (use
   entire onion)
2 Tbsp. minced fresh parsley
   or 2 tsp. dried parsley
½ tsp. cornstarch
¾ lb. linguine, cooked al
   dente
Parmesan cheese, freshly
   grated

Combine butter and oil in large skillet over medium heat. Add shallots and garlic and sauté until garlic is golden and shallots soft. Add clam juice, minced clams and their liquid, green onion and parsley. Reduce heat and simmer until clams are heated, about 3 minutes. Combine cornstarch with a little water and add to sauce to thicken slightly. Add linguine and toss thoroughly. Sprinkle with freshly grated Parmesan cheese and serve immediately.
          Serves 2 as main course
                4 as first course

Variations: May use different types of pasta or substitute
          oysters for clams.

FETTUCCINE AND SPINACH

1 pkg. (8 oz.) fettuccine, cooked and drained
1 pkg. (10 oz.) frozen chopped spinach, thawed and drained
1 clove garlic, finely chopped
¼ cup vegetable oil
1 tsp. Wyler's Chicken Flavor Instant Onion Soup mix
½ cup water
1 cup small curd cottage cheese
½ tsp. basil
½ tsp. salt
¼ cup grated Parmesan cheese
¼ cup grated Romano cheese
1 Tbsp. chopped parsley

In a large skillet, cook spinach and garlic in oil, stirring frequently. Dissolve soup mix in water. Stir soup mixture, cottage cheese, basil and salt into skillet with spinach. Stir over low heat until blended. Toss spinach mixture with hot noodles, Parmesan and Romano cheeses. Serve in heated dish, garnished with parsley.   Serves 6-8

BAKED NOODLES

8 oz. thin egg noodles, cooked and drained
½ cup small curd cottage cheese
1 cup sour cream
1 sm. onion, diced
1 Tbsp. Worcestershire sauce
½ cup grated Parmesan cheese

Preheat oven to 350°. Butter a 2½-3-quart casserole dish. Mix noodles with all other ingredients and place in casserole. Bake uncovered for 30-45 minutes. Can be assembled 1-2 hours ahead.   Serves 8

 Butter a 2½-3-quart glass casserole dish. Place noodles and other ingredients in dish. Cook, uncovered, 10-12 minutes, turning every 3-4 minutes.

LINGUINE WITH VEGETABLES

1 cup ricotta cheese
⅓ cup grated Romano
   cheese, plus additional
   for dusting
3 tsp. salt, divided
1 med. head of cauliflower,
   cut into flowerets
1 med. bunch of broccoli,
   cut into flowerets
1 cup olive oil
6 cloves garlic, minced
1 lb. fresh mushrooms, sliced
½ tsp. crushed red pepper
1 lb. linguine noodles

Combine ricotta and Romano cheeses. To large pot of boiling water, add 1 tsp. salt, cauliflower, and broccoli. Cover and return to a boil. Then uncover and cook until crisp-tender, about 7 minutes. Remove vegetables to a colander with a slotted spoon. Reserve liquid for cooking linguine.

Heat olive oil and garlic in large skillet. When garlic is lightly browned, stir in mushrooms, 2 tsp. salt and red pepper. Sauté about 5 minutes. Stir in vegetables and continue cooking a few more minutes. If mixture becomes too dry, add some of the reserved liquid.

Meanwhile, heat reserved cooking liquid to boiling. Add more water if necessary. Add linguine and cook for 10-12 minutes; drain. Combine linguine and vegetables. Divide among shallow individual serving bowls. Top with cheese mixture and dust with additional Romano cheese.   Serves 10

CURRIED NOODLES

1 lb. med. noodles, cooked and drained
½ cup butter
⅓ cup flour
1 Tbsp. curry powder
1 Tbsp. salt
¼ tsp. pepper
6 cups milk
1 cup sour cream
½ cup prepared chutney, chopped

Preheat oven to 375°. Melt butter in saucepan; remove from heat. Whisk into melted butter the flour, curry powder, salt and pepper. Gradually stir in milk. Return mixture to heat; bring to a boil, stirring with whisk. Remove from heat. Stir in sour cream and chutney. Combine noodles and sauce; mix well. Place in a 3-quart casserole dish. Bake covered for 20–30 minutes or until bubbly. Can make sauce well ahead. Reheat in double boiler and toss with cooked noodles just before serving, or bake as above.   Serves 10-12

 You may use the microwave for the last step by placing noodles and sauce in a glass 3-quart casserole. Cook on High, uncovered 5–6 minutes, stirring after 3 minutes until bubbly.

HERBED SPINACH NOODLES

1 lb. spinach noodles
4 Tbsp. butter
1 Tbsp. dill
1 tsp. Spice Islands Fines Herbes
½ tsp. onion salt
½ tsp. garlic salt
Freshly ground pepper to taste
Grated Parmesan cheese

Cook noodles in a large pot of gently boiling, salted water for 12–15 minutes, depending on type of noodles or package directions. Drain. Return to pot. Toss with butter, dill, Fines Herbes, salt and pepper. Pass Parmesan cheese.
Serves 10–12

Variation: May use tomato noodles.
Helpful Hint: May use more butter and/or other herbs.

PARMESAN CREAM NOODLES

2 Tbsp. butter, softened
1 clove garlic, finely
    chopped
4 oz. cream cheese, softened
½ cup hot water
2-3 Tbsp. white wine
1 Tbsp. fresh lemon juice
1 tsp. chopped sweet basil
    or ½ tsp. dry basil
1 Tbsp. chopped parsley
Salt and pepper to taste
½ cup freshly grated
    Parmesan cheese (do not
    use canned Parmesan
    cheese)
6-8 oz. egg noodles, cooked
    and buttered (should
    equal 4 cups)

In a medium-sized heavy sauce-pan, over medium heat, melt butter with garlic until garlic just begins to brown, about 4 minutes. Add cream cheese slowly, stirring constantly until it begins to melt. Stir in hot water, wine and lemon juice. Add basil, parsley, salt and pepper. Stir in Parmesan cheese until mixture is smooth and creamy. Pour over hot buttered noodles and serve immediately.   Serves 4

Helpful Hint: Recipe may be "put on hold" by turning off heat and covering saucepan after Parmesan cheese is added. If mixture dries out, add equal parts water and white wine, while heating to achieve desired consistency before putting on noodles.

SPAGHETTI CARBONARA

makes an excellent main dish or side dish

4 Tbsp. butter
1 lb. spaghetti, cooked and
    drained
2 eggs
½ lb. bacon, cooked and
    crumbled
¼ cup grated Parmesan
    cheese
Salt and pepper to taste
Garlic salt to taste

Melt butter in a large pan. Add cooked spaghetti. Break eggs into spaghetti and stir vigorously. Add bacon and Parmesan cheese. Season with salt, pepper and garlic salt to taste.
                Serves 4

PASTA PRIMAVERA

as created by Charity Suczek

2 tomatoes, peeled and sliced
1 Tbsp. olive oil
⅓ tsp. chopped garlic
½ cup chopped parsley
Salt and pepper to taste
10 mushrooms, sliced
1 cup zucchini, sliced
1 cup snow peas
1 cup green peas
1½ cups broccoli stems and flowers, sliced
¾ tsp. chopped garlic
2 Tbsp. olive oil
1 lb. spaghetti or other pasta
1 Tbsp. olive oil
½ pt. whipping cream
½ cup butter, melted
½ cup grated Parmesan cheese
⅓ cup chopped fresh basil (or 2 Tbsp. dried basil)
½ cup pine nuts

Blanch zucchini, snow peas, green peas and broccoli and drain. Sauté tomatoes in 1 Tbsp. olive oil with garlic, parsley, salt and pepper. Set aside. In another skillet heat 2 Tbsp. olive oil and sauté mushrooms, zucchini, snow peas, green peas and broccoli just long enough to heat vegetables.

Cook pasta according to package directions, adding 1 Tbsp. olive oil to cooking water. Drain. In saucepan, heat cream, butter, Parmesan and basil. With a fork, slowly mix in cooked pasta.

Place pasta on a large, deep platter. Top with vegetables. Pour tomato mixture over vegetables and top with pine nuts. Serve at room temperature.

Serves 8–10

CAVIAR AND SMOKED SALMON PASTA

may be served as a course by itself before the entrée

1 lb. box bow-shaped noodles
1½ cups whipping cream
½ lb. salmon lox or salmon butter
1 Tbsp. grated Parmesan cheese
Nutmeg to taste
1 jar (3 or 4 oz.) caviar

Prepare noodles according to package directions. Warm the cream. Break up salmon and add it to the cream. Add Parmesan cheese and nutmeg to taste. Drain noodles and return to pan or serving dish. Pour cream and salmon mixture over noodles and toss lightly. Carefully add caviar and serve immediately.

Serves 6–8

CHEESE POTATOES

3 lg. potatoes, peeled and
　sliced
Salt and cracked pepper to
　taste
4 slices bacon, cooked crisp
　and crumbled
½–1 lg. onion, sliced
½ lb. American cheese,
　cubed (about 2 cups)
½ cup butter
2½-foot square piece of
　heavy-duty aluminum foil

Preheat oven to 350°. Mix together potatoes, salt, pepper,
bacon, onion, cheese and butter
in heavy-duty aluminum foil.
Leave hole in top of package for
steam to escape. Bake at 350° for
1 hour **or** place on grill over hot
coals for 1 hour.　　Serves 6

DILLY ESCALLOPED POTATOES

2 lbs. lg. baking potatoes
½ cup cooked and crumbled
　bacon
½ cup sliced onion
3 Tbsp. butter
3 Tbsp. flour
½ tsp. seasoned salt
½ tsp. white pepper
¼ tsp. dill seed
1¾ cups milk
1 cup shredded sharp
　cheddar cheese

Preheat oven to 350°. Peel
potatoes and cut into thin slices.
Layer potatoes, bacon and onion
in a greased, shallow 2-quart
casserole. In medium saucepan,
melt butter. Add flour, seasoned
salt, pepper and dill seed. Cook,
stirring frequently. Gradually
add milk, stirring constantly, until sauce is thickened. Add
cheese and stir until melted.
Pour sauce evenly over potatoes.
Bake covered 45–60 minutes.
Uncover and bake for an additional 15–20 minutes. Can be
assembled 1–2 hours before baking.　　Serves 6–8

 Layer potatoes; make sauce; pour over potatoes.
Sprinkle with paprika. Cook on High, covered
for 20–25 minutes, rotating casserole twice.
Remove from oven and let stand at least 5
minutes before serving.

POTATOES DELUXE

2 lbs. frozen hash brown
   potatoes
¼ cup diced onion
1 can (10¾ oz.) cream of
   chicken soup, undiluted
2 cups sour cream
½ cup butter, melted
8 oz. sharp cheese, grated
Salt and pepper to taste
Paprika

Let potatoes thaw for 30 minutes. Preheat oven to 375°. Mix onion, soup, sour cream, butter and cheese. Combine with potatoes in large bowl. Add salt and pepper to taste. Pour into a greased 9x13 pan. Sprinkle with paprika. Bake uncovered for 1 hour.

Serves 8–10

AUNT GINNY'S ROQUEFORT DICED POTATOES

very rich, but superb

5 Tbsp. butter
5 Tbsp. flour
2 cups coffee cream, scalded
⅔ cup chicken broth
5 Tbsp. grated Parmesan
   cheese
1 tsp. salt
½ tsp. white pepper
2 lbs. all-purpose **or** new
   potatoes, cooked, peeled
   and diced
1 pkg. (4 oz.) Roquefort
   cheese, or less to taste
4 Tbsp. butter, or more to
   taste, melted
Paprika

Preheat oven to 425°. Melt butter in top of double boiler. Add flour and cook about 2 minutes over low heat, stirring constantly. Remove from heat and gradually stir in scalded cream and then chicken broth. Return to burner and cook sauce, stirring constantly, until thick and smooth. Stir in Parmesan cheese, salt and white pepper. Fold in potatoes. Pour into lightly greased 9x13 casserole and sprinkle generously with crumbled Roquefort, melted butter and paprika. Bake uncovered for 15 minutes at 425° until cheese bubbles.   Serves 6–8

Helpful Hints: Use Pam to grease casserole. Potatoes may be boiled ahead, but should be room temperature when added to sauce.

 Scald coffee cream in microwave by placing in glass measuring cup and microwaving 3–5 minutes on Medium.

KING ARTHUR POTATOES

6 med. potatoes, unpeeled
6 med. cooking onions
½ cup butter, melted
1 clove garlic, crushed
¾ tsp. salt
¼ tsp. pepper
¼ tsp. celery seeds
¼ tsp. paprika

Preheat oven to 400°. Cut potatoes and onions into ¼-inch slices. In a single layer alternate slices, slightly overlapping, in a 13x9x2 baking dish. Combine butter, garlic, salt, pepper, and celery seeds; drizzle over potato and onion slices. Cover and bake at 400° for 40 minutes. Sprinkle with paprika, and bake uncovered another 20 minutes. Can be assembled 1 hour before baking.   Serves 6–8

NEW POTATOES IN MUSTARD AND WATERCRESS SAUCE

18 sm. new potatoes
3 Tbsp. butter
3 Tbsp. flour
1 cup coffee cream
1 cup milk
2½ Tbsp. prepared mustard
1 cup chopped watercress
Salt and pepper to taste

Boil potatoes in their skins. Combine butter, flour, cream, and milk in top of a double boiler. Cook until thickened to the consistency of heavy cream. Add mustard and salt and pepper to taste. Peel cooked potatoes and add to sauce. Add watercress. Serve very hot.
Serves 5–6

BAKED & STUFFED POTATO VARIATIONS

Baking Instructions

Bake the potatoes until tender at any convenient temperature between 350° and 450° for 50-60 minutes.

Pierce medium baking potato in several places. Place on paper towel in center of oven. Bake on high 4-4½ minutes, turning over half-way through cooking time. Potatoes are cooked if you can push their sides in slightly. Remove from oven, wrap in foil, and let stand 10 minutes before serving or preparing stuffing.

Ideas For Stuffing Potatoes

Slit the baked potatoes lengthwise and scoop out the pulp. Mash thoroughly, adding 1 tsp. milk or cream for each potato. Season with salt and pepper. Blend in any of the following suggestions. Refill potato skins. Brush with butter. Place on baking sheet and reheat at 450° for 8-10 minutes.

1. Sour cream, grated Romano cheese, crumbled bacon and chopped green onions.
2. Grated cheddar cheese, sour cream, snipped fresh parsley and chopped chives.
3. Sour cream, cream cheese, cooked chopped spinach, chopped green onions and nutmeg.
4. Sautéed mushrooms, chopped chives and grated Parmesan cheese.
5. Grated Swiss cheese and diced ham.
6. Butter and crumbled bleu cheese.
7. Chopped green onions, nutmeg and unpeeled chopped tomatoes.
8. Chopped spinach, sautéed mushrooms, minced onions and grated cheddar cheese.

Ideas For Topping Potatoes

Slit baked potatoes and top with any of the following:

1. Chili, grated cheddar cheese and chopped green onions.
2. Cooked and crumbled spicy bulk sausage, grated American cheese, chopped green chilies, shredded lettuce and chopped tomato.
3. Sautéed onions, minced garlic, shredded zucchini, grated Parmesan cheese and chopped tomatoes.
4. Guacamole, crumbled bacon and chopped tomatoes.
5. Cream cheese, chopped pecans, chopped green onions, and flaked crab meat.
6. Any appropriate Stouffers or other prepared frozen entrée.
7. Sour cream and caviar.

MINIATURE POTATO PANCAKES

may also be served as an hors d'oeuvre

6 med. potatoes (2 lbs.), peeled and cut up
2 eggs
1 sm. onion, quartered
⅓ cup flour
1 tsp. salt
Bacon fat or cooking oil for frying

Serve With: A side dish of sour cream, lingonberry preserves or applesauce.

Serves 6

Preheat oven to 300°. Using the shredding blade of a food processor, put the potatoes (a few at a time) into the tube. Press down with the plunger and continue adding potatoes until all are grated. Place grated potatoes in a mixing bowl and cover with cold water to prevent discoloration. Put the steel blade in the food processor. Put eggs, onion, flour, and salt into food processor and blend for 10 seconds. Drain potatoes, pat dry, and return to mixing bowl. Stir the batter into the potatoes.

Put the bacon fat or cooking oil in skillet and heat. When the oil is hot (approximately 375°), add batter by teaspoons. Cook on both sides until crisp and lacy. Make a few at a time and transfer to a heat-proof platter in a 300° oven to keep warm.

CANDIED PECAN YAMS

6 med. yams, baked, peeled
   and sliced
¼ cup butter, melted
½ cup light corn syrup
3 Tbsp. dark brown sugar
¼ cup chopped pecans

Preheat oven to 375°. Place sliced yams in a greased 1½-quart baking dish. Mix together butter, syrup, sugar and pecans, and pour over yams. Bake uncovered at 375° for 30–40 minutes, basting frequently.

Serves 6–8

Poke each yam several times with a fork. Place yams on a paper towel, in a circle, 2 inches apart in microwave. Bake 15–20 minutes or until you can push in on sides of potato. Remove from oven; wrap in foil for at least 10 minutes. Melt butter on High for 30–45 seconds. Add corn syrup, brown sugar and pecans. Peel and slice yams. Place sliced yams in round or oblong baking dish. Pour butter mixture over yams. Cook on High, covered by wax paper, 6–8 minutes turning halfway through cooking time. Baste every 2–3 minutes while cooking.

LEMON RICE

¼ cup butter
1 cup thinly sliced celery
¼ cup sliced green onion
¼ cup chopped parsley
2 tsp. grated lemon peel
½ tsp. salt
Pepper
3 cups hot cooked rice

Melt butter. Stir together with celery, onion, parsley, lemon peel, salt and pepper. Toss with rice and serve.   Serves 4

Serve With: Shrimp in Mornay Sauce

Timely Tip:
1 tsp. lemon juice to each quart of water will keep rice fluffy when cooking.

SWEET POTATO SOUFFLÉ
old southern recipe

1 lg. can (2 lb. 8 oz.) sweet
    potatoes, whole cut
⅓ cup white sugar
½ cup brown sugar
2 Tbsp. butter
½ cup milk

Topping
4 Tbsp. butter
½ cup brown sugar
¼ cup flour
½ cup chopped pecans

Preheat oven to 350°. Heat sweet potatoes in pan on stove. Simmer until fork tender if necessary. Drain sweet potatoes. Mash and add white and brown sugars, butter and milk. Beat until smooth. Place mixture in 8-inch casserole.

Topping
Melt butter. Mix in brown sugar, flour and pecans. Sprinkle over sweet potato mixture.

Bake uncovered at 350° for 30 minutes. May be assembled ahead and refrigerated or frozen. Bring to room temperature before baking.
Serves 8–10

GREEN RICE

2 eggs, well-beaten
1 sm. onion, grated or
    chopped
1 cup grated cheddar cheese
½ tsp. sugar
½ tsp. salt
¼ cup butter, melted
1 cup whipping cream
3 cups cooked rice (either
    hot or cold)
3-4 Tbsp. minced parsley

Preheat oven to 375°. Combine all ingredients and mix thoroughly. Place in a 1½-quart glass or porcelain casserole, and bake uncovered for 1 hour or until top is browned. Serves 8–10

Place cooked rice and other ingredients in a round or oblong glass casserole dish. Sprinkle with paprika and cook on High, uncovered, 15-18 minutes, or until set in the center.

SPECIAL RICE CASSEROLE

½ cup butter
1 sm. can (2½ oz.)
    mushrooms, sliced
1 can (8 oz.) water chestnuts,
    sliced
1 cup uncooked rice
1 can (10¾ oz.) onion soup,
    undiluted

Preheat oven to 350°. Drain mushrooms and water chestnuts, reserving liquids. Sauté mushrooms and water chestnuts in butter. Add onion soup and reserved liquids plus water to equal 1 cup. Add rice and mix well. Place in 1-quart casserole dish and bake covered for 1 hour. Can be assembled ahead and refrigerated or frozen. Bring to room temperature before reheating.   Serves 6

Helpful Hint: May substitute a package of dehydrated onion soup mix plus 1 cup water for the can of soup.

TURMERIC RICE

wonderful with Spicy and Sweet Chicken

⅓ cup sliced green onions
1 Tbsp. butter
1½ cups uncooked long-
    grain rice
3 cups water
1 Tbsp. lemon juice
1½ tsp. beef bouillon
    granules
¼ tsp. salt
¼ tsp. ground turmeric
½ cup raisins
Parsley

In a large saucepan, cook onion in butter until tender. Add rice and cook until golden. Add water, lemon juice, beef bouillon, salt and turmeric. Heat until boiling. Reduce heat, cover and simmer 15 minutes. Remove from heat, add raisins and let stand for 10 minutes. Garnish with parsley.   Serves 8

Variations: Add water chestnuts or nuts (peanuts or cashews).

WILD RICE WITH MUSHROOMS AND ALMONDS

2 Tbsp. butter
½ cup uncooked long-grain
   wild rice
¼ cup slivered almonds
1 Tbsp. chopped chives or
   scallions
1½ lbs. fresh mushrooms,
   sliced
1½ cups chicken broth

Preheat oven to 300°. Put butter, rice, almonds, chives or scallions and mushrooms in a frying pan and cook over medium heat, stirring occasionally, until almonds are lightly browned. Put heated mixture in 1-quart casserole and add broth. Cover and bake at 300° for about 2 hours. Stir with fork several times during baking and just before serving. Serves 4–6

RICE AND CHEESE FLORENTINE

3 cups cooked rice, cooled
1 pkg. (10 oz.) frozen
   chopped spinach, thawed
   and drained
4 eggs, slightly beaten
2 cups creamed cottage
   cheese
⅓ cup grated Parmesan
   cheese
½ tsp. salt
⅛ tsp. pepper
3 Tbsp. dry bread crumbs
¼ cup chopped pecans

Preheat oven to 350°. Combine rice, spinach, eggs, cottage cheese, Parmesan cheese, salt and pepper. Turn into a buttered 13x9 pan. Sprinkle with crumbs. Top with pecans. Bake at 350° for 20 minutes, or until set. Serves 6

 Place ingredients in a glass or microwave 9x13 dish, cooking on High 10–12 minutes, turning dish every 3–4 minutes.

You may divide ingredients into two round 9-inch glass dishes. Cook each separately, on High 6–8 minutes, turning every 3 minutes.

GARLIC GRITS

1 cup quick grits
6 oz. Merkt's Cheddar
   Cheese with Garlic
½ cup butter
2 eggs
½ cup milk
Pepper
Garlic powder
Parmesan or Romano cheese

Preheat oven to 350°. Cook grits according to package directions. Stir in cheese and butter and remove from heat. Allow to cool. Stir in well-beaten eggs and milk. Season with pepper and garlic powder to taste. Pour into 2-quart buttered casserole and dust with grated Romano or Parmesan cheese. Bake uncovered at 350° for 1 hour or until it has the consistency of a baked custard.   Serves 6

Variation: Can use grated sharp cheddar cheese and 1 clove of garlic, crushed.

BAKED APPLE SLICES
side dish for ham and pork

6-8 apples
1 Tbsp. butter
½ cup sugar
¼ tsp. cinnamon
1 tsp. flour
¼ tsp. allspice

Preheat oven to 350°. Core and slice apples. Place in buttered, oven-proof casserole. Dot apples with butter. Mix sugar, spices and flour. Sprinkle on apples. Cover apples and bake at 350° for one hour.   Serves 6

Variation: Can fry apples in butter, add sugar and spices, and top with whipped cream.

 Prepare as above and microwave on High 8–10 minutes, rotating dish every 2–3 minutes. Let stand 2–3 minutes.

MUSHROOM STUFFING

use as a side dish or turkey stuffing

¼ cup butter
1½ cups chopped onion
1 cup diced celery
2 lbs. mushrooms, chopped
Salt and pepper to taste
1 pkg. (8 oz.) stuffing mix
½ cup chopped parsley

Preheat oven to 350°. Melt butter in a large skillet over medium heat. Sauté onion and celery 3–4 minutes. Add mushrooms, salt and pepper. Cook, stirring, for 5 minutes. Prepare stuffing according to package directions. Add vegetables and parsley. Mix thoroughly. Place in greased casserole and bake covered 45 minutes to 1 hour at 350°.

Will stuff a 12–15 lb. turkey.

Use microwave for final cooking step. Bake covered on High 10–12 minutes.

Timely Tip:
For a no-baste crispy skinned turkey, wash and dry fowl. Rub inside and out with Hellmann's mayonnaise.

APRICOT DATE CHUTNEY

improves with age

¾ cup coarsely chopped
  dates
½ cup coarsely chopped
  dried apricots
½ cup white vinegar
⅓ cup brown sugar, firmly
  packed
¼ tsp. garlic powder
¼ tsp. ground cloves
⅛ tsp. ground ginger
1 sm. tart apple, peeled and
  coarsely chopped

In a stainless steel or enameled saucepan (DO NOT USE ALUMINUM because of vinegar), slowly simmer all ingredients, except apple, for 10 minutes, stirring occasionally. Add apple and simmer 4–5 minutes longer. Cool to room temperature, and store refrigerated in glass jar 6–8 weeks.   Yields 1½ cups

Serve With: Excellent accompaniment to all curries, pork roast, chops and roast chicken. Also superb over cream cheese as an hors d'oeuvre.

CHUTNEY PEACHES

excellent garnish with meat

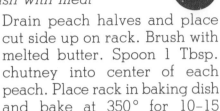

Canned peach halves
Bottled chutney
Butter, melted

Drain peach halves and place cut side up on rack. Brush with melted butter. Spoon 1 Tbsp. chutney into center of each peach. Place rack in baking dish and bake at 350° for 10–15 minutes or until heated through.

Helpful Hint: Nice way to served chutney with a curry dish.

MANDARIN ORANGE CASSEROLE

½ cup butter, softened
1 cup sugar
4 eggs
1 can (8 oz.) crushed
   pineapple
1 can (11 oz.) mandarin
   oranges
6 slices Pepperidge Farm
   white bread, cubed with
   crusts on

Preheat oven to 350°. Cream butter and sugar. Add eggs one at a time. Add undrained oranges and pineapple. Fold in bread cubes. Place in a greased 2-quart casserole. Bake un-covered 50–60 minutes at 350°.
Serves 6

ESCALLOPED PINEAPPLE

1 cup butter
1 cup brown sugar
½ cup sugar
3 eggs
4 cups cubed cinnamon
   raisin bread
1 can (20 oz.) pineapple
   chunks, drained

Preheat oven to 350°. Mix but-ter, sugar and eggs. Fold in bread cubes and pineapple. Turn into 2-quart glass dish. Bake uncovered at 350° for 30 minutes. Serves 8–10

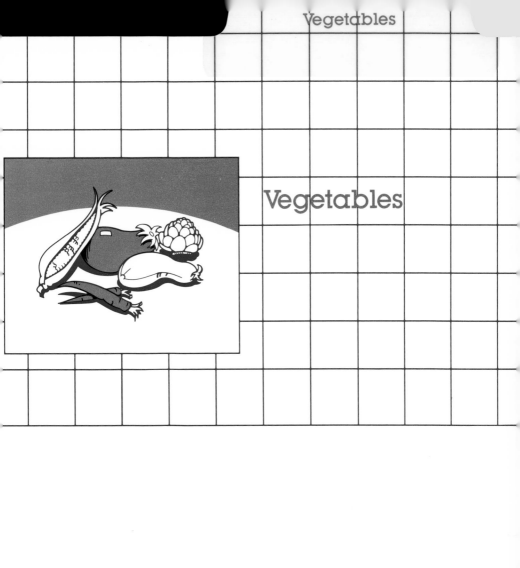

Vegetables

Vegetables

BAKED ACORN SQUASH VARIATIONS

use your imagination

½ acorn squash per person

Orange Filling
6 halves acorn squash
3 Tbsp. butter
4½ tsp. grated lemon peel
4½ tsp. grated orange peel
4½ tsp. orange juice
4½ tsp. lemon juice
4½ tsp. sherry

Brown Sugar
6 halves acorn squash
6 Tbsp. butter
6 Tbsp. brown sugar

Apple
6 halves acorn squash
1 can (1 lb.) sliced apples
¾ cup brown sugar
Nutmeg to taste

Honey
6 halves acorn squash
¼ cup honey
2 Tbsp. butter
1 Tbsp. Worcestershire
    sauce
¼ cup chopped nuts

Vegetable
Fill cooked squash with
    buttered peas or your
    favorite vegetable

Preheat oven to 350°. Split and seed squash. Place split squash upside down on a buttered baking pan. Bake at 350° about 40 minutes. Turn squash over and prick with a fork, being careful not to break the skin. Combine ingredients of your favorite filling and spoon into cavity of squash. Return to oven for 15–20 minutes or until hot.

Split squash and scoop out seeds. If squash is hard to cut, microwave whole squash 1–2 minutes on High. Arrange 3 squash halves on round glass platter. Cover with wax paper and cook 8–10 minutes. Repeat with rest of squash halves. Prick with fork and fill with favorite filling. Cover with wax paper and microwave on High an additional 2–3 minutes.

ANNIE'S ARTICHOKES

2 cans (8½ oz. each)
artichoke hearts, drained
2 pkgs. (10 oz. each) frozen
French-cut green beans,
thawed
1 can (10¾ oz.) mushroom
soup, undiluted
1 can (8 oz.) water
chestnuts, drained and
sliced
1 can (4 oz.) mushrooms,
drained
½ cup Italian dressing
½ cup butter, melted

Preheat oven to 350°. Combine all ingredients except melted butter. Pour into buttered casserole dish. Drizzle melted butter over top of casserole. Bake uncovered 30 minutes.

Serves 8–10

Variation: If artichokes come marinated, may use the marinade instead of Italian dressing.
Helpful Hint: May vary amount of ingredients according to preference.

ASPARAGUS CASSEROLE

1½ lbs. fresh asparagus, or
3 pkgs. frozen tips
2 Tbsp. butter
½ cup mayonnaise
¼ tsp. salt
⅛ tsp. pepper
⅛ tsp. dry mustard
Juice from half a lemon
½ cup buttered bread
crumbs
½ cup grated Parmesan
cheese

Preheat oven to 375°. Cook asparagus until just tender. Do not overcook. Drain and place in a greased 8x8x2 pan. Melt butter until just brown. With a whisk, blend in mayonnaise, seasonings, and lemon juice until smooth. Pour over asparagus. Top with bread crumbs and sprinkle with Parmesan cheese. Bake uncovered 20–30 minutes. Can be assembled in the morning and baked before serving. Serves 6

 Cook each package of asparagus on High 3–4 minutes. Bake entire recipe on High 3–4 minutes or until bubbly.

ASPARAGUS SESAME

1 bunch asparagus, cut in 1″ diagonal slices
2 Tbsp. oil
¼ cup sesame seeds, toasted

Heat oil over high heat in wok or skillet. Be careful not to burn oil. Stir fry asparagus quickly, keeping it slightly crunchy. Remove from heat, toss with sesame seeds, and serve immediately.   Serves 2

Variation: Add onions to taste.

BATTER FOR DEEP FRYING VEGETABLES

1 cup flour
1 tsp. baking powder
1 Tbsp. soy sauce
¾ tsp. Tabasco
1 Tbsp. salad oil
1 cup stale beer

Combine all ingredients. Allow batter to stand 30 minutes or more to thicken. Dip assorted vegetables in batter and deep fry until golden. Drain and lightly salt. Keep vegetables warm in 200° oven while frying remainder. If batter gets too thick, add a little more beer.
                   Yields 2 cups

Variations: Great for onion rings, mushrooms, cauliflower and/or zucchini.
Helpful Hint: Vegetables must be washed and thoroughly dried before frying.

BAKED BEANS

¼ lb. bacon
1 can (46 oz.) B & M Baked Beans
2 Tbsp. dried chopped onion
2 Tbsp. prepared mustard
¾ cup brown sugar
1 cup ketchup

Preheat oven to 350°. Brown, drain and crumble bacon. Combine all ingredients and pour into a casserole or bean pot. Cover. Bake 1½ hours, uncovering last 15–20 minutes. Make ahead.   Serves 10

SWEET AND SOUR GREEN BEANS

tastes best when reheated on the second or third day

2 lbs. fresh green beans cut into 1" pieces
5 slices bacon cut into ½" strips
¾ cup sugar
1 cup vinegar
½ tsp. salt
¼ cup chopped onion

Cook beans in a small amount of water in a covered saucepan until tender, 15–20 minutes. Drain. Fry bacon pieces until crisp. Remove pan from heat and add sugar to the bacon and drippings. Stir in vinegar and salt. Heat until sugar is dissolved. Add bacon mixture and the onion to the green beans. Simmer 5 minutes.   Serves 8

DILLED BEETS WITH SOUR CREAM

1 bunch of beets (1½–2 cups, cooked and diced)
3 Tbsp. butter
⅓ cup very thinly sliced green onions, including tops
½ rounded tsp. dill weed
½ tsp. salt to taste
Dash fresh ground pepper
1 dollop sour cream per serving

In lightly salted water, gently boil beets in their skins until tender, about 35–45 minutes. Peel, cool and dice into ½-inch cubes. Melt butter in saucepan. Add beets, onion, dill, salt and pepper, stirring to mix. Heat thoroughly. Serve with a generous dollop of sour cream. Can be made ahead. Serves 4

Helpful Hint: Peeled, cooled whole beets can be refrigerated up to 48 hours before dicing.

BEETS L'ORANGE

even if you don't like beets, you will love these

1½ tsp. cornstarch
⅓ cup sugar
Pinch salt
⅓ cup orange juice
  concentrate
2 Tbsp. butter
2 cans (16 oz. each) sliced
  beets, drained, reserving
  2 Tbsp. juice

Combine cornstarch, sugar and salt. Mix well with wire whisk until all lumps are dissolved. Add orange concentrate and stir until smooth. Cook mixture over medium heat, stirring constantly until thickened. Add butter and simmer 6 minutes. Stir in beets and juice. Heat thoroughly. Can be made ahead 2 or more days.   Serves 6–8

BROCCOLI CASSEROLE

good for a luncheon

2 pkgs. (10 oz. each) frozen
  chopped broccoli, thawed
  & drained well
1 pint small curd cottage
  cheese
½ lb. sharp cheddar cheese,
  grated
6 Tbsp. flour
4–5 Tbsp. chopped onion
1 tsp. salt
Pepper to taste
¼ cup butter, melted
6 eggs

Preheat oven to 350°. Mix all ingredients except eggs and smooth into a casserole. Recipe may be prepared to this point up to 2 days ahead, covered and refrigerated. Beat eggs and pour over casserole. Bake uncovered one hour until eggs are firm.
          Serves 6

 Frozen vegetables may be defrosted in the microwave. If vegetables are wrapped in foil, remove foil and place vegetables in glass dish in microwave. If vegetables are packaged in a paper box, pierce box and place it in the microwave. Cook 10 oz. packages on High for 3–5 minutes.

BROCCOLI DUCHARME

1½ lbs. broccoli
10 Tbsp. butter, divided
3 Tbsp. flour
1¼ tsp. granulated chicken
   bouillon mix
1¼ cups milk
¼ cup sherry
½ cup water
1½ cups Pepperidge Farm
   stuffing mix
½ cup chopped walnuts

Preheat oven to 350°. Cut broccoli into flowerets with 1½ inch stems. Cook to crisp stage only. Drain broccoli and place in a 1½-quart baking dish.

Melt 6 Tbsp. butter in a saucepan over low heat. Make a roux by adding flour and bouillon granules. Stir until ingredients are blended smoothly, without lumps. Allow to bubble. Slowly add milk and cook, stirring constantly, until thickened. Add sherry and mix well.

Pour sauce over broccoli. Melt 4 Tbsp. butter. Add water, then stuffing and toss to mix well. Blend in walnuts. Spread stuffing on top of broccoli and sauce. Bake uncovered for 30 minutes.
Serves 6

CARROTS AND GRAPES

4 cups sliced carrots
3 Tbsp. sugar
½ cup butter
Salt to taste
¾ cup halved white seedless
   grapes
Snipped parsley to garnish

Preheat oven to 300°. Blanch carrots in ½ cup very lightly salted boiling water. They should be quite crisp. Drain and place in casserole with remaining ingredients except parsley. Bake in 300° oven until thoroughly heated, about 20–30 minutes. Sprinkle with fresh snipped parsley and serve.
Serves 8

DILLED CABBAGE

8 cups finely shredded white
    cabbage
½ cup minced onion
4 Tbsp. butter
6 oz. Philadelphia cream
    cheese, softened, cut into
    small bits
3 Tbsp. dill
Salt and pepper to taste

In large pot, blanch shredded cabbage in enough boiling salted water to cover for 3 minutes. Drain cabbage in colander and refresh under cold water. Return to pot. Sauté onion in butter until softened. Add to cabbage, toss well. Add cream cheese and cook over low heat until cheese has melted. Stir in dill weed, check for salt and pepper and toss well. Simmer 2 minutes more.   Serves 6–8

CARROTS WITH PISTACHIOS AND COINTREAU

5 Tbsp. butter, divided
½ cup natural pistachio
    nuts, shelled and skinned
1 lb. carrots, cut diagonally
    into ¼" slices
3 Tbsp. water
1 tsp. salt
¼ cup Cointreau

Melt 2 Tbsp. butter in medium skillet over medium-high heat. Add nuts and sauté 1 minute. Remove from heat and set aside. Combine carrots, 3 Tbsp. butter, water and salt in large saucepan, and bring to a boil over medium-high heat. Reduce heat to medium-low, cover and cook 5 minutes until carrots are tender.

Transfer carrots to heated serving bowl using slotted spoon, and keep warm. Boil cooking liquid until reduced to 2 Tbsp. Pour over carrots. Add nuts and Cointreau. Toss gently and serve. Can be prepared earlier and reheated in microwave.
                    Serves 6

DILL CARROTS

a simple, elegant complement for dinner

6 med. carrots, thinly sliced
2 heaping Tbsp. butter
2 tsp. sugar
⅛ tsp. salt
3–4 oz. water
2 tsp. dill

Combine all ingredients in top of double boiler and cover. Bring bottom water to a boil and reduce to medium–low. Simmer about 45 minutes, or until carrots are tender when tested with a fork. Be sure not to let water boil dry in bottom of double boiler. Reheats well.

Serves 6–8

CELERY CASSEROLE

4 cups celery cut in 1″
  pieces
1½ cups grated mild
  cheddar cheese
1 can (10¾ oz.) cream of
  chicken or celery soup,
  undiluted
½ cup toasted sliced
  almonds

Preheat oven to 325°. Parboil celery in lightly salted water for 5 minutes. Drain and put in 8x11 baking dish. Sprinkle cheese over top and spread on soup. Top with sliced almonds. Bake uncovered 35 minutes or until it bubbles in the center.

Serves 6

 Bake casserole in a microwave dish on High 7–8 minutes, rotating once or twice until bubbly.

CORN PUDDING

old Southern recipe

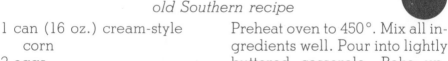

1 can (16 oz.) cream-style
  corn
2 eggs
2 Tbsp. flour
4–6 Tbsp. butter
¼ cup sugar, or to taste
Pinch of salt

Preheat oven to 450°. Mix all ingredients well. Pour into lightly buttered casserole. Bake uncovered 20–30 minutes. Let set 3–4 minutes before serving.

Serves 6–8

LAYERED EGGPLANT BAKE

1 Tbsp. vegetable oil
1 lg. onion, coarsely chopped
1 lg. green pepper, cut in 1" squares
1 sm. eggplant, peeled and cut in 1" cubes
½ lb. mushrooms, sliced
1 lg. tomato, chopped
1 tsp. thyme
1 tsp. salt
Dash pepper
1 cup packaged herb-seasoned stuffing
2 cups grated Swiss cheese, divided

Preheat oven to 350°. In a large skillet, heat oil over medium heat. Add onion and green pepper and sauté 3 minutes. Add eggplant and mushrooms, and sauté 3 minutes more. Stirring constantly, add tomato, thyme, salt and pepper, and cook 1 minute.

Spread stuffing over bottom of buttered 9x13 casserole. Layer half the vegetable mixture and 1 cup cheese over stuffing. Top with remaining vegetables. Bake uncovered at 350° for 30 minutes. Sprinkle with the remaining cheese, and bake uncovered another 10 minutes.

Serves 8

 In a 10-inch Corning skillet, heat oil 30–45 seconds. Add onion and green pepper and sauté, covered, 3 minutes. Add eggplant and mushrooms and sauté, covered, 3 minutes more. Stir in tomato, thyme, salt and pepper and cook 2 minutes.

Spread stuffing over bottom of buttered 9x13 glass casserole. Layer half vegetable mixture and 1 cup cheese over stuffing. Top with remaining vegetables. Loosely cover with wax paper. Cook on High for 7–10 minutes, rotating dish every 2–3 minutes. Sprinkle with remaining cheese and cook an additional 1–2 minutes until cheese melts.

RATATOUILLE

¼ cup olive oil
4 cloves garlic, crushed
1 bay leaf
1 med. onion, chopped
Salt and pepper to taste
1 sm. eggplant, peeled and
  cubed
3 Tbsp. Burgundy wine
½ cup tomato juice
1 tsp. basil
1 tsp. marjoram
½ tsp. oregano
Dash crushed rosemary
2 sm. or 1 med. zucchini,
  cubed
2 green peppers, cut into
  strips or cubes
2 med. tomatoes, cut into
  chunks
2 Tbsp. tomato paste
½ cup chopped fresh
  parsley

Heat olive oil in large heavy cooking pot. Add garlic, bay leaf and onion. Salt lightly. Sauté over medium heat until onion begins to turn transparent. Add eggplant, wine, tomato juice and herbs. Stir well, cover and cook over low heat 10–15 minutes. When eggplant is fork tender, add zucchini and peppers. Cover and simmer 10 minutes. Add tomatoes and tomato paste, salt and pepper and mix well. Continue to stew until all vegetables are tender. Before serving, remove bay leaf and stir in parsley.   Serves 4–6

MINTED PEAS

2 pkgs., 10 oz. each frozen
  peas, or 3 cups fresh
  peas
3 Tbsp. mint jelly
Salt and pepper to taste
2 Tbsp. butter

Cook peas. Melt mint jelly in saucepan over low heat. Add drained hot peas and toss. Add salt, pepper and butter to taste.
          Serves 8

 Cook each package of frozen peas in microwave for 5 minutes on High. Melt mint jelly in a glass dish on Medium for 30–45 seconds. Add peas and toss; add salt and pepper to taste.

MUSHROOM CASSEROLE

6 slices white bread
½–¾ cup butter, divided
1½ lbs. mushrooms, sliced
½ cup chopped onions
½ cup chopped celery
½ cup chopped green
   pepper
2 eggs
¼ cup milk
½ cup Hellmann's
   mayonnaise
1 can (10¾ oz.) cream of
   mushroom soup,
   undiluted
¾ cup grated cheddar
   cheese

Remove crusts and butter 6 slices of bread on both sides. Cut into 1 inch cubes. Sauté sliced mushrooms in remaining butter. Combine mushrooms, onions, celery, green pepper and mayonnaise.

In ovenproof pan, place layer of cubed bread. Cover with mushroom mixture. Mix eggs and milk and pour over top. Refrigerate 2 hours or overnight.

Preheat oven to 350°. Before baking, spread casserole with cream of mushroom soup and top with cheddar cheese. Bake uncovered at 350° for 50–60 minutes. Serves 8–10

BAKED MUSHROOMS

a great winter vegetable dish

½ lb. mushrooms
2 Tbsp. white wine
2 cans (8½ oz. each)
   artichoke hearts, drained
6 slices bacon, cooked and
   crumbled
2 cans (8 oz. each) tomato
   sauce
2 Tbsp. pine nuts
2 Tbsp. chopped parsley
2 Tbsp. grated Parmesan
   cheese

Preheat oven to 350°. Wash mushrooms, trim tough ends from stems. Remove stems, slice them and set aside. Sprinkle a buttered, shallow baking dish with wine. Arrange mushroom caps and artichoke hearts alternately in dish. Sprinkle with bacon. Combine tomato sauce, sliced mushroom stems and pine nuts. Mix well. Pour over vegetables. Sprinkle with parsley and cheese. Bake uncovered 30 minutes. Serves 4

MUSHROOM CHEESE CASSEROLE

good for a light supper

1 lb. mushrooms, sliced
1 med. onion, thinly sliced
8 Tbsp. butter
2 eggs
1 cup milk
3 cups whole wheat bread,
　cut into ¾" cubes
2 cups grated mozzarella
　cheese
2 cups grated cheddar
　cheese
1 tsp. salt
¼ tsp. pepper
2 tsp. parsley flakes
½ tsp. thyme

Preheat oven to 325°. Grease a 2-quart casserole. Sauté mushrooms and onions in butter. In separate bowl, beat eggs and stir in milk.

Place 1½ cups bread cubes in the casserole. Top with 1 cup of each cheese and one-half of the sautéed mushrooms and onions. Sprinkle with ½ tsp. salt, ⅛ tsp. tsp. pepper, 1 tsp. parsley flakes and ¼ tsp. thyme. Repeat layer. Pour egg-milk mixture over layers. Bake covered for 45 minutes, and then uncovered for 15 minutes until brown and crusty on top.　　　　Serves 6

CHEESE ONION BAKE

6 med. onions, thinly sliced
¼ cup butter
¼ cup flour
½ tsp. salt
2 cups milk
2 cups grated cheddar
　cheese

Preheat oven to 350°. Place sliced onions in lightly greased 2-quart casserole. Set aside. Over low heat, melt butter in saucepan. Add flour and salt, stirring until smooth. Cook one minute, stirring. Gradually add milk and cook over medium heat, stirring until thickened. Add cheese, stirring until melted and smooth. Pour sauce over onions. Bake uncovered one hour. Can make a day prior to baking. Remove from refrigerator one hour before baking.
　　　　Serves 8

HERB-SPINACH BAKE

always gets "raves", even from anti-spinach people

1 pkg. (10 oz.) frozen
   chopped spinach, thawed
   and drained well
1 cup cooked rice
1 cup grated sharp cheddar
   cheese
2 eggs, slightly beaten
2 Tbsp. butter, softened
⅓ cup milk
2 Tbsp. chopped onion
½ tsp. Worcestershire sauce
1 tsp. salt
¼ tsp. crushed thyme

Preheat oven to 350°. Mix all ingredients. Pour into greased 8 × 8 × 2 baking dish. Bake uncovered 20 minutes.

Serves 4–5

BLANCHE'S SPINACH PIE

¼ cup butter
1 lb. carton small curd
   cottage cheese
3 eggs, beaten
½ lb. cheddar cheese, grated
1 pkg. (10 oz.) frozen
   chopped spinach, thawed
   and drained well
3 Tbsp. flour
Salt and pepper to taste

Preheat oven to 350°. Cut butter into small pieces. Mix all ingredients in a bowl. Pour into a greased 9-inch pie plate. Bake uncovered for 60–75 minutes, or until set and bubbly.

Serves 6–8

SPINACH CASSEROLE

1 med. onion, chopped
¼ cup butter
2 pkgs. (10 oz. each) frozen
   chopped spinach, thawed
   and squeezed dry
2 cups sour cream
½ cup grated Parmesan
   cheese
1 can (14 oz.) artichoke
   hearts, chopped

Preheat oven to 325°. Sauté onions in butter. Stir in spinach, sour cream, Parmesan cheese and artichoke hearts. Place in 9-inch square dish and bake uncovered 25 minutes.

Serves 6–8

BAKED TOMATOES WITH SPINACH

served at the 1983 JLD annual meeting

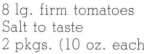

8 lg. firm tomatoes
Salt to taste
2 pkgs. (10 oz. each) frozen
  chopped spinach, thawed
  and squeezed dry

Butter Topping
1 cup butter, softened
2 Tbsp. minced shallots
2 cloves garlic, crushed
2 Tbsp. minced parlsey
½ tsp. salt
Freshly ground pepper

1 cup grated Parmesan
  cheese
½ cup bread crumbs

Preheat oven to 350°. Slice tops off and remove center core and some seeds, leaving all pulp. Sprinkle with salt. Fill with spinach. Mix all Butter Topping ingredients. Spread thickly on tomatoes. Top with Parmesan mixed with bread crumbs. Bake uncovered about 15 minutes or until soft. Place briefly under broiler to brown. Can assemble up to one day ahead. Remove from refrigerator one hour before baking.   Serves 8

CREOLE ESCALLOPED TOMATOES

7 Tbsp. butter, divided
2 sm. green peppers, thinly
  sliced
1 lg. onion, coarsely
  chopped
½ lb. mushrooms, sliced
2 cups Pepperidge Farm
  stuffing
6 lg. tomatoes, each peeled
  and cut into 8 pieces
1 Tbsp. sugar
1 tsp. salt
Paprika
¼ cup buttered bread
  crumbs
2 Tbsp. grated Parmesan
  cheese

Preheat oven to 400°. Melt 3 Tbsp. butter in skillet. Sauté peppers, onion and mushrooms.

In greased 2-quart baking dish, layer half of the stuffing, half of the tomatoes and half of the sautéed mixture. Sprinkle layer with sugar, salt, paprika and dot with 2 Tbsp. butter. Repeat with other half of ingredients for second layer, topping with buttered bread crumbs. Sprinkle with cheese. Bake uncovered at 400° for 30–40 minutes or until bubbly.   Serves 6-8

BROILED TOMATO SLICES

1 Tbsp. butter
2 lg. firm tomatoes, cut into 6 thick slices
½–¾ cup bottled Italian dressing
2 Tbsp. buttered bread crumbs
1 Tbsp. grated Parmesan cheese
Chopped fresh parsley (optional)

Preheat browning dish 4½ minutes on High in microwave. Add butter to dish. Dip tomato slices in dressing and place in dish. Cook 1 minute, turn slices over and cook 1 minute more. Remove from pan. Sprinkle with bread crumbs, cheese and parsley.

To make bread crumbs:
Crumble 1 slice lightly toasted bread in small dish; add 1–2 tsp. butter, stir and cook 45 seconds on High.

Conventional Method
Heat butter in a heavy skillet. Dip tomatoes in dressing and place in the skillet. Cook 1–2 minutes; turn and cook 1 minute more. Remove from pan and sprinkle with bread crumbs, cheese and parsley.

To make bread crumbs:
In a small saucepan, crumble lightly toasted bread; add 1–2 tsp. butter and cook 2–3 minutes. Serves 6

SHERRY TOMATOES

1 whole tomato
1 Tbsp. sherry
2 tsp. mayonnaise
2 Tbsp. grated cheddar cheese

Core tomato. Pour sherry into tomato. Mix mayonnaise and grated cheddar cheese, and stuff tomato with mixture. Bake uncovered at 350° until bubbly, about 20–30 minutes. Serves 1

AMY'S SEVEN VEGETABLE CASSEROLE

a vegetable gardener's delight

4 sm. or 2 med. zucchini, sliced ¼" thick
1 lg. carrot, sliced very thin
1 lg. stalk celery, destringed, cut diagonally ¼" thick
½ each lg. red and lg. green peppers, cut into ½" pieces
1 banana pepper, finely chopped (optional)
1 lg. tomato, peeled and diced
½ sm. onion, coarsely chopped
½ cup chicken broth or defatted chicken essence
Salt to taste
1½ cups grated sharp cheddar cheese, divided

Preheat oven to 350°. Combine vegetables, chicken broth and ¾ cup cheese in a mixing bowl. Season with salt, if necessary. Place in ungreased casserole. Bake covered 1-1½ hours at 350°. Fork test carrots for tenderness. Top with remaining ¾ cup cheese for last 15 minutes of baking. Serve in saucers or drain well with slotted spoon. Can be assembled up to 5 days ahead, covered and refrigerated. Bring to room temperature and bake before serving.

Serves 4-6

SUMMER CASSEROLE

1 med. onion, chopped
1 green pepper, chopped
4 Tbsp. butter, divided
6 ears of corn, kernels cut from cob
6 med. tomatoes, cut in ½" slices
3 sm. zucchini, cut in ⅓" slices
2 tsp. salt, divided
½ tsp. dried basil, divided
Pepper to taste
4 Tbsp. brown sugar, divided
1 cup buttered bread crumbs

Preheat oven to 350°. Sauté onions and green pepper in 2 Tbsp. butter. In greased 2-quart baking dish, layer half corn, tomatoes, zucchini, onions and green pepper. Sprinkle with 1 tsp. salt, ¼ tsp. dried basil, pepper to taste and 2 Tbsp. brown sugar. Repeat for second layer. Dot with remaining 2 Tbsp. butter. Top with bread crumbs. Bake uncovered 35 minutes at 350°.

Serves 8

FRESH SUMMER AND FALL VEGETABLE SAUTÉ

6-7 cups of assorted fresh
  vegetables
A good mix would be:
  3 yellow squash
  2 zucchini
  2 carrots
  6 mushrooms
  10 pea pods to shell
  20 chinese pea pods
  4 asparagus spears
  4 green onions
4 Tbsp. butter
Freshly ground pepper to
  taste

Cut each vegetable, except pea pods and peas, into a very fine julienne. The ingredients can be varied according to what looks the best in the market. Melt butter in a very large skillet or wok; sauté vegetables until just crisp. Do not overcook. Season lightly with freshly ground pepper. Serve immediately.   Serves 8

MONTEREY ZUCCHINI CASSEROLE

1 cup uncooked rice
1 can (4 oz.) green chilies,
  chopped and drained
1 lb. Monterey Jack cheese,
  divided
3 med. zucchini, sliced ¼ "
  thick, parboiled
3 lg. tomatoes, peeled and
  sliced
2 cups sour cream
1 tsp. oregano
1 tsp. garlic salt
4 Tbsp. chopped green
  onion
4 Tbsp. chopped green
  pepper
1 Tbsp. chopped parsley

Preheat oven to 350°. Cook rice. Place in a 9x13 baking dish. Layer chopped chilies on top of rice. Thinly slice half of the cheese and place on chilies. Layer on zucchini and tomatoes. Mix sour cream with spices, green pepper, onion and parsley. Spoon over tomatoes. Grate remaining cheese and sprinkle over casserole. Bake uncovered 30 minutes at 350° or until bubbly. Can be assembled ahead and refrigerated. Add 15 minutes to baking time.

Serves 10-12

ZUCCHINI CASSEROLE

½ cup butter, melted
1 pkg. (8 oz.) Pepperidge
  Farm stuffing mix
4 med. zucchini, thinly
  sliced
2 carrots, shredded
1 med. onion, grated
2 oz. pimentos (optional)
1 can (10¾ oz.) cream of
  chicken soup, undiluted
1 cup sour cream

Preheat oven to 350°. Melt butter in frying pan, and stir in all of the stuffing mix. Set aside ½ cup buttered stuffing mix. Combine remaining stuffing mix with all other ingredients. Smooth into buttered casserole and top with reserved ½ cup stuffing mix. Bake, uncovered for 25 minutes or until browned. Can be assembled ahead.

Serves 6–8

Variation: Can substitute 2 cans cream of chicken soup instead of sour cream.

ZUCCHINI ROUNDS

good for brunch

⅓ cup Bisquick
¼ cup grated Parmesan
  cheese
⅛ tsp. pepper
2 eggs, slightly beaten
2 cups unpeeled, shredded
  zucchini (2 med.
  zucchini)
2 Tbsp. butter

In a mixing bowl, stir together Bisquick, cheese and pepper. Add eggs and mix until moistened. Stir in zucchini. Melt butter in 10-inch skillet over medium heat. Use 2 Tbsp. of mixture for each round. Fry 4 rounds at a time, 2–3 minutes on each side. Keep cooked rounds warm in a low-heated oven while cooking remaining rounds. Serves 4–6

Variations: Add seasoning salt and garlic powder.
Helpful Hint: Have skillet very warm before cooking the rounds.

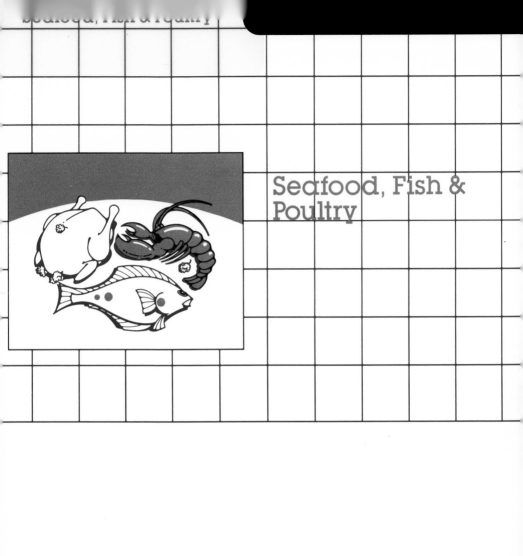

Seafood, Fish & Poultry

DEVILED CRAB

good luncheon dish

1 med. onion, chopped
1 green pepper, chopped
1 cup sliced fresh
  mushrooms
4 Tbsp. butter, divided
2 Tbsp. flour
1-1½ cups milk
Salt and pepper to taste
1 can (7 oz.) crab meat,
  drained (if possible use
  only King Crab, not
  Snow Crab meat)
1 cup grated cheddar cheese
Paprika

Preheat oven to 350°. Sauté onion, green pepper and mushrooms slightly with 2 Tbsp. butter. Set aside. To prepare white sauce, melt 2 Tbsp. butter in saucepan. Blend in flour. Slowly add milk, stirring constantly until it boils and thickens. Add salt and pepper. Add sautéed vegetables and crab meat to white sauce, but do not cook longer.

Put into four individual baking shells. Top with grated cheese and paprika. Bake uncovered at 350° for 25-30 minutes or until slightly browned and bubbly. Can be frozen before baking or assembled a day ahead and refrigerated.   Serves 4

SCALLOPS À L'AVONELLE

6 Tbsp. butter, divided
1 tsp. chopped chives
½ tsp. parsley flakes
⅛ tsp. tarragon
1/16 tsp. garlic salt
1/16 tsp. black pepper
¾ tsp. lemon juice
½ cup soft bread crumbs
¼ tsp. salt
48 scallops (2 lb. bag)

Preheat oven to 500°. Soften 3 Tbsp. butter. Add chives, parsley, tarragon, garlic salt, pepper and lemon juice. Set aside. Melt 3 Tbsp. butter and toss with bread crumbs. Sprinkle scallops with salt. In 6-8 small individual casseroles or baking shells, arrange 6-8 scallops. Top each portion with 1 tsp. herbed butter and sprinkle bread crumbs on top. Bake uncovered for 5-8 minutes. Can be assembled ahead.   Serves 6-8

OYSTERS FRIED IN BATTER

1 cup flour, divided
½ tsp. salt
1 Tbsp. butter, melted
1 egg, slightly beaten
½ cup beer
1 egg white
Oil
2 dozen oysters, shucked

Sift ½ cup flour and salt into a mixing bowl. Stir in the butter and egg. Pour the beer in gradually and mix only until the batter is fairly smooth. **Don't overmix.** Let the batter sit at room temperature for an hour.

When ready to fry the oysters, beat the egg white until stiff peaks form. Fold the egg white into the batter gently until no streaks of white remain.

Heat at least 3 inches of oil until it registers 375° on a deep-frying thermometer. Dip oysters in rest of flour. Shake off any excess and dip in batter. Drain off excess batter. Fry oysters 5 or 6 at a time for 3–4 minutes until they are puffed and golden brown. Drain on paper towels and keep warm in oven at 200° until all oysters have been fried. Serve at once.   Serves 4

SCAMPI ROSSI A' LA HUDKINS

2 lbs. raw shrimp, shelled
    and deveined
⅓ cup olive oil
½ cup dry vermouth
2 cloves garlic, crushed
¾ tsp. salt
½ tsp. freshly ground
    pepper
3 Tbsp. chopped parsley
3 Tbsp. lemon juice

Sauté shrimp in hot olive oil. Add vermouth, garlic, salt and pepper. Cook until liquid is almost gone. Sprinkle with parsley and lemon juice and serve.   Serves 4–5

VEGETABLE SCALLOP PRIMAVERA

2 Tbsp. cooking oil
1 lb. scallops
1 cup diced zucchini
1 cup sliced mushrooms
½ cup julienned carrots
½ cup chopped scallions
1 cup (¼" cut) asparagus
    pieces
¾ cup chicken broth
1 cup whipping cream
Freshly ground pepper
½ cup chopped fresh basil
½ lb. linguine, cooked
    according to pkg.
    directions
½-¾ cup freshly grated
    Parmesan cheese

Place cooking oil in hot wok. Swirl to cover wok. Stir fry scallops until opaque, approximately 4-5 minutes. Set aside. Stir fry each vegetable separately until crisp, 2-3 minutes, adding more oil as needed. Set each vegetable aside after cooking. Add chicken broth, cream, pepper and basil to wok and bring to boil, stirring until flavors blend. Adjust seasonings to taste. Add vegetables and scallops to wok. Mix in linguine and toss with Parmesan cheese.

Serves 4-6

Variations: Many fresh vegetables may be substituted.
Helpful Hint: Vegetables should be crisp, as they will cook more when ingredients are mixed at end.

SHRIMP RICE PARISIENNE

½ cup butter
1 clove garlic, crushed
3 Tbsp. bread crumbs
2 Tbsp. chopped chives
2 Tbsp. cooking sherry
2 tsp. chopped parsley
½ tsp. paprika
1½ lbs. cooked shrimp,
    shelled and deveined
2-3 cups hot cooked rice

Melt butter in large skillet. Stir in garlic, bread crumbs, chives, sherry, parsley and paprika. Add cooked shrimp. Cook over low heat for 10-15 minutes. Do not overcook shrimp. Serve over hot, buttered rice.   Serves 4

Variation: Use clams.
Helpful Hint: Low heat is important so that you do not overcook shrimp.

COQUILLES ST. JACQUES

Court Bouillon
1 cup water
1 sm. onion, sliced
1 stalk celery, sliced
1 bay leaf
3 slices lemon
½ cup dry white wine
1 lb. scallops, washed and
   drained

Sauce
¼ cup finely chopped onion
¼ lb. fresh mushrooms,
   sliced
¼ cup butter
¼ cup flour
Dash pepper
1 cup coffee cream
1 cup grated Gruyére cheese
2 Tbsp. dry white wine
Parsley, chopped

Mashed Potatoes
2 lbs. white potatoes, cooked
¼ cup butter
¼ cup milk
1 egg yolk
¼ cup Parmesan cheese
Salt and white pepper to
   taste

Court Bouillon
Prepare a Court Bouillon by combining water, sliced onion, celery, bay leaf and lemon in a medium saucepan. Bring to a boil, then reduce heat and simmer for 10 minutes. Add wine and scallops. Cover and simmer for 6 minutes, or until scallops are tender. Drain and reserve liquid.

Sauce
Saute´ chopped onions and mushrooms in butter for 5 minutes. Remove from heat and stir in flour and a dash of pepper. Slowly add cream. Bring to a boil, stirring constantly. Reduce heat and stir until thick, about 4-5 minutes. Add Gruyére; cook and stir until melted. Blend in wine, ½ cup Court Bouillon and scallops. Sprinkle lightly with parsley.

Potatoes
Mash potatoes. Add remaining ingredients. Put mixture in a pastry bag or cookie press.

Assembly
Divide scallop mixture among individual baking shells. Pipe mashed potatoes around edges. Place shells on cookie sheet and broil 4 inches from heat until golden brown and hot, about 2-3 minutes.   Serves 4

CRAB MEAT CASSEROLE

a tasty luncheon dish

1 can (14 oz.) artichoke
    hearts, drained and sliced
1 lb. crab meat, fresh or
    frozen, rinsed and
    drained
6 Tbsp. butter, divided
½ lb. mushrooms, sliced
2½ Tbsp. flour
1 cup whipping cream
½ tsp. salt
1 tsp. Worcestershire sauce
¼ cup med. dry sherry
Paprika and cayenne to taste
¼ cup grated Parmesan
    cheese

Preheat oven to 375°. Place artichoke hearts in bottom of baking dish. Cover with crab meat. Sauté mushrooms in 2 Tbsp. butter, and spread over crab meat. Melt 4 Tbsp. butter in saucepan. Stir in remaining ingredients except cheese, stirring well after each addition. Heat until slightly thickened. Pour over mushrooms. Sprinkle with cheese. Bake at 375° for 20 minutes.   Serves 4

SHRIMP ALMONDINE

2 cups water
1 cup rice
½ tsp. salt
1 tsp. curry
2 Tbsp. butter
1 pkg. (10 oz.) frozen
    French-cut green beans,
    thawed and drained
1-1½ lb. cooked shrimp,
    shelled and deveined
1 can (10¾ oz.) cream of
    mushroom soup,
    undiluted
½ soup can milk
2 egg whites
1 cup mayonnaise, scant
¾ cup thinly sliced almonds

Preheat oven to 400°. Put first 5 ingredients in saucepan; bring to a boil and simmer for about 10 minutes or until most of the water is absorbed by the rice. Rice will continue to cook in the oven.

In a greased 9x13 shallow casserole, layer rice, beans and shrimp. Mix soup with milk and pour over mixture in casserole. Beat eggs white until stiff; fold in mayonnaise and spread on top of casserole. Sprinkle almonds on top. Bake uncovered for 30 minutes at 400°.

Serves 6-8

SHRIMP CREOLE

8 Tbsp. butter, divided
2 cups chopped onion
1 cup chopped green pepper
1 cup chopped celery
1 clove garlic, finely minced
1 can (32 oz.) peeled Italian
   tomatoes
9 Tbsp. tomato paste (¾ of a
   6 oz. can)
Salt and pepper to taste
1 tsp. Worcestershire sauce
3 sm. slices lemon peel
2 whole cloves
½ tsp. sugar
½ tsp. thyme
1 bay leaf
¼ cup olive oil
1 sm. eggplant, diced with
   skin on
1½ lbs. raw shrimp, peeled
   and deveined
1 Tbsp. capers
4 Tbsp. finely chopped
   parsley
4 cups hot cooked rice

Melt 6 Tbsp. butter in large skillet. Add onion, green pepper and celery, and sauté until onion is translucent. Add garlic and tomatoes, plus liquid from can. Chop tomatoes into smaller pieces with spoon. Add tomato paste, salt, pepper, Worcestershire, lemon peel, cloves, sugar, thyme and bay leaf. Simmer 10 minutes, stirring occasionally.

Heat oil in separate skillet and sauté eggplant until browned. Add eggplant to sauce and cook 10 minutes. Add shrimp and simmer 5 minutes more. Discard lemon peel, bay leaf and cloves. Stir in remaining 2 Tbsp. butter and capers. Transfer to serving dish and sprinkle with parsley. Serve very hot with freshly cooked rice.   Serves 6

MARINADE FOR FRESH SALMON

1 clove garlic, minced
¼ cup salad oil
3 Tbsp. lemon juice
½ tsp. dried thyme
¼ tsp. salt

About 50 minutes before serving, place all ingredients in a shallow dish. Place fish in marinade and refrigerate for 30 minutes, turning occasionally. Drain before broiling.
                Yields scant ½ cup

STUFFED SALMON

can be served as an appetizer or a main dish

1 cup olive oil
2 cups chopped onions
6 cloves garlic, minced
8 oz. mushrooms, coarsely
    chopped
2 cups chopped Italian
    parsley
½ cup dry white wine
½ lb. Feta cheese, cut into
    small pieces
4 slices bread, toasted and
    finely crumbled
5-6 lb. whole salmon
    (prepared for stuffing)
Lemon juice

Preheat oven to 450°. Pour oil in skillet and brown onions; add garlic, mushrooms and parsley. Add wine. Remove from heat; add Feta cheese and bread crumbs. Stuff salmon. Bake uncovered at 450° 10 minutes per inch of thickness. Baste with oil, lemon juice or white wine.

Serves 6-8

SHRIMP CURRY

1 lb. shrimp, cooked and
    cleaned
7 Tbsp. butter, divided
½ cup chopped onion
1 cup chopped carrots
1 cup chopped celery
3 Tbsp. flour
2 tsp. curry powder
½ tsp. salt
½ tsp. sugar
1½ cups milk
Freshly ground pepper, to
    taste
2 cups cooked white rice
1 cup chopped peanuts
1 cup currants
1 cup shredded coconut
1 cup crumbled crisp bacon
Chutney

Cut shrimp into bite-sized pieces. Melt 4 Tbsp. butter in skillet and sauté onion until limp. Add carrots and celery and sauté until heated through but still crisp. Set aside. In a saucepan melt 3 Tbsp. butter. Stir in flour, curry powder, salt and sugar. Gradually add milk while stirring. Continue to stir until thickened. Add sauce to sautéed vegetables. Add shrimp and heat through. Season with pepper. Serve over rice with peanuts, currants, coconut, bacon and chutney as condiments. Serves 4

GRILLED SHRIMP AND ITALIAN SAUSAGE

32 bite-sized pieces Italian
  sausage
16 raw jumbo shrimp,
  shelled and deveined
⅓ cup olive oil
Juice of ¼ lemon
1 clove garlic, crushed
2 leaves fresh basil
1 bay leaf
2 pinches salt
1 pinch white pepper
8 wooden skewers

Cook the sausage and set aside to cool. Slice shrimp in half down the back and place in a bowl. Combine olive oil, lemon juice, garlic, basil, bay leaf, salt and pepper. Pour over shrimp, toss well, and allow to marinate for at least one hour. Soak the skewers in water (to prevent them from burning on the grill).

Skewer one end of a shrimp half, then a piece of sausage, then the other end of shrimp, so that shrimp is wrapped around sausage. Place four shrimp and four pieces of sausage on each skewer. Grill, turning occasionally for even cooking. Shrimp are done when firm and brown around the edges.

Serves 4

MUSTARD SAUCE FOR FISH

unforgettable — a little goes a long way

½ cup Hellmann's
  mayonnaise
½ cup sour cream
2 Tbsp. prepared mustard
1 Tbsp. horseradish
2 tsp. dry mustard

Blend all ingredients.
Yields approx. 1¼ cups

PIXILATED FISH

4 Tbsp. butter
1½–2 lbs. fish filets
   (flounder preferred, but
   may use haddock, cod or
   scrod)
¼ tsp. salt
⅛ tsp. pepper
½–1 Tbsp. lemon juice
2 Tbsp. dry white wine
2 tsp. paprika to sprinkle
2 Tbsp. grated Parmesan
   cheese

Preheat oven to 400°. Put butter in 9x13 shallow casserole and place in oven to brown. Season filets with salt and pepper. When butter has browned, remove the casserole from oven. Place filets in casserole flesh side down. Bake at 400° for 15 minutes. Remove from oven. Turn filets over and baste with butter. Combine lemon juice and wine and sprinkle over the fish, then sprinkle with paprika. Return to oven for no more than 2 minutes. Remove from oven and sprinkle with Parmesan cheese. Serves 4

SHRIMP IN MORNAY SAUCE

3 Tbsp. butter
2 Tbsp. chopped green
   onion
3 Tbsp. flour
1 cup whipping cream
½ cup milk
½ tsp. salt
Dash white pepper
Dash nutmeg
1 cup (¼ lb.) grated Swiss
   cheese
1 lb. shrimp, cooked and
   cleaned
½ tsp. lemon juice
Paprika

Preheat oven to 400°. In saucepan, cook onion in butter over medium heat several minutes until soft. Sprinkle with flour and blend well. Gradually stir in cream and milk. Stir constantly until mixture thickens and comes to a boil. Stir in salt, white pepper and nutmeg. Remove from heat and stir in Swiss cheese until melted.

Place shrimp in shallow casserole and sprinkle with lemon juice. Pour sauce over shrimp and dust with paprika. Bake uncovered at 400° for 15 minutes or until brown and bubbly. Serves 4

Serve With: Lemon Rice

STEVENSON'S SHRIMP

works well for buffet

6½ Tbsp. butter, divided
4½ Tbsp. flour
¾ cup milk
¾ cup whipping cream
¼ cup dry sherry
1 Tbsp. Worcestershire
    sauce
Salt and white pepper to
    taste
2 cans (8 oz. each) artichoke
    hearts, drained
2 lbs. cooked shrimp
1 lb. mushrooms, sliced
¼ cup grated Parmesan
    cheese
Paprika
Parsley

Preheat oven to 375°. Melt 4½ Tbsp. butter in saucepan; stir in flour, browning slightly as for a roux. Add milk and cream, stirring with wire whisk. Cook until mixture becomes very thick. Do not boil. Stir in sherry and Worcestershire. Continue to stir over low heat until well-blended. Remove from heat.

Cut artichoke hearts into halves or quarters and place in casserole. Arrange shrimp on top of artichokes. Lightly saute´ mushrooms in remaining 2 Tbsp. butter. Place on top of shrimp. Spoon white sauce over mushrooms. Sprinkle Parmesan and then paprika over all. Bake uncovered 30 minutes or until bubbly. Garnish with parsley. Can be made ahead.   Serves 6–8

FISH IN MUSHROOM WINE SAUCE

Sauce
3 Tbsp. butter
2 Tbsp. flour
1 can (10¾ oz.) cream of
    mushroom soup,
    undiluted
½ cup white wine
2 Tbsp. grated Parmesan
    cheese
2 Tbsp. chopped parsley
½ lb. mushrooms, sliced and
    sautéed in butter (optional)
1-1⅓ lbs. fresh fish

Preheat oven to 375°. Melt butter in saucepan over medium heat. Stir in flour; add soup and wine. Cook, stirring constantly, until mixture boils and thickens. Add cheese, parsley and sautéed mushrooms if desired. Grease shallow baking dish. Arrange fish in a single layer in dish. Pour sauce over fish. Bake uncovered for 25 minutes.
                        Serves 4

TEMPURA PAGEL

1 cup cornstarch
½ cup flour
1½ tsp. salt
¼ tsp. garlic powder
1 tsp. sugar
2 Tbsp. baking powder
⅛ tsp. pepper
1 egg, beaten
¼ cup salad oil
¾ cup water, no more
2 lbs. lg. raw shrimp in
    shells
Enough salad oil for deep
    frying (about 1 gal.)

Dipping Sauce
1 bottle (14 oz.) ketchup
1 bottle (5 oz.) horseradish

Mix first 7 ingredients. Blend egg and oil and mix with dry ingredients. Beating constantly, add water slowly to avoid lumps until it reaches the consistency of heavy cream. Shell and devein shrimp, leaving on the tail. Cut nearly through the length of the vein side to butterfly. Lay on paper towels to dry.

Bring frying oil to 375°. It should be about 4 inches deep. Hold bowl of batter close to hot oil. Dip one shrimp at a time into batter and drop into oil. Drop only enough shrimp into pot so they are not touching each other. Fry until golden, about 2–3 minutes, turning if necessary. Remove shrimp to drain on paper towels and newspaper. Keep warm in oven. Continue cooking the shrimp, maintaining 375° temperature of oil. If batter thickens, stir in a little more water. Cooked batter should be light and crystallized.

Dipping Sauce
Combine ketchup with drained horseradish to taste.   Serves 4

Timely Tip:
Unless otherwise specified, never put lemon on fish before broiling or baking. It will make the fish mushy.

SEAFOOD CASSEROLE SUPREME

1 cup whole milk
1 can (10¾ oz.) condensed cream of mushroom soup, undiluted
1 lb. Velveeta cheese, cubed
1 can (6 oz.) shrimp
1 can (6 oz.) tuna
1 can (6 oz.) clams
1 can (6 oz.) crab meat
1 can (6 oz.) sliced mushrooms
1 can (5 oz.) sliced water chestnuts
1 cup half and half
4 cups cooked rice
1 tsp. chopped parsley
2 Tbsp. butter
1 pkg. (2⅞ oz.) slivered almonds
⅓ cup sherry

Preheat oven to 350°. Combine milk, soup and cheese in a large saucepan. Cook over medium heat, stirring frequently, until cheese melts and mixture is smooth. Drain cans of seafood, mushrooms and water chestnuts. Add to soup mixture. Stir in half and half, rice and parsley. Turn mixture into buttered 8x12 pyrex dish. Melt butter in a skillet and saute´ almonds. Sprinkle on top of seafood. Pour sherry over all. Bake uncovered for 45–50 minutes. Let sit 5–10 minutes before serving.   Serves 6–8

Combine 2 Tbsp. butter and almonds in shallow baking dish. Cook on High uncovered 5–6 minutes, stirring after 2 minutes. Combine milk, soup and cheese in large dish. Cook on Medium–High for 3–5 minutes, stirring several times, until cheese melts and mixture is smooth. Drain cans of seafood, mushrooms and water chestnuts. Add to soup. Cook on High for 1 minute. Stir in half and half, rice and parsley and cook for 1 minute. Turn mixture into buttered 8x12 pyrex dish. Sprinkle with almonds. Pour sherry over all. Bake uncovered on High 10–12 minutes or until heated through. Let stand 4–5 minutes before serving.

SALMON WITH AVOCADO BUTTER

Avocado Butter
4 Tbsp. butter, softened
⅓ cup mashed ripe avocado
1 Tbsp. lemon juice
1 Tbsp. mayonnaise
½ tsp. Worcestershire sauce
⅛ tsp. salt
1 sm. clove garlic, minced
3 drops Tabasco
2 Tbsp. chopped parsley

4 salmon steaks (6-8 oz.
   each and 1″ thick or
   equal amount)
1 lime, quartered

In small bowl, cream butter until smooth. Add avocado, lemon juice, mayonnaise, Worcestershire, salt, garlic and Tabasco. Cream until smooth. Stir in parsley. Refrigerate, covered, for 1 hour. Remove avocado butter 10 minutes before serving to soften.

Preheat broiler. Place salmon steaks 4-5 inches from broiler. Broil 5-7 minutes on each side. When done, fish will flake easily when tested with fork. Sprinkle steaks with lime juice and serve with avocado butter. Butter may be prepared 1-2 days ahead.   Serves 4

EXTRAVAGANT SEAFOOD BAKE

1 lb. cooked crab meat and
   cooked lobster meat,
   combined
1 lb. shrimp, cooked and
   deveined
1 cup mayonnaise
½ cup chopped green
   pepper
¼ cup minced onion
1½ cups finely chopped
   celery
½ tsp. salt
1 Tbsp. Worcestershire
   sauce
2 cups potato chips, finely
   crushed or bread crumbs,
   buttered
Paprika

Preheat oven to 400°. Combine first 8 ingredients. Put in greased medium casserole. Cover with crushed potato chips or bread crumbs. Sprinkle with paprika. Bake uncovered at 400° for 25 minutes.
          Serves 6-8

FILET OF SOLE EN PAPILLOTE

8 med. sole filets
11 med. fresh mushrooms
(2 chopped and 9 sliced)
3 Tbsp. sour cream
1 egg white
1 Tbsp. chopped fresh
parsley
3 Tbsp. lemon juice, divided
2 Tbsp. chopped fresh
tarragon, divided (may
substitute ½ tsp. dried
tarragon)
1 tsp. chopped garlic,
divided
6 Tbsp. butter, divided
Herb salt
Freshly ground pepper
2 med. tart apples, coarsely
chopped
1 Tbsp. chopped chives

Variation: Mayonnaise may
be used for sour
cream and egg
white.

Preheat oven to 350°. Pat filets dry with paper towel. Cut two filets into 1-inch strips and place in work bowl of food processor. Set remaining filets aside. Add 2 chopped mushrooms, sour cream, egg white, parsley, 1 tsp. lemon juice, 1 tsp. fresh tarragon and ½ tsp. garlic to food processor. Mix until well-blended.

Cut six 12-inch squares of aluminum foil or parchment. Place one filet on each square, skin side up. Sprinkle each filet with lemon juice (about 2 Tbsp. in all), and top each with a spoonful of mushroom mixture. Fold fish over end to end. Melt 2 Tbsp. butter and brush over filets.

In small skillet, melt 1 Tbsp. butter. Add 9 thinly sliced mushrooms, 1 tsp. lemon juice, herb salt and pepper to taste. Stir and cook for 2 minutes. Spread over each filet. In same skillet, melt 1 Tbsp. butter and sauté apples for 2 minutes. Spread on top of mushrooms. In same skillet, combine 2 Tbsp. butter, ½ tsp. garlic, remaining tarragon, chives, salt and pepper to taste. Top each filet.

Fold foil over each filet and seal well. Arrange on baking sheet and bake 20–25 minutes. Cut slit in center of each package and serve immediately.   Serves 6

HUNGARIAN WHITEFISH

an unusual fish dish everyone loves

4 whitefish filets
8 Tbsp. butter, divided
Salt
Paprika
1 cup sliced fresh
   mushrooms
1 can (10¾ oz.) cream of
   mushroom soup,
   undiluted
1 cup sour cream

Preheat oven to 350°. Place filets in a single layer in a greased 9x13 baking dish. Cut 6 Tbsp. butter into small pieces and place on fish. Sprinkle with salt and paprika. Sauté mushrooms in 2 Tbsp. butter. Spoon over fish, and bake uncovered for 15 minutes.

Combine soup and sour cream in saucepan. Heat, stirring constantly, until mixture just begins to bubble. Pour sauce over fish. Bake uncovered another 15–20 minutes. Fish will flake when it is done. Sprinkle top with more paprika and serve. Serves 4–6

 Place fish in greased 9x13 glass baking dish. Dot with 6 Tbsp. butter and sprinkle with paprika and salt. Melt 2 Tbsp. of butter in small dish on High for 45 seconds. Add mushrooms and stir to coat mushrooms with butter. Cook, covered, for 2–3 minutes or until tender. Stir after first minute. Spoon mushrooms over fish. Loosely cover with wax paper and cook on High for 3–4 minutes. Mix soup and sour cream together in medium sized dish. Cook on Medium for 2–3 minutes or until heated through. Stir after 1 minute. Pour sauce over fish and sprinkle with paprika. Bake uncovered on High 2–3 minutes more.

CHICKEN ALMONDINE

great "do ahead" for company

4 whole chicken breasts,
split, boned and skinned
(8 pieces)
1 cup sour cream
3 Tbsp. flour
½ lb. fresh mushrooms,
sliced
⅔ cup white wine
1 can (10¾ oz.) cream of
mushroom soup,
undiluted
Sliced or slivered almonds
Salt and pepper to taste

Preheat oven to 325°. Arrange chicken breasts in a single layer in a 9x13 glass casserole. Combine sour cream, flour, mushrooms, white wine and soup. Add salt and pepper to taste. Pour mixture over chicken breasts, sprinkle with almonds. Bake uncovered at 325° for 1–1½ hours. Do not overcook. May be assembled earlier in the day and refrigerated.

Serves 6–8

Serve With: Best served over wild rice or pilaf.

 Place chicken in 9x13 glass casserole, placing the thickest part of the chicken to outside of dish. Cover with wax paper. Microwave on High 3-5 minutes, rotating dish halfway through cooking time. Combine sour cream, flour, mushrooms, white wine and soup. Rearrange chicken and pour sauce over the top. Sprinkle with almonds. Microwave 5-7 minutes uncovered, rotating dish several times. Chicken is cooked when it is fork tender and no longer pink.

CANTONESE CHICKEN WITH CHERRIES

½ cup flour
1½ Tbsp. garlic salt
1½ Tbsp. paprika
2 whole chicken breasts,
boned and split
¼ cup cooking oil
1 can (1 lb.) pitted dark
sweet cherries, reserve
juice
1 cup sauterne wine
4 cups hot cooked rice

Mix flour, garlic salt and paprika. Coat chicken with flour mixture. Brown in oil in skillet. Drain cherries, reserving ½ cup cherry syrup. Add cherries, cherry syrup and wine to chicken. Cover and simmer until chicken is tender, about 1 hour. Serve over hot cooked rice. May be made ahead.

Serves 4

PLUM SAUCE FOR CHICKEN

1 med. onion, finely
  chopped
2 Tbsp. butter
1 can (6 oz.) frozen
  lemonade concentrate
1 jar (12 oz.) plum preserves
3 Tbsp. brandy
⅔ cup chili sauce
1 tsp. powdered ginger
2 tsp. prepared mustard
2 tsp. marjoram

Sauté onion in butter until tender. Add remaining ingredients, mixing well. Simmer, stirring occasionally, for 15 minutes. Serve with baked or broiled chicken lightly seasoned with garlic, salt and pepper. Can be made ahead.

Yields about 3 cups

CHICKEN BREASTS CANNELLONI

it's worth the effort!

4 whole chicken breasts,
  split, skinned, boned and
  flattened (8 pcs.)
Grey Poupon Dijon mustard
Italian seasoning
Ground pepper
8 oz. mozzarella cheese
Flour
Salt
Pepper
3 Tbsp. olive oil
3 Tbsp. butter
1 bunch green onions,
  chopped
1 cup sliced mushrooms
3 tomatoes, peeled, seeded,
  cored, chopped
1 cup dry vermouth

Spread mustard on boned side of each piece of chicken. Sprinkle with Italian seasoning and pepper. Add 1 slice of cheese to each breast. Roll up, tucking sides in to enclose filling. Roll each breast in flour mixed with salt and pepper. Sauté in olive oil and butter over medium heat for about 10 minutes — keep turning. Remove from pan and keep warm. In same pan, sauté onions and mushrooms in olive oil. Add tomatoes and dry vermouth. Add chicken breasts and heat through.

Serves 8

Helpful Hint: Use toothpicks to hold chicken together.
Serve With: Rice or spaghetti.

CRAB-STUFFED CHICKEN

4 lg. chicken breasts, halved, boned and skinned
4 Tbsp. butter, divided
¼ cup all purpose flour
¾ cup milk
¾ cup chicken broth
⅓ cup dry white wine
¼ cup chopped onion
1 can (7½ oz.) crab meat, drained and flaked, or the comparable amount of fresh or mock crab
1 can (3 oz.) mushrooms, drained and chopped
½ cup coarsely crumbled Saltine or Ritz crackers (about 10 crackers)
2 Tbsp. snipped parsley
½ tsp. salt
¼ tsp. pepper
1 cup grated Swiss cheese (4 oz.)
½ tsp. paprika

Pound each piece of chicken between wax paper until about ⅛ inch thick.

In a saucepan, melt 3 Tbsp. butter, blend in flour. Add milk, broth and wine, all at once. Cook and stir until mixture thickens and bubbles. Set aside. In skillet cook onion in 1 Tbsp. butter until tender, but not brown. Stir in crab, mushrooms, cracker crumbs, parsley, salt and pepper. Stir in 2 Tbsp. of the sauce.

Preheat oven to 350°. Top each chicken piece with about ¼ cup crab mixture. Fold sides in and roll up. Place seam side down in baking dish. Pour remaining sauce over all. Bake covered in 350° oven for 1 hour or until tender. Uncover, sprinkle with cheese and paprika. Bake 2 minutes longer, or until cheese melts. May be made ahead. Freezes well.   Serves 8

Helpful Hint: If using whole crab legs, do not add them to the sauce. Place crab leg on chicken breast, top with sauce and roll up around crab leg.

Timely Tip:
Whisk in 1 Tbsp. of boiling water to white sauce or other sauces that start to separate. This will correct the problem.

CHICKEN DASHINGTON

2 Tbsp. butter
½ cup chopped fresh
    mushrooms
2 Tbsp. flour
½ cup coffee cream
¼ tsp. salt
⅛ tsp. cayenne
1½ cups grated medium to
    sharp cheddar cheese
6 whole chicken breasts,
    boned and skinned
2 eggs, slightly beaten
¾ cup bread crumbs
Oil

Sauce
1 Tbsp. butter
¼ cup flour
½ cup milk
Pinch salt
6 oz. grated cheddar cheese
Dill
Paprika

Melt butter, sauté mushrooms. Stir in flour until smooth. Stir in cream. Add salt and cayenne pepper. Stir until thick. Stir in cheese until melted. Pour into medium sized pie plate. Cover and chill 1 hour.

Place chicken breasts between wax paper and pound from the center out, forming ¼-inch cutlets. Remove cheese mixture from refrigerator and cut into 6 pieces. Form each piece into a stick. Place a stick on each breast. Roll up breasts, tucking in sides well. Dust each breast with flour. Dip into beaten eggs and then into bread crumbs. Cover and chill 1 hour.

Preheat oven to 325°. Fry chicken rolls in hot oil for 5 minutes. Place in a shallow baking pan and bake uncovered 30–40 minutes at 325°.

Sauce
Melt butter in saucepan, add flour and stir 1–2 minutes. Remove from heat and add milk and salt. Whisk until smooth. Return to heat and add cheese. Heat until cheese melts and sauce bubbles. Pour sauce over chicken. Sprinkle with dill and paprika and serve.   Serves 6

SHERRIED CHICKEN

3 whole chicken breasts,
  split, boned and skinned
  (6 pieces)
6 slices of Swiss cheese
1 can (10¾ oz.) cream of
  chicken soup, undiluted
¼ cup white wine or sherry
2 cups Pepperidge Farm
  stuffing
¼ cup butter, melted

Preheat oven to 375°. Place chicken breasts on the bottom of a 10-inch square pan or 9x12 pyrex dish. Layer cheese over chicken breasts. Combine soup and wine and pour over chicken and cheese. Put stuffing over soup mixture. Dribble melted butter over the top. Bake at 375° uncovered for 45 minutes. Can be assembled ahead.

Serves 4-6

CHICKEN AUX HERBES

4 whole chicken breasts,
  split, boned and skinned
  (8 pieces)
2-3 lemons
Salt and pepper
1½-2 pkgs. **softened** herb
  cheese (Rondelle,
  Boursin, Allouette, etc.)
  Note: cheese with herbs
  — **not** au poivre
¾ + cup flour
2 eggs
2 Tbsp. water
1 + cup unseasoned bread
  crumbs, crushed
1 cup butter
½ cup oil

Pound each piece of chicken between wax paper until about ⅛ inch thick. Score several times in each direction with a sharp knife. Sprinkle with lemon juice, salt and pepper in that order. Spread softened herb cheese over chicken. Roll chicken, tucking in sides to enclose cheese. Can be done to this point the night before and refrigerated covered.

Lightly flour chicken. Lightly beat eggs and water and dip chicken in mixture. Coat chicken with bread crumbs. Refrigerate **at least** one hour.

In a heavy skillet, fry cold chicken in oil and butter approximately 5 minutes a side until golden.   Serves 4-6

CHICKEN DELUXE

6 Tbsp. butter
6 Tbsp. flour
1 cup whipping cream
1 cup sour cream
Few drops Worcestershire
    sauce
Salt and pepper to taste
¼ - ½ cup white wine
6-8 whole chicken breasts,
    boned
Slivered almonds

Preheat oven to 350°. In a saucepan make a roux of butter and flour. Cook a few minutes. Add cream and continue cooking until thick. Remove from heat and add sour cream, Worcestershire sauce, salt and pepper. Sauce can now be covered and refrigerated 4-5 days.

Layer bottom of 9x13 pyrex dish with chicken. Add desired amount of wine to thin sauce and pour over chicken. Sprinkle with slivered almonds. Bake uncovered at 350° for 45 minutes.

Serves 6-8

Variation: Especially good with grapes, mushrooms and artichoke hearts to taste.

 Make sauce using directions above. Make a single layer of chicken in a 9x13 glass casserole. Use two dishes if necessary. Cover with wax paper and cook on High 3-5 minutes, turning dish halfway through cooking time. Pour sauce over chicken and sprinkle with almonds. Bake, uncovered, on High for 10-12 minutes, giving dish half turns every 2-3 minutes.

Timely Tip:
Freeze left over chicken broth in ice cube trays or paper cups. When frozen remove from trays or cups, and place in plastic bag in freezer. Use for seasoning rice, noodles, etc.

CHICKEN DIVINE

easier than Chicken Cordon Bleu

8 oz. thinly-sliced Canadian
    bacon or boiled ham
3 whole chicken breasts,
    split, boned and skinned
    (6 pieces)

Sauce
4 Tbsp. butter
4 Tbsp. flour
¼ tsp. white pepper
½ tsp. salt
1 cup milk
1 cup whipping cream

8 oz. sliced Swiss cheese
Oregano

Preheat oven to 350°. Divide Canadian bacon or ham into 6 portions and lay in a 9x13 pyrex dish. Lay chicken on top of bacon or ham, tucking under any uneven edges.

Sauce
Melt butter in sauce pan. Add flour, pepper and salt. Stir 1–2 minutes. Remove from heat, gradually add milk and cream. Return to heat and cook until thickened, stirring constantly. Pour over chicken.

Sprinkle with oregano to taste (approximately ¼ tsp. per breast). Divide cheese into 6 portions and place on top of each breast. Bake uncovered at 350° for 50 minutes. Can prepare one day ahead.

Serves 4–6

GROUSE WITH CURRANT GLAZE

1 grouse per person
1 apple per grouse
Salt and pepper
Butter
Currant jelly
Brandy

Preheat oven to 350°. Stuff grouse cavity with quartered apple. Rub salt and pepper onto outside of grouse. Bake uncovered in 350° oven for 45 minutes, basting with butter. Mix currant jelly with enough brandy to liquify and add to pan. Baste for 15 additional minutes.

Yields 1 grouse per person

Variations: Excellent with duck or pheasant.

FRENCH CHICKEN WITH VEGETABLES

2 whole chicken breasts,
  split and skinned
3 whole chicken legs,
  separated and skinned (or
  equivalent of above)
Salt and pepper to taste
Flour (approx. 1 cup)
¼ lb. salt pork, diced
¼ tsp. thyme
Pinch marjoram
1½ cups diced carrots
½ cup white pearl onions,
  raw, peeled
1½ cups diced raw potatoes
½ lb. fresh mushrooms,
  sliced
1½ cups chicken stock (or
  chicken broth)
½ bay leaf
1 sprig parsley
1 clove garlic, minced

Preheat oven to 350°. Wash and dry chicken. Season with salt and pepper, roll in flour. Fry salt pork until crisp. Skim out pork and drain on paper towels. Brown chicken in the fat. Place chicken in a large covered casserole. Sprinkle with thyme and marjoram. Mix vegetables together and add to the casserole. To chicken stock (or broth) add bay leaf, parsley, garlic, salt and pepper to taste and the drained salt pork. Pour over vegetables. Cover casserole and bake in 350° oven for 1½ hours or until chicken is tender and vegetables are done. Just as good (or better) if done a day ahead and reheated.

Serves 6

CHICKEN WITH OYSTER SAUCE

6 chicken breasts
3 slices ginger root
1 clove garlic
3 Tbsp. soy sauce
3 Tbsp. oyster sauce
1 Tbsp. brown sugar
2 tsp. sherry
Dash 5-spice powder
1 cup chicken broth

Put all ingredients in a large frying pan. Bring to a boil and simmer, covered, until cooked through, about 30 minutes. Remove lid and boil to reduce sauce to a glaze.   Serves 4–6

Variation: Use Spice Parisienne instead of 5 spice powder (see Special Sections pg. 254).

CURRANT SAUCE

for duck or game

6 Tbsp. currant jelly
3 Tbsp. sugar
2 Tbsp. Port wine
Grated orange rind
2 Tbsp. lemon juice
2 Tbsp. orange juice
¼ tsp. salt

Beat jelly, sugar and wine for 5 minutes. Add remaining ingredients and stir until blended. Can be made ahead.

Yields 1 cup

WILLETT'S EASY CHICKEN KIEV

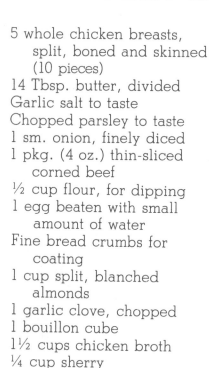

5 whole chicken breasts,
   split, boned and skinned
   (10 pieces)
14 Tbsp. butter, divided
Garlic salt to taste
Chopped parsley to taste
1 sm. onion, finely diced
1 pkg. (4 oz.) thin-sliced
   corned beef
½ cup flour, for dipping
1 egg beaten with small
   amount of water
Fine bread crumbs for
   coating
1 cup split, blanched
   almonds
1 garlic clove, chopped
1 bouillon cube
1½ cups chicken broth
¼ cup sherry
½ cup dry white wine
Salt and pepper to taste

Place chicken between 2 sheets of wax paper. Flatten with rolling pin. Cut 1 stick butter into 10 equal strips and arrange on chicken. Sprinkle chicken with garlic salt, parsley and diced onion. Place 1-2 thin strips of corned beef over the seasonings. Roll up chicken. Dip chicken in flour. Refrigerate for at least 1 hour.

Dip chicken in egg and roll in bread crumbs. Brown gently in 4 Tbsp. melted butter. Remove from pan. Add remaining butter to pan drippings and brown the almonds. Add garlic, bouillon cube, 1 Tbsp. flour, chicken broth, sherry, white wine, salt and pepper.

Preheat oven to 350°. Arrange chicken in a 9x13 pyrex dish or 3-quart casserole. Pour sauce over chicken. Cover and bake 30–45 minutes at 350°. May assemble in advance and refrigerate or freeze **before** or **after** baking. Serves 8

POULET MARENGO

½ cup flour
1 tsp. salt
½ tsp. pepper
1 tsp. dried tarragon
1 roasting chicken (3 lbs.)
   cut up, or 3–4 chicken
   breasts, split
¼ cup olive oil
¼ cup butter
1 cup dry white wine
2 + cups canned tomatoes
1 clove garlic, chopped
Chopped parsley

Preheat oven to 350°. Mix flour, salt, pepper and tarragon and dredge chicken in it. Reserve remaining flour mix. In a large skillet, heat olive oil and butter. Add chicken and brown on all sides. Remove chicken to a heavy 3-quart covered casserole. Add the reserved flour to fat remaining in skillet. Gradually stir in the wine. When the sauce is thickened and smooth, pour it over the chicken and add the tomatoes, garlic and parsley. Cover and bake at 350° at least 45 minutes. Can be made ahead. Freezes well.

Serves 6–8

Helpful Hint: When making this in quantity, add more tomatoes and tarragon so that the chicken can stew for a long time (up to 2 hours) and become really tender and flavorful.

 Use microwave for final cooking step. Cook chicken in covered glass casserole on High, 10–12 minutes, giving dish quarter turns every 2–3 minutes.

SCOTCH COLLOP SAUCE

1 cup sour cream
2 Tbsp. honey
Dash of nutmeg
1½ oz. Scotch
Broken walnut pieces to
   garnish

Warm sour cream over low heat, but do not boil or heat too long as it will curdle. Add honey and nutmeg. Stir well. Just before serving, add Scotch. Stir until hot. Pour over boneless sautéed chicken or veal medallions. Sprinkle with broken walnuts.

Yields 1¼ cups

Variation: Also delicious mixed with chicken pieces and rolled in crepes.

CRANAPPLE PEAR SAUCE

wonderful with holiday turkey or ham

2 pears, peeled, cored and diced
2 lbs. fresh cranberries
3 apples, peeled, cored and diced
2 cups golden raisins
2 cups sugar
1 cup fresh orange juice (about 3 oranges)
2 Tbsp. grated orange peel
2 tsp. ground cinnamon
¼ tsp. ground nutmeg
½ cup Cointreau or Grand Marnier

Heat all ingredients, except liqueur, in a huge saucepan to boiling. Reduce heat and simmer uncovered, stirring frequently until mixture thickens, about 45 minutes. Stir in liqueur. Refrigerate, covered, 4 hours or overnight. Keeps for weeks in the refrigerator.

Yields 6 cups

HOT ORIENTAL SALAD

3 lg. whole chicken breasts, boned, skinned and cut into 1" pieces.
¼ cup corn starch
¼ cup corn oil
Dash garlic powder
1 lg. tomato, cut into chunks
⅓ cup sliced water chestnuts
1 can (8 oz.) sliced mushrooms, drained
1 cup coarsely chopped green onion
1 cup diagonally sliced celery
1 green pepper diagonally sliced
1 tsp. M.S.G.
¼ cup soy sauce
2 cups finely sliced lettuce
3 cups hot cooked rice

Roll chicken pieces in cornstarch. Heat oil over medium high. Add chicken. Quickly sauté to light brown. Sprinkle with garlic powder. Add tomato, water chestnuts, mushrooms, green onion, celery and green pepper. Sprinkle with M.S.G. Stir in soy sauce. Cover, reduce heat and simmer 5 minutes, or until vegetables are tender crisp. When ready to serve, toss with lettuce. Serve hot over rice.

Serves 4-6

Variation: Snow peas, cashews, fresh mushrooms and a little white wine.

CHICKEN PARMIGIANA

6 lg. chicken breasts, split, skinned, boned (12 pcs.)
Salt to taste
¼ tsp. pepper
Flour
3 eggs, beaten
2¾ cups Ritz cracker crumbs
7 Tbsp. olive oil, divided
3 med. onions, chopped
3 med. cloves garlic, minced
3 lg. tomatoes, cut up **or** 1 can (28 oz.) whole tomatoes, drained and cut up
⅓ cup dry red wine
1 bay leaf, crushed
½ tsp. oregano
1 lb. mozzarella cheese (12 slices)
3 Tbsp. freshly grated Parmesan cheese

Preheat oven to 375°. Flatten chicken breasts slightly between two sheets of wax paper. Sprinkle with salt and pepper. Dip in flour, then eggs, then coat with cracker crumbs. Brown slowly in 5 Tbsp. hot oil until golden brown on both sides and cooked through. Remove and keep warm.

Heat 2 Tbsp. oil in saucepan. Add onions and garlic and sauté until golden brown. Stir in tomatoes, wine, bay leaf, oregano and salt to taste. Bring to boil, stirring constantly. Reduce heat and simmer 10 minutes, stirring occasionally.

Spoon half of sauce into 9x13 pan. Arrange chicken in pan. Tuck cheese between and over chicken. Spoon over rest of sauce and sprinkle with Parmesan cheese. Bake uncovered at 375° for 15–20 minutes. Can be assembled a day or two ahead before baking.
Serves 8–10

Timely Tip:
Combine honey and mustard and use as a barbecue glaze.

DOUG'S CHICKEN PICCATA

4 whole chicken breasts
  skinned, boned and
  halved (8 pieces)
½ cup flour
1½ tsp. salt
¼ tsp. freshly ground
  pepper
¼ tsp. Accent
¼ cup clarified butter
1 Tbsp. olive oil
4 Tbsp. Madeira wine, or
  more to taste
3 Tbsp. lemon juice
2 Tbsp. apple juice
Lemon slices, at least 8
¼ cup minced fresh parsley
  (optional garnish)

Place chicken breasts between 2 sheets of wax paper and pound them until thin (about ¼ inch). Combine flour, salt, pepper and Accent in a bag. Add breasts and coat well; shake off excess. Heat butter and olive oil in large skillet until bubbling. Sauté chicken breasts 2–3 minutes on each side. (Do not overcook). Drain on paper towels and keep warm. Drain off all but 2 Tbsp. butter and oil. Stir wine into drippings, scraping bottom of skillet to loosen any browned bits. Add fruit juices and heat briefly. Return chicken to skillet, interspersing with lemon slices, and heat until sauce thickens. Sprinkle with minced parsley.

Serve With: Fettuccine.

Serves 4–6

SPICY 'N SWEET CHICKEN

3 whole chicken breasts,
  split and skinned
Garlic powder to taste
5 Tbsp. soy sauce, divided
½ cup dry sherry, divided
⅓ cup hot chutney, coarsely
  chopped
¼ cup orange marmalade
1½ tsp. ground ginger

Preheat oven to 350°. Place chicken breasts, meat side down, in a casserole. Sprinkle with garlic powder, 4 Tbsp. soy sauce and ¼ cup dry sherry. Bake at 350° for 30 minutes. In a small bowl mix chutney, marmalade, ¼ cup sherry, ginger and 1 Tbsp. soy sauce. Turn chicken over and baste with this sauce several times during the last 15-20 minutes of cooking. Ladle sauce over chicken for serving.

Serve With: Turmeric Rice.

Serves 4–6

SUPRÊMES DE VOLAILLE MILANAISE

4 whole chicken breasts,
  boned
¼ tsp. salt
Dash pepper
1 cup flour
½ cup freshly grated
  Parmesan cheese
½ cup fine white bread
  crumbs
1 egg plus dash salt and ½
  tsp. olive oil beaten
  together in soup bowl
8 Tbsp. clarified butter,
  divided
3 Tbsp. minced parsley
1 Tbsp. lemon juice

Season the chicken breasts with salt and pepper. One at a time roll in the flour and shake off the excess. Combine Parmesan cheese and bread crumbs. Dip chicken one piece at a time in egg, salt and oil mixture and then in crumb mixture. Lay the chicken on wax paper and allow cheese and bread crumbs to set for 10-15 minutes.

In 4 Tbsp. clarified butter, sauté chicken 3-5 minutes on each side and remove to serving dish. Add 4 Tbsp. clarified butter to skillet, and set over moderately high heat a minute or so. Immediately remove from heat and add parsley and lemon juice. Pour over chicken breasts and serve. May be prepared in the morning and cooked just before serving.   Serves 4

ORIENTAL CHICKEN À L'ORANGE

6-8 chicken legs with thighs
  and/or breasts
Salt and pepper to taste
3-4 Tbsp. butter

Sauce
1¼ cups orange juice (or
  more)
½ cup currants
¼ cup chutney
½ tsp. cinnamon
½ tsp. curry

Preheat oven to 425°. Salt and pepper chicken in baking dish. Pat each piece with butter. Place chicken in oven uncovered at 425° for 15 minutes. Combine sauce ingredients in pan and simmer for 10 minutes. Pour onto chicken and lower temperature to 350°. Bake for 1 hour. Keep spooning sauce over chicken throughout cooking time.
                    Serves 6-8

CHICKEN AND CASHEWS

1 lb. chicken breasts, boned and cubed

Marinade
1 tsp. sherry
⅛ tsp. pepper
⅛ tsp. M.S.G. (optional)
2 slices ginger root, minced
2½ Tbsp. soy sauce
1 Tbsp. corn starch

3 Tbsp. sesame oil, divided
1 cup raw cashews
½ sm. onion, diced
1 cup diced celery
½ cup diced water chestnuts
1 cup diced green pepper
½ cup water
1 Tbsp. soy sauce
1 tsp. cornstarch in 1 Tbsp. water
2-3 cups cooked rice

Put all marinade ingredients together in large bowl. Marinate chicken for ½ hour or longer.

Heat wok to high temperature. Add 2 Tbsp. oil. Stir fry raw cashews and remove with slotted spoon. Add 1 more Tbsp. oil. Stir fry chicken until golden, remove, keep warm. Stir fry diced onion 2 minutes. Add other vegetables. Stir fry for 1 minute. Add water, soy sauce, and cornstarch mixture. Return chicken and nuts. Mix thoroughly and serve with rice.

Serves 4

Variations:
Add bean sprouts, 1 clove garlic minced, peapods.

CHICKEN AND PINEAPPLE YAKI-TORI

1 can (15¼ oz.) pineapple chunks
½ cup soy sauce
⅓ cup sugar
1 clove garlic, minced
¼ tsp. ground ginger
4 whole chicken breasts, boned, skinned and cut into chunks
2 green peppers, cut into chunks
2 cans (8 oz. each) whole water chestnuts
1 pt. cherry tomatoes

Drain pineapple, reserving ⅓ cup syrup. Combine reserved syrup, soy sauce, sugar, garlic and ginger in saucepan. Bring to a boil, then let cool. Marinate chicken in sauce at least 4 hours.

Alternate pineapple, chicken, peppers, tomatoes and water chestnuts on skewers or hibachi sticks. Marinate again for 15 minutes before cooking. Grill or broil six inches from heat turning slowly, 15-20 minutes.

Serves 6

KING RANCH CHICKEN
Mexican party must

3-4 lbs. chicken
1 onion
1-2 stalks celery
Salt and pepper to taste
1 pkg. frozen tortillas or
  canned
1 med. onion, chopped
1 lg. green pepper, chopped
½ lb. cheddar cheese,
  grated
1 can (10¾ oz.) cream of
  chicken soup, undiluted
1 can (10¾ oz.) cream of
  mushroom soup,
  undiluted
Chili powder
Garlic salt
1 can tomatoes and chilies
  undrained

Boil chicken until tender in water seasoned with onion, celery, salt and pepper. Cool. Cut chicken into bite-sized pieces. Reserve all stock. Soak tortillas in hot stock until wilted. Combine the soups.

Preheat oven to 375°. Layer casserole with ½ tortillas, chicken, onion, green pepper and soups. Sprinkle liberally with chili powder; add garlic salt and grated cheese. Repeat the layer. Cover casserole with tomatoes and chilies and all the juice. Juices in the casserole should be about half the depth of the dish. If not, add a little more stock. Bake casserole un-covered at 375° for 30 minutes. Assemble at least 24 hours ahead and refrigerate so that the flavors will blend. May be assembled and frozen.

Serves 8

CHICKEN TERIYAKI

2 lg. whole chicken breasts,
  boned and skinned
¼ cup soy sauce
¼ cup honey
¼ cup vinegar
2 Tbsp. blended whisky
1 clove garlic
¼ tsp. powdered ginger
1 cube chicken bouillon

Cut chicken into 2-inch square pieces. Marinate overnight in combined remaining ingre-dients. Remove chicken from marinade and place on skewers. Grill about 3-4 minutes a side, or until tender.   Serves 2-4

CHICKEN LASAGNA

good as a luncheon dish,
but heavy enough for dinner

8 oz. noodles, cooked and drained
1 pkg. (8 oz.) cream cheese, softened
1½ cups cottage cheese
2 cans (10¾ oz. each) mushroom soup, undiluted
1 cup whole milk
¾ tsp. salt
½ tsp. poultry seasoning
⅓ cup chopped green pepper
⅓ cup chopped onion
¼ cup minced parsley
4 cups cubed, cooked chicken
1½ cups buttered bread crumbs

Preheat oven to 375°. Beat together cheeses, soup, milk, salt and poultry seasoning. Stir in green pepper, onion and parsley. Layer ½ the noodles, chicken, and soup mixture in casserole. Repeat. Top with bread crumbs. Bake casserole uncovered at 375° for 1 hour. Let stand a few minutes before serving. Can be made ahead. Freezes well.   Serves 8

Cook onion, parsley and green pepper in 1 tsp. oil for 1-2 minutes on High. Beat together cheeses, soup, milk, salt and poultry seasoning in glass dish. Heat by microwaving on High 2-4 minutes, stirring after 2 minutes. Stir in green pepper, onion and parsley. Layer half the noodles, chicken and soup mixture in glass casserole. Repeat. Top with bread crumbs. Bake uncovered on High 12-15 minutes, giving quarter turns every 3-4 minutes. Lasagna is cooked when bubbly and hot in center.

Meats

Meats

FAVORITE FLANK STEAK

¼ cup soy sauce
3 Tbsp. honey
3 Tbsp. vinegar
1 tsp. ground ginger
1 clove garlic, crushed
1 green onion, finely
  chopped
¾ cup salad oil
1 flank steak (approximately
  1½ lbs.), scored

Mix together soy sauce, honey and vinegar. Stir in ginger. Blend in garlic, chopped green onion and oil. Place meat in an oblong glass dish and pour marinade over. Refrigerate, covered, 4 hours or overnight, turning meat occasionally.

Grill over hot coals or broil in oven until cooked to your liking, basting with marinade if desired. Let stand a few minutes and then cut very thin slices diagonally across the grain.

Serves 4

JOHNSTON'S PEPPER STEAK

1 lb. round steak, ½" thick
1 Tbsp. paprika
2 Tbsp. butter
3 cloves garlic, crushed
1½ cups beef broth
1 cup sliced green onions,
  including tops
2 green peppers, cut in
  strips
2 Tbsp. cornstarch
¼ cup water
¼ cup soy sauce
2 fresh tomatoes, cut in
  eighths
3 cups cooked rice

Pound steak to ¼-inch thickness. Then cut into ¼-inch wide strips. Sprinkle meat with paprika and allow to stand while preparing other ingredients or longer.

In a large skillet, brown meat in butter. Add garlic and beef broth. Cover and simmer for 30 minutes. Stir in onions and peppers. Cover and cook 5 more minutes.

Blend together cornstarch, water and soy sauce. Stir into meat mixture. Cook and stir until liquid is clear and thickened, about 2 minutes. Add tomatoes and stir gently. Serve over rice.

Serves 6

GRILLED FLANK STEAK WITH RED WINE SAUCE

1-1¼ lb. flank steak
Soy sauce
Salt (optional)
Freshly ground black pepper
1 tsp. dried thyme, crushed
1¼ cups chopped shallots or
    green onions and tops
1¼ cups red wine
½ cup butter
2 Tbsp. finely chopped
    parsley

Variation:
Add sautéed, sliced mush-
rooms to sauce.

Brush steak with soy sauce and sprinkle well with salt, pepper and thyme. Let stand for at least 1 hour. Brush again with soy sauce and grill over a brisk fire, 3-5 minutes on each side for medium-rare steak.

Meanwhile, make sauce by combining the shallots or green onions with red wine. Heat just to the boiling point. Add butter and salt to taste, and stir until butter is melted. Add parsley. Carve steak diagonally into thin slices and spoon sauce over steak.

Sauce can be made ahead and reheated. Any remaining sauce can be used on hamburger or other form of beef.

Serves 3

BAKED BEEF STEW

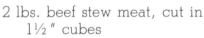
make at noon, enjoy your afternoon

2 lbs. beef stew meat, cut in
    1½ " cubes
2 tsp. salt
2½ Tbsp. minute tapioca
1 Tbsp. sugar
3 med. onions, peeled and
    sliced
6 carrots, cubed
5 med. potatoes, cubed
1½ cups chopped celery
¾ cup V-8 juice

Preheat oven to 250°. Trim fat from meat and place in roasting pan. Mix salt, tapioca and sugar. Sprinkle over meat. Add onions, carrots, potatoes and celery to pan. Pour V-8 juice over all. Cover roasting pan and seal tightly. Bake for 5 hours. **No peeking.** Serves 6

SWISS POT ROAST

4 lb. beef rump roast
¼ cup butter
1 med. onion
4 cloves
2 lbs. fresh mushrooms, sliced
Salt and pepper
Dry white wine
Sour cream (optional)

Remove all strings, fat and gristle from roast. Heat butter until brown in a heavy casserole or Dutch oven. Brown meat on all sides in butter over high heat. Stud onion with cloves and tuck down in pot beside meat. Add sliced mushrooms, salt and pepper.

Reduce heat and cover casserole with a tightly fitting lid. Simmer over lowest possible heat for 2–3 hours, or until meat is very tender. Moisture from the mushrooms should create enough juice to cook roast. Check occasionally and, if necessary, add enough white wine to keep pan juices from scorching.

When done, remove meat and onion from pan. If desired, sour cream may be added to mushrooms and juices. Slice roast against the grain to serve.

Serves 6

MADEIRA SAUCE

3 Tbsp. butter
1½ Tbsp. flour
¾ cup beef stock
1 tsp. Kitchen Bouquet
¼ cup Madeira

Melt butter, stir in flour. Whisk over medium heat for 5 minutes. (Removes pasty flour taste.) Slowly add beef stock, Kitchen Bouquet and wine. Serve over Beef Wellington, tenderloin, or any beef. Can be made ahead.

Yields 1 cup

Variation: Fresh sliced mushrooms may be added.

STEAK IN A BAG

2-3 lbs. top sirloin steak,
2½" thick
Seasoned salt and pepper to
taste
4 Tbsp. vegetable oil
4 Tbsp. butter, softened
1 cup fine bread crumbs
4 oz. sharp cheddar cheese,
shredded
Brown paper grocery bag
Fresh parsley, chopped
(optional)

Preheat oven to 375°. Remove excess fat from steak and sprinkle with seasoned salt and pepper. Spread oil and then butter on steak. Combine bread crumbs and cheese. Press this mixture onto steak, coating well. Place steak in bag and fold over ends securely. Place bag on a rimmed baking sheet. Bake in oven 30-40 minutes for medium-rare meat.

Remove steak from bag and let stand for 5 minutes before slicing. If desired, sprinkle steak with parsley before serving. Prepared steak may be refrigerated in bag for several hours. Bring to room temperature before cooking.   Serves 4-6

STEAK DIANE

2 boneless club steaks, 8-10
oz. each
Salt and pepper
Clarified butter
3 Tbsp. brandy
2 Tbsp. butter
½ lemon
½ tsp. Dijon mustard
1 Tbsp. finely minced chives
2 tsp. finely minced parsley
2 tsp. Worcestershire sauce

Sprinkle steaks with salt and pepper and sauté in clarified butter until lightly browned on both sides. Heat brandy, add to sauté pan and set ablaze. When flames subside, remove steaks to a hot platter. Add butter to liquid in pan. Squeeze lemon into pan. Add mustard, chives, parsley and Worcestershire sauce. Stir well. Heat to bubbling and spoon over the steaks.   Serves 2

STEAK SICILIANO

2½ lbs. sirloin or round
   steak, about 1½" thick
Seasoned meat tenderizer
1 cup Burgundy wine
1 sm. clove garlic
1 Tbsp. Worcestershire
   sauce
1 sm. onion, minced
2 Tbsp. minced parsley
2 Tbsp. prepared
   horseradish
2 Tbsp. prepared mustard
1 Tbsp. sugar
2 Tbsp. butter
1 tsp. salt
¼ tsp. pepper
¼ tsp. oregano

Sprinkle all surfaces of steak evenly with meat tenderizer. Pierce deeply and generously with fork. Let stand at room temperature for 1 hour.

Combine remaining ingredients in small saucepan. Heat until butter melts, then cool to room temperature. Pour sauce over steak and marinate several hours, or overnight in the refrigerator, turning steak occasionally.

Remove steak from sauce. Strain sauce, reserving solids and liquid. Broil steak on one side, basting with marinade liquid. Turn steak, spread top surface with solids from sauce. Broil to desired degree of doneness. Cooking time will be approximately 5 minutes per side for rare, 7 minutes per side for medium-rare, 8 minutes per side for well-done. Slice steak to serve. Extra sauce can be served on the side.   Serves 6

Variation: Sauce also makes good marinade for shish-kabob.

Timely Tip:
As an alternative to clarified butter, use two parts butter to one part oil or unsalted margarine. The oil allows sautéing at a higher temperature without burning the butter.

SIMPLY ELEGANT STUFFED TENDERLOIN

3 lg. onions, thinly sliced
6 Tbsp. olive oil
4 Tbsp. butter
2 cloves garlic, minced
1 can (14½ oz.) ripe olives, chopped
½ cup chopped prosciutto ham
1 tsp. freshly ground black pepper
1 tsp. thyme
Salt to taste
2 egg yolks, beaten
2 Tbsp. chopped parsley
1 whole beef tenderloin (about 6 lbs.)
Additional parsley for garnish

Preheat oven to 300°. Sauté onions in olive oil and butter until limp. Add garlic, olives, ham, pepper, thyme and salt. Cook until well-blended. Remove from heat and stir in egg yolks and parsley. Return skillet to heat and cook a few minutes, stirring until blended.

Cut filet **almost** through to bottom into 8-10 thick slices. Spoon stuffing mixture between the slices. At the tail end, fold the meat back over some stuffing and use a skewer to secure.

Roast for 50 minutes, or until meat thermometer inserted in center reaches the desired temperature. Let stand for 10 minutes. Slice through and serve on platter decorated with fresh parsley.   Serves 8-10

Variation: Filet may be prepared and refrigerated up to 1 day ahead. Bring to room temperature before roasting. If tenderloin is too long to fit on a pan, cut in half.

MR. FOSTER'S STEAK SAUCE

½ cup butter
¼ cup snipped parsley
¼ cup minced onion
2 tsp. Worcestershire sauce
½ tsp. dry mustard
½ tsp. freshly ground pepper

In a small saucepan, combine all ingredients. Heat until butter melts. Serve with broiled sirloin steak. Can be made ahead.
                Yields scant 1 cup

FOOL PROOF BEARNAISE SAUCE

½ cup butter, softened
¼ cup water or dry white
   wine
3 Tbsp. tarragon vinegar
2 tsp. chopped green onions
¼ tsp. salt
Dash pepper
3 egg yolks
½ cup mayonnaise

Combine all ingredients except mayonnaise in blender. Blend until smooth. Combine with mayonnaise until smooth and heat over medium heat until thick, stirring constantly. May be served at room temperature.

Yields 1½ cups

Variation: More herbs may be added to taste.
Helpful Hints: Do not make ahead. Make sure all lumps are out of the mayonnaise.

BORDELAISE SAUCE

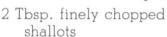

superb sophisticated sauce

2 Tbsp. finely chopped
   shallots
¾ cup Gallo Hearty
   Burgundy
½ bay leaf
Pinch of thyme
1 cup sliced mushrooms
2–3 Tbsp. butter
1½ Tbsp. flour
1 cup beef stock

Put shallots, wine, bay leaf and thyme in a saucepan and simmer until reduced to ¼ cup. Strain mixture by scraping through sieve as much as possible for smooth texture. Set aside.

Sauté mushrooms in butter. Stir in flour. Add beef stock. Cook over medium heat stirring constantly until mixture boils and thickens. Add wine mixture, simmer for 5 minutes. Keep warm and covered until ready to serve. Can be made ahead.

Yields 1¾ cups

Helpful Hints: Double or triple recipe and store in covered container in refrigerator. Do not salt as it is salty by itself.
Serve With: Filet or flank steak sliced diagonally.

CORNISH PASTIES

takes time, but ohhh so good

Filling

2 lbs. beef (top round or sirloin) cut into ½″ cubes

1½–2 cups ½″ diced raw potatoes

1½ cups ½″ diced raw rutabaga

1 med. onion, coarsely chopped

2 lg. carrots, finely diced

Salt and pepper to taste

Pastry

3 cups flour

1 Tbsp. salt

1 cup ground suet at room temperature

1 cup iced water, or less

1+ tsp. ground suet per pasty

Serves 9

Filling

Mix ingredients together in a large bowl.

Pastry

Using hands, mix flour, salt and suet together until suet is incorporated with flour. Add iced water by the Tbsp. until mixture sticks together. Shape into 9 balls. On a well-floured surface roll each ball into a circle as thin as pie crust.

Assembly

Preheat oven to 425°. As each circle is rolled place ¾ packed cup filling on ½ of circle. Place generous tsp. of suet on top of filling. Fold dough over to form a half circle shape. Dampen edges and fold pastry edge towards inside for tight seal. Further seal with fork tines. Make a 1–1½ inch vent in top of pastry.

Place pasty on a cookie sheet sprayed with Pam. Bake 30 minutes at 425° till brown. Turn oven down to 325° and bake another 30 minutes.

The pasties are ready to be eaten, or cool on a rack and freeze. Thaw for 3 hours — not in microwave. To reheat, bake 1 pasty 15 minutes at 350° or 4 pasties for 30 minutes.

Variations: Use mushrooms, peas, celery, chicken or turkey. Substitute rendered chicken fat for suet.

Helpful Hints: When preparing rutabaga, cut in half, then slice flat side down. Peel after slicing, before dicing.

BEEF STROGANOFF

¾ lb. fresh mushrooms,
   sliced
1 sm. onion, minced
1 clove garlic, minced
2-4 Tbsp. butter, divided
2 lbs. beef tenderloin, sliced
   in strips
½ cup canned beef bouillon
¼ cup dry vermouth
1 Tbsp. Worcestershire
   sauce
1 tsp. paprika
Salt and pepper to taste
1½ cups sour cream, room
   temperature

In large skillet, lightly brown mushrooms, onion and garlic in 1-2 Tbsp. butter. Remove from skillet and keep warm. Brown beef strips in 1-2 Tbsp. butter quickly over high heat. Cook meat in batches so that each piece is browned evenly. Meat should be rare to medium-rare. Remove meat from skillet, combine with mushroom mixture, and keep covered.

To pan drippings, add beef bouillon and vermouth. Simmer for 5 minutes. Add Worcestershire, paprika, salt and pepper. Simmer 1 more minute. Cover and reduce to warm for no more than 20-25 minutes.

Just before serving, add sour cream to warm wine gravy. Simmer and whisk over low heat until blended. Add meat and mushroom mixture, and heat to serving temperature. Serve immediately over rice or lightly buttered noodles.   Serves 4

BEEF STROGANOFF WITH DILL

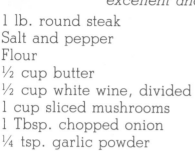

excellent and easy company dish

1 lb. round steak
Salt and pepper
Flour
½ cup butter
½ cup white wine, divided
1 cup sliced mushrooms
1 Tbsp. chopped onion
¼ tsp. garlic powder
2 tsp. dill
1 beef bouillon cube
½–1 cup sour cream

Slice meat in ⅛-inch strips across the grain. Sprinkle with salt and pepper, and toss in flour. In a heavy frying pan, melt 2 Tbsp. butter and brown meat, a few pieces at a time. Use more butter with each batch of meat. Remove meat to a 2-quart **enameled** casserole. Lift the glaze in frying pan with ¼ cup wine and pour over meat.

Use more butter to brown mushrooms. Add chopped onion, and sauté until translucent. Add these to meat and again "wash" out pan with ¼ cup wine. Add water to not quite cover meat in casserole. Stir in garlic powder, dill and bouillon cube. Simmer on top of the stove until meat is tender. Thicken sauce with flour and water if necessary.

Just before serving, remove casserole from heat and stir in sour cream, whisking carefully to blend. May be prepared ahead up to addition of sour cream.

Serves 4

Serve With: Buttered noodles.

GREEN ONION CHOPPED STEAK

2 lbs. ground beef (round or sirloin)
½ cup soy sauce
1 cup Burgundy
1 Tbsp. chopped green onion
1 Tbsp. chopped parsley
1 tsp. celery salt
1 tsp. garlic powder
1 tsp. ground pepper

Form meat into patties and place in glass dish. Combine remaining ingredients. Pour over meat. Cover and refrigerate for at least 2-3 hours, preferably overnight. Use your favorite method to cook the patties.   Serves 6-8

BEST IN THE WEST BEANS

¼ lb. ground beef
¼ lb. bacon, chopped
¼ onion, chopped
2 Tbsp. ketchup
2 Tbsp. barbecue sauce
¼ tsp. salt
1 Tbsp. prepared mustard
1 Tbsp. molasses
1 tsp. chili powder
Very scant ¼ tsp. pepper
1 can (8 oz.) red kidney beans
1 can (8 oz.) pork and beans
1 can (8 oz.) butter beans

Preheat oven to 350°. Brown ground beef, bacon and onions. Drain off excess fat. Combine ketchup, barbecue sauce, salt, mustard, molasses, chili powder and pepper and add to meat mixture, stirring well. Add beans and combine thoroughly. Transfer to casserole and bake uncovered 1 hour. May be made ahead. Freezes.

Serves 5-6

Helpful Hint: Recipe can be doubled or quadrupled.

 Combine ground beef, bacon and onion in a small glass dish. Loosely cover with waxpaper. Cook mixture for 3-4 minutes on High, stirring after 2 minutes. Drain. Combine ketchup, barbecue sauce, salt, mustard, molasses, chili powder and pepper. Add meat mixture and beans, and combine thoroughly. Transfer to a 3-quart casserole and cook, covered, for 12-15 minutes or until heated thoroughly. Rotate dish several times during cooking process. Let stand 5 minutes.

CANNELONI

16 manicotti shells, cooked and drained

Filling
¼ cup finely chopped onion
2 cloves garlic, finely chopped
2 Tbsp. olive oil
1 pkg. (10 oz.) frozen chopped spinach, thawed and squeezed dry
2 Tbsp. butter, divided
1 lb. ground round
2 chicken livers
5 Tbsp. grated Parmesan
2 Tbsp. whipping cream
2 eggs, lightly beaten
½ tsp. oregano
Salt and ground black pepper to taste

White Sauce
4 Tbsp. butter
4 Tbsp. flour
1 tsp. salt
⅛ tsp. white pepper
1 cup milk
1 cup whipping cream

Topping
3 cups tomato sauce
4 Tbsp. grated Parmesan cheese
2 Tbsp. butter, cut into tiny pieces

Preheat oven to 375°.

Filling
Saute onion and garlic in olive oil until soft, but not brown. Stir in spinach and cook until all moisture has boiled away. Transfer to large mixing bowl. Brown the ground round in 1 Tbsp. butter; drain and add to the spinach mixture. Cook chicken livers in 1 Tbsp. butter until light brown and firm but still pink inside. Chop livers coarsely and add to spinach mixture. Add remaining filling ingredients, mix well and set aside.

White Sauce
In saucepan, melt butter and stir in flour, salt and pepper. Stir until bubbly. Add milk and cream, stirring constantly over medium to high heat until thickened.

Assembly
Fill cooked manicotti shells with spinach-beef mixture. Pour a film of tomato sauce into two 9x13 shallow glass dishes. Place manicotti shells side by side in one layer on the tomato sauce. Pour white sauce over shells, and spoon tomato sauce on top. Sprinkle Parmesan cheese over tomato sauce and dot cheese with butter. Bake uncovered for 20 minutes. Broil for 30 seconds to brown top.   Serves 6-8

BEEF MANICOTTI

superb for a buffet

1 lb. ground beef
2 cups water
2 cans (6 oz. each) tomato
  paste
½ cup chopped onion
1 can (4 oz.) sliced
  mushrooms, drained
6 Tbsp. chopped parsley,
  divided
2 tsp. crushed oregano
1½ tsp. salt
1 tsp. sugar
1 lg. clove garlic, minced
24 oz. ricotta or cream style
  cottage cheese, drained
½ cup grated Parmesan
  cheese
2 eggs, slightly beaten
½ tsp. salt
8 manicotti shells

Preheat oven to 350°. In Dutch oven, brown meat and drain. Add water, tomato paste, onion, mushrooms, 2 Tbsp. parsley, oregano, 1½ tsp. salt, sugar and garlic. Simmer uncovered for 30 minutes, stirring occasionally.

In separate bowl, combine ricotta or cottage cheese, Parmesan, eggs, 4 Tbsp. parsley and ½ tsp. salt.

Cook manicotti shells in boiling water just until tender, about 20 minutes, drain. Rinse in cold water and drain.

Stuff each shell with ⅓–½ cup cheese mixture, using small spoon. Pour half the tomato sauce into a 9x13 baking dish. Arrange stuffed shells in a row. Drizzle with remaining sauce. Bake in 350° oven for 30–35 minutes. Let stand 10 minutes before serving. Sprinkle with additional Parmesan cheese. May be made ahead up to baking. If refrigerated, add 5–10 minutes to baking time.

Serves 4–6

 Ground beef can be cooked in heavy duty plastic strainer with glass dish underneath for 4½–5 minutes on High, stirring once or twice.

STEVE'S CHILI

1 lb. green peppers (about 4), seeded and coarsely chopped
1½ Tbsp. salad oil
1½ lbs. onions, coarsely chopped
2 cloves garlic, crushed
½ cup finely chopped parsley
½ cup butter
3½ lbs. ground beef chuck
⅓ cup chili powder
5 cups canned tomatoes
Salt to taste
2 tsp. pepper
2 tsp. cumin seed
1½ tsp. M.S.G.
3 Tbsp. vinegar
2 hot Jalapeno peppers, finely chopped
2 dashes Tabasco sauce

Saute peppers slowly in salad oil for 5 minutes. Add onions and cook until tender, stirring frequently. Add garlic and parsley. In a large skillet, melt butter and cook ground beef for about 15 minutes. Add the meat to onion mixture. Stir in chili powder and cook another 10 minutes.

Simmer tomatoes for 5 minutes in a 6-quart kettle. Add the meat mixture to the tomatoes and season with salt, pepper, cumin seed, M.S.G., vinegar, Jalapeno peppers and Tabasco. Cover and simmer for 3 hours. Skim fat from top before serving. May be made ahead. Freezes.

Yields 4 quarts

EASY VENISON STEW
no gamey taste — children love it!

2 lbs. venison, cubed
2 onions, quartered
1 raw potato, cut into bite-sized pcs.
½ lb. mushrooms, sliced
1 can (10¾ oz.) mushroom soup, undiluted
½ soup can dry red wine
1 tsp. salt
Cracked pepper, to taste
¼ tsp. thyme
¼ tsp. marjoram
Brown Sauce, as needed

Preheat oven to 275°-300°. Combine all ingredients in a casserole and bake, covered, at 275°-300° for about 4 hours. Thicken juices with flour if desired. Add Brown Sauce for color, if necessary. Can be made ahead.   Serves 4-6

Serve With:
Flavored noodles or rice (preferably rice mix)

MEXICAN CASSEROLE
like a Mexican lasagna

½ cup chopped onion
2 cloves garlic, minced
1 Tbsp. oil
1 lb. lean ground beef
1 can (28 oz.) stewed
   tomatoes
1 pkg. (1¼ oz.) taco
   seasoning mix (or more to
   taste)
1 can (4 oz.) diced green
   chilies
1 can (2½ oz.) chopped
   black olives
1 pkg. (15-16 oz.) cheese
   flavored tortilla chips,
   lightly crushed
½ lb. mozzarella cheese,
   grated
2 cups sour cream
½ cup grated cheddar
   cheese

Preheat oven to 350°. Sauté onion and garlic in oil. Add ground beef and cook until brown. Blend in tomatoes, taco seasoning, green chilies and olives. Simmer for 10 minutes.

Grease a 9x13 baking dish. Spread half of crushed tortilla chips in bottom of dish. Add all of meat mixture. Layer mozzarella cheese, then sour cream on top. Add remaining tortilla chips.

Bake uncovered about 30 minutes, or until heated through. Sprinkle with cheddar cheese and continue baking until cheese melts.   Serves 6-8

BARBECUE SAUCE
great for grilled chicken or pork

1 med. onion, finely
   chopped
1 clove garlic, minced
¼ cup oil
2 Tbsp. vinegar
⅓ cup firmly packed brown
   sugar
2 cups ketchup
1 cup water
4 tsp. Worcestershire sauce
1 Tbsp. prepared mustard
1½ tsp. chili powder
Cayenne pepper (optional)
Tabasco (optional)

In saucepan, cook onion and garlic in oil for 5 minutes. Add vinegar, brown sugar, ketchup, water, Worcestershire sauce, mustard and chili powder. Add cayenne or tabasco if desired. Simmer, uncovered, for 30 minutes. Can be made ahead. Freezes well.

Yields 3 cups

NORWEGIAN MEAT BALLS

1 lb. ground round
½ lb. ground pork
1 sm. onion, grated
1½ carrots, grated
¼-½ cup bread crumbs
3 Tbsp. flour, divided
Salt and pepper to taste
Pinch of mace
¾-1 cup milk
Butter
1½-2¼ cups water
1 beef bouillon cube

Thoroughly combine ground round, pork, onion, carrots, bread crumbs, 2 Tbsp. flour, salt, pepper and mace. Add enough milk to soften without making mixture mushy. Shape into meatballs the size of a quarter.

Brown meatballs in butter. Add 1½-2 cups water and bouillon cube. Cover and simmer gently for 20-30 minutes, until meat is done but not tough. Combine 1 Tbsp. flour with ¼ cup water. Stir into liquid in pan to thicken gravy. May be made ahead. Freezes.   Serves 4

ZUCCHINI AND BEEF CASSEROLE

1 lb. ground beef
1 cup chopped onions
1 cup chopped green pepper
4 cups sliced zucchini
2 tsp. salt
1 tsp. oregano
¼ tsp. nutmeg
½ tsp. basil
½ tsp. cumin
½ tsp. garlic powder
½ tsp. pepper
1½ cups beef broth
1 can (16 oz.) tomatoes
1 cup uncooked long grain
   rice
1 cup grated mozzarella
   cheese, divided

Preheat oven to 350°. Brown the ground beef and drain it. Add all other ingredients except for ½ cup of mozzarella cheese. Bring the mixture to a boil and simmer until rice is almost tender (15-20 minutes). Transfer mixture to a greased 9x13 baking dish. Sprinkle remaining cheese on top. Bake uncovered for 45 minutes. May be assembled ahead.   Serves 6

MARGARET'S MEAT AND SPINACH CASSEROLE

2 pkgs. (10 oz. each) frozen, chopped spinach, thawed and drained well
½ lb. bulk pork sausage
1 lb. lean ground beef
1 lg. onion, chopped
1 clove garlic, minced
1 can (15 oz.) tomato sauce
1 can (6 oz.) tomato paste
½ cup water
1 cup Burgundy
¼ tsp. rosemary
¼ tsp. basil
¼ tsp. marjoram
¼ tsp. oregano
¼ tsp. black pepper
¼ tsp. savory
1½ tsp. salt
8 oz. bow tie noodles, cooked and drained
2 cups sour cream
1 cup grated Parmesan cheese

Crumble pork sausage and ground beef in skillet. Cook over medium heat until pink (not brown). Add onion and garlic and cook until meat is falling apart. Drain. Blend tomato sauce, tomato paste, water, Burgundy and seasonings into meat mixture. Simmer 30–40 minutes, until thick.

Preheat oven to 350°. Add cooked noodles to meat mixture while meat is still hot. Spread half of meat mixture in a 3-quart casserole dish. Add half of spinach on top of meat, then half of the sour cream, and half of the cheese. Repeat layers. Bake uncovered for 30–40 minutes. May be assembled ahead.

Serves 8–10

FIESTY PORK CHOPS

3 Tbsp. brown sugar
2 Tbsp. flour
1 Tbsp. vinegar
1 tsp. mustard
½ bottle (12 oz.) chili sauce
6–8 pork chops, well trimmed

Preheat oven to 350°. Combine brown sugar, flour, vinegar, mustard and chili sauce. Spread this mixture on bottom of 9x12 baking dish. Place pork chops on top. Bake, uncovered, for 1 hour, turning meat once. Sauce can be made ahead.

Serves 4–6

PICCADILLO

a Key West favorite

1½-2 lbs. ground beef
2 onions, diced
2 green peppers, diced
3-4 Tbsp. oil
2 Tbsp. Worcestershire
   sauce
½ tsp. M.S.G.
¼ tsp. oregano
½ tsp. salt
¼ tsp. ground black pepper
½ tsp. garlic powder
½ tsp. celery salt
¼ tsp. paprika
1 can (15 oz.) Hunt's tomato
   sauce
1-2 Tbsp. capers, drained
½ cup raisins
½-¾ cup halved stuffed or
   pitted ripe olives, drained
6-8 cups cooked saffron or
   white rice

Sauté meat, onions and peppers. Stir in seasonings. Add rest of ingredients, except rice, and cook 40 minutes over slow heat. Serve over rice.　　Serves 8

HAM LOAF

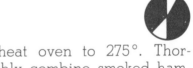

1 lb. ground smoked ham
1 lb. ground fresh pork
2 eggs, slightly beaten
1 cup crushed graham
   crackers
¾ cup milk
1 can (10¾ oz.) tomato
   soup, undiluted
½ cup vinegar
½ cup water
1 cup brown sugar
1 tsp. dry mustard

Preheat oven to 275°. Thoroughly combine smoked ham, pork, eggs, graham crackers and milk. Shape into loaf in a shallow 8½x11 glass pan. Leave some room around edges of pan. Combine the tomato soup, vinegar, water, brown sugar and dry mustard in a saucepan and bring to a boil. Pour sauce over the meatloaf and bake uncovered for 2 hours. Can be made ahead. Freezes.　　Serves 6

BAKED HAM À L'ORANGE

⅓ cup Triple Sec or Cointreau
⅓ cup fresh orange juice
½ tsp. fresh grated orange rind
⅓ cup currant jelly
1 Tbsp. cornstarch
1 cup brown sugar, divided
½ cup water
1 Tbsp. dry hot mustard
1 cup or more raisins
1 can (8 oz.) unsweetened crushed pineapple, undrained
Pinch of salt
Pinch of allspice
Ginger ale
7 lb. ham
Cloves

Preheat oven to 350°. Combine Triple Sec, orange juice, orange rind and currant jelly in a saucepan. Heat to boiling and set aside. Dissolve cornstarch and ¼ cup brown sugar in water and slowly add to orange juice mixture. Return pan to medium heat, and stir until ingredients are well-blended and slightly thickened. Add remaining sugar, mustard, raisins, pineapple, salt, allspice and ½ cup ginger ale. Stir to blend.

Score ham in a diamond pattern and stud with cloves. Place in roaster or pyrex baking dish. Pour sauce over top of ham. Bake uncovered for 1 hour, basting frequently (every 10–15 minutes). Add more ginger ale to sauce as it bakes away. Reduce heat to 300°. Continue basting ham, and cook until done, 30–45 more minutes. Remove cloves before serving. Spoon sauce over sliced ham. Sauce can be frozen.

Serves 14–18

Variation: Garnish before baking with pineapple rings with cherries in the center.

HAM ORIENTALE

3½ cups diced cooked ham
1 med. onion, thinly sliced
    and separated into rings
1 green pepper, cut into ½″
    squares
¾ cup pineapple chunks,
    drained (reserve ½ cup
    juice)
½ cup raisins
½ cup orange juice
⅓ cup vinegar
½ cup packed brown sugar
3 Tbsp. cornstarch
2 tsp. dry mustard
¼ tsp. salt
1 tsp. Worcestershire sauce
1 Tbsp. soy sauce
4 cups hot cooked rice

Preheat oven to 350°. In a baking dish, layer ham, onions, green pepper, pineapple and raisins in that order. Combine pineapple juice, orange juice and vinegar in a saucepan. Combine brown sugar, cornstarch, mustard and salt and add to mixture in saucepan. Heat and stir until dissolved and thickened. Add Worcestershire and soy sauce. Pour sauce over ham mixture. Bake uncovered for 45 minutes. Serve on bed of rice. Can be made ahead.

Serves 6–8

 Bake, loosely covered with wax paper, on High for 10–12 minutes, rotating every 3–4 minutes.

CEN'S PORK CHOPS

4 thick pork chops
1 clove garlic, minced
¼ cup bourbon, or more as
    needed
2 Tbsp. soy sauce, or more
    as needed

Preheat oven to 325°. Brown pork chops in skillet. Remove to casserole. Saute´ garlic in same skillet. Stir in bourbon and soy sauce, and scrape pan to loosen browned bits. Pour liquid from skillet over chops. Cover and bake for 20–30 minutes. As an alternative, you may wish to return chops to skillet in which you made the sauce, cover and simmer 15–20 minutes. Can be made ahead.

Serves 4

NORDIC MACARONI BAKE

great family week night dinner

2 cups ham, cubed
2 Tbsp. butter
½ cup chopped green
  pepper
½ cup chopped onion
2 Tbsp. flour
2½ cups milk, divided
4 cups cooked sm. macaroni
  shells (½ lb. uncooked)
1 cup cubed Jarlsberg
  cheese
1 cup chopped tomatoes
1 tsp. dry mustard
½ tsp. salt
¼ tsp pepper
½ cup grated Jarlsberg
  cheese

Preheat oven to 350°. In sauce-pan, brown ham lightly in but-ter. Add green pepper and onion; cook until translucent, about 5 minutes. Add flour, mix thoroughly, cook about 2 min-utes. Remove from heat, grad-ually stir in 2 cups of the milk. Return to heat and cook, stirring until thickened and smooth. Remove from heat, add cooked macaroni shells, cubed cheese, tomato, dry mustard, salt and pepper. Mix well.

Pour into greased 2-quart bak-ing dish. Bake at 350° for 20 minutes. Remove from oven and check moisture content; if too dry, add remaining ½ cup of milk. Sprinkle with grated cheese. Return to oven for 10 minutes or until mixture bubbles and cheese begins to brown.

Serves 6–8

GRAM'S MUSTARD SAUCE

great with ham

2 Tbsp. dry mustard
1 cup brown sugar
1 heaping Tbsp. flour
3 eggs, beaten
⅓ cup water
1 Tbsp. butter
⅔ cup vinegar

Mix all dry ingredients in 2-quart saucepan. Add remain-ing ingredients and stir con-stantly while heating on medium heat to thicken. Will keep sev-eral weeks in refrigerator.

Yields 1 pint

BEST PORK ROAST YOU'VE EVER EATEN

6 rib center cut pork loin
    roast
⅓ cup honey
⅓ cup Dijon mustard
¼ tsp. garlic powder, or to
    taste
½ tsp. rosemary
1 cup water, divided
½ beef bouillon cube
Salt and pepper to taste
2-3 Tbsp. Marsala (optional)
    or
1 Tbsp. cornstarch (optional)
3 Tbsp. water (optional)

Preheat oven to 400°. Place roast in shallow metal pan. Combine honey and Dijon mustard. Coat top and sides of roast with this mixture. Sprinkle garlic powder and rosemary over entire coated surface. Roast meat for 15 minutes at 400°, then remove from oven and add ⅓ cup water to bottom of pan.

Reduce oven heat to 325°, and roast meat 35 minutes per pound, or until meat thermometer reaches 175°. Check occasionally and add a little more water to pan to keep honey drippings from scorching.

When meat is done, remove from oven and place on carving board. Scrape pan and pour juices into saucepan. Add ½ cup water, ½ beef bouillon cube, salt and pepper to taste. Add Marsala, if desired, and simmer long enough to cook away alcohol smell. Skim off any grease and serve. Or thicken with 1 Tbsp. cornstarch dissolved in 3 Tbsp. water. Serves 6

Timely Tip:
Molasses or honey are less likely to stick if you dip the measuring cup in hot water before measuring.

BREADING FOR CHOPS

½ cup unseasoned dry
  bread crumbs
¼ cup grated Parmesan
  cheese
1 tsp. salt
1 tsp. crushed basil
¼ tsp. crushed thyme
1 tsp. paprika
½ cup butter, melted

Mix bread crumbs, cheese and spices. Dip chicken or pork chops in butter, then in crumb mixture. Bake according to individual preference.

Variation: Also good on chicken.

PORK CHOP MARINADE
lots of flavor

1½ cups salad oil
¾ cup soy sauce
¼ cup Worcestershire sauce
2 tsp. dry mustard
2¼ tsp. salt
1 Tbsp. pepper
½ cup wine vinegar
1½ tsp. chopped fresh
  parsley
2 cloves garlic, crushed
⅓ cup lemon juice

Put all ingredients in blender until well mixed. Pour marinade over pork chops. Cover and refrigerate overnight, turning occasionally. Cook on grill according to thickness of chops, 10-20 minutes or until done.

Yields 3½ cups

PORK CHOPS CHARCUTIERE

from the Pontchartrain Wine Cellars

1 lg. onion, thinly sliced
5 Tbsp. lard or margarine, divided (do not use butter)
1 tsp. flour
1 cup beef stock or bouillon
½ cup white wine
Salt and pepper
6 lg. pork chops
2 Tbsp. coarsely chopped gherkins
1 tsp. Dijon mustard
2 Tbsp. chopped parsley

Sauté onions in a saucepan with 2 Tbsp. lard or margarine until tender. Do not brown. Stir in flour. When the flour has disappeared, add the beef stock and wine. Stir until thick. Season to taste with salt and pepper. Bring sauce to boil and skim if necessary. Let simmer 30 minutes.

Meanwhile, brown pork chops in remaining 3 Tbsp. lard or margarine. Reduce the heat. Cover and cook until tender. Skim the sauce again if need be and add gherkins and mustard. Pour the sauce over the cooked chops and sprinkle with chopped parsley. Serve immediately.

Serves 6

PORK CHOPS ITALIANO

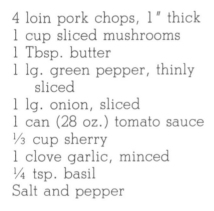

4 loin pork chops, 1" thick
1 cup sliced mushrooms
1 Tbsp. butter
1 lg. green pepper, thinly sliced
1 lg. onion, sliced
1 can (28 oz.) tomato sauce
⅓ cup sherry
1 clove garlic, minced
¼ tsp. basil
Salt and pepper

Preheat oven to 350°. In large skillet, brown chops and mushrooms in butter. Place pork chops in 8-inch square baking dish and distribute mushrooms on top. Sauté green pepper and onion in same skillet. Add tomato sauce, sherry, garlic and basil. Add salt and pepper to taste. Simmer for 5 minutes. Pour sauce evenly over chops. Cover with foil and bake for 1 hour. Remove cover and cook ½ hour longer, until chops are done and sauce has cooked down. Can be assembled ahead. Freezes.

Serves 4

CHUTNEY PORK CHOPS

2 Tbsp. cooking oil
6 thick pork chops
1 can (14½ oz.) sliced
   pineapple
Water
½ cup chopped chutney
2-3 tsp. curry
1 tsp. instant beef bouillon
2 tsp. salt
2¼ cups uncooked Minute
   rice

Heat oil in a 12-inch heavy skillet and cook pork chops over medium heat for 15–20 minutes. Remove chops.

Drain pineapple, reserving syrup. Set aside three slices and chop remaining pineapple. Add enough water to syrup to measure 2¼ cups.

In skillet, combine pineapple syrup, chutney, curry, bouillon and salt. Bring to a boil. Stir in uncooked rice and chopped pineapple. Place pork chops on top of rice. Quarter reserved pineapple slices and place atop chops. Cover, reduce heat, and simmer 5 minutes.   Serves 6

PORK CHOPS TERIYAKI

4 thick pork chops
½ cup teriyaki sauce
½ cup apple juice
1 Tbsp. cornstarch
1 Tbsp. water

Brown pork chops. Add teriyaki sauce and apple juice to skillet. Cover and simmer until chops are tender. Remove chops from pan. Blend 1 Tbsp. cornstarch with 1 Tbsp. water and stir into skillet juices. Stir until thickened. Return chops to skillet to glaze.   Serves 4

THE EMBERS' ORIGINAL ONE POUND PORK CHOP

2 cups soy sauce
1⅓ cups water, divided
1 cup brown sugar, divided
1 Tbsp. dark brown molasses
1 tsp. salt
6 pork chops, 1 lb. each
1 Tbsp. dry mustard
1 bottle (14 oz.) Heinz
    ketchup
1 bottle (12 oz.) Heinz chili
    sauce
(Do not substitute for Heinz
    ketchup or chili sauce)

To make marinade, combine soy sauce, 1 cup water, ½ cup brown sugar, molasses and salt in saucepan and bring to a boil. Let cool. Place pork chops in a bowl bone-side up. Pour marinade over chops and refrigerate overnight.

Preheat oven to 375°. Remove chops from marinade and place in baking pan. Cover tightly with foil. Bake about 2 hours, until tender.

To make sauce, mix dry mustard, ⅓ cup water and ½ cup brown sugar together, stirring to remove any lumps. Add ketchup and chili sauce and bring mixture to a boil. Set aside.

When pork chops are tender, remove from oven and reduce heat to 350°. Dip the chops in sauce. Return to oven for 30 minutes, or until lightly glazed. Marinade and sauce may be made ahead and frozen.   Serves 6

Variations: Finished pork chops may be grilled slowly for a few minutes.
If desired, ½ lb. pork chops can be used: Divide remaining ingredients in half and cut cooking time in half.
Helpful Hints: Marinade and sauce can be reused if brought to a boil and stored in refrigerator or freezer.

MUSHROOM AND SAUSAGE STRUDEL

2 lbs. sweet Italian sausage
2 lbs. mushrooms, minced
¼ cup minced shallots or
  green onions
6 Tbsp. butter
2 Tbsp. oil
Salt and freshly ground
  pepper to taste
2 pkgs. (8 oz. each) cream
  cheese
8 sheets phyllo dough
  (16x22)
¾ cup butter, melted
Bread crumbs

Preheat oven to 400°. Remove sausage meat from casings and brown until no longer pink. Crumble and drain well. Sauté mushrooms and shallots in butter and oil over moderately high heat, stirring frequently. Cook until pieces separate and liquid has evaporated. Season to taste with salt and pepper. Combine with sausage and blend in cream cheese.

Spread a sheet of phyllo dough on a damp towel, narrow end towards you. Brush with melted butter and sprinkle with bread crumbs. Repeat procedure with second and third sheets of phyllo. Butter fourth sheet, but **do not** sprinkle with crumbs. Put half the sausage and mushroom mixture on narrower edge of phyllo dough, leaving a 2-inch border at sides. Fold in sides. Then, using the end of the towel, roll. Put phyllo roll on a buttered baking sheet. Brush with melted butter. Repeat for second strudel. Bake, uncovered, in a 400° oven about 20 minutes or until browned. Cut with shears for serving.   Serves 8

BARBECUED LEG OF LAMB

1 leg of lamb, butterflied
½ cup olive oil
¼ cup lemon juice
½ cup chopped onion
¼ cup snipped parsley
1 clove garlic, minced
1 tsp. salt
1 tsp. marjoram
1 tsp. thyme
½ tsp. pepper

Place leg of lamb in large, shallow pan. Combine remaining ingredients and pour over lamb. Marinate overnight in refrigerator or 6 hours at room temperature, turning meat occasionally. Grill on barbecue as you would a steak. It is best cooked until pink and served thinly sliced.   Serves 8

LAMB SHANKS

6 lamb shanks
3 Tbsp. flour
1 tsp. salt
Dash pepper
Salad oil
1 cup dry white wine
¼ cup wine vinegar
½ cup orange juice
3 Tbsp. lemon juice
1 Tbsp. Worcestershire
    sauce
1 Tbsp. brown sugar
¾ tsp. Kitchen Bouquet

Preheat oven to 300°. Wipe lamb shanks with damp cloth. Combine flour, salt and pepper. Roll shanks in seasoned flour, then brown in salad oil in a large skillet. Remove lamb shanks to large casserole dish.

To prepare gravy, reduce heat under skillet. Add any remaining seasoned flour and stir. Add wine, wine vinegar, orange juice, lemon juice and Worcestershire sauce to skillet. Cook until thick. Add brown sugar and Kitchen Bouquet. Pour gravy over shanks. Cover and bake for 3 hours, turning meat once. Can be made ahead.
                Serves 6

Variation: Up to ⅓ cup more brown sugar and 1 cup more orange juice can be added to taste.

LAMB STEW

3 lbs. lamb shoulder, cut in
   1" cubes
⅓ cup flour
1 cup butter
3 cloves garlic, crushed
Salt and pepper
¼ cup sugar
1½ cups beef bouillon
1 can (12 oz.) tomatoes
½ tsp. rosemary
1-2 cups frozen artichoke
   hearts (optional)
2 cups baby carrots
   (optional)
1 cup sliced fresh
   mushrooms, sautéed
   (optional)

Dredge lamb in flour, then brown in butter and garlic. Add salt and pepper to taste. Pour sugar over lamb and stir until carmelized. Add bouillon, tomatoes and rosemary. Cover and simmer for 1 hour. Skim off fat. Add frozen artichokes, carrots and mushrooms and heat through. Can be made ahead. Freezes.   Serves 6–8

BLEU CHEESE SAUCE

a change from gravy

¾ cup Madeira or sherry
2 Tbsp. chopped green
   onions
1 cup whipping cream
½ cup beef broth
6 oz. bleu cheese, softened
¼ lb. unsalted butter,
   softened
Cayenne to taste
Paprika

Serve With:
As sauce for beef, lamb, or fish.

Yields 1½ cups

In saucepan, combine Madeira with green onions and reduce mixture over moderately high heat to 2 Tbsp. Mixture reduces rapidly. Add cream and beef broth and reduce liquid over moderate heat to 1 cup which takes about 10–15 minutes.

In a bowl or food processor, cream together bleu cheese and butter until smooth. Whisk cheese mixture, a little at a time, into the saucepan and simmer sauce for about 3 minutes. Strain into bowl. Add cayenne to taste. Transfer to pitcher or gravy boat and sprinkle with paprika.

ROGER'S GREEK ROAST LEG OF LAMB

Leg of lamb
1 tsp. salt
1 Tbsp. black pepper
1 Tbsp. oregano
3 cloves garlic, sliced
⅓ cup butter
Juice of 1 large lemon
2 onions, chopped
5 mushrooms, dried or fresh
6 sprigs of parsley
2 cups water, divided

Preheat oven to 500°. Place lamb, skin side up, on rack in open roasting pan. Rub meat with mixture of salt, pepper and oregano. Make slashes with knife in meat surface, and insert slices of garlic ½ inch into meat. Melt butter. Add lemon juice and pour over meat. Place onions, mushrooms, parsley and 1 cup water in pan. Roast lamb uncovered at 500° for 30 minutes. Add another 1 cup of water to pan and lower oven temperature to 350°. Roast uncovered to desired degree of doneness, basting occasionally. Will take approximately 3 hours for medium–well meat.   Serves 8

BURGUNDY LAMB KEBOBS

2 Tbsp. salad oil
⅓ cup Burgundy wine
1 onion, thinly sliced
1 clove garlic, crushed
2 bay leaves
½ tsp. tarragon
½ tsp. oregano
1 tsp. salt
¼ tsp. freshly ground
    pepper
1 lb. lamb, cut in 1-2" cubes
2 med. green peppers, cut in
    1" chunks
8 sm. boiling onions or 2
    med. onions, quartered
12 mushroom caps
8 cherry tomatoes

Prepare marinade by combining first 9 ingredients. Pour over lamb and refrigerate overnight.

Thread lamb cubes on skewers, alternating with pieces of green pepper, onions, mushrooms and cherry tomatoes. Grill over hot coals to desired degree of doneness.   Serves 4

ROAST RACK OF LAMB PROVENCAL

from the Golden Mushroom

7 lb. rack of lamb
Kosher salt
Freshly ground pepper

Persillade
⅔ cup bread crumbs
6 cloves garlic, mashed
½ cup chopped parsley
Fresh or dried oregano to taste
2 Tbsp. olive oil
Good pinch of savory
Good pinch of thyme
Good pinch of rosemary

Dijon mustard
Salt and pepper

Have butcher split rack of lamb lengthwise and remove all spinal bones, leaving the ribs only. Remove cap and blade and trim fat down to a ¼-inch cover. Draw a line across the rib bones, 1 inch from edge of the eye (heart of meat) and cut away all fat and tissue above the line on top and between the bones.

Persillade
Combine all ingredients.

Preheat oven to 450°. Season meat with kosher salt and freshly ground pepper on all sides. Wrap bare bones with foil to protect them from burning. Place under broiler and brown all sides. Using a table knife, spread Dijon mustard on the rack. Coat the rack well with the Persillade, packing it down. Place the rack on a cookie sheet or sizzling platter in 450° oven and roast to desired doneness (25 minutes for medium-rare). To carve, slice between the ribs.

Serves 4

MOUSSAKA

2 eggplants
Vegetable oil
Salt and pepper
2 cloves garlic, crushed
1½ lbs. ground lamb or beef
1 cup chopped onion
2 cans (8 oz. each) tomato
   sauce
¼ cup dry red wine
1 tsp. oregano
1 tsp. parsley
1 tsp. cinnamon
Salt and pepper to taste
2 Tbsp. butter
2 Tbsp. flour
2 cups milk
2 eggs
½ cup sour cream, room
   temperature
1 cup grated Monterey Jack
   cheese
Grated Parmesan cheese

Cut unpeeled eggplants into ½-inch slices. Brush each slice with oil and sprinkle with salt. Broil until golden brown.

In a large skillet, sauté garlic in a small amount of oil. Add meat and onions and sauté for a few more minutes. Blend in tomato sauce, red wine, oregano, parsley, cinnamon, salt and pepper to taste. Simmer, uncovered, for 30 minutes or until relatively thick.

To prepare custard, melt butter in medium saucepan. Blend in flour over low heat, then slowly add milk. Cook and stir until a thick white sauce. Remove from heat. Beat eggs in a small bowl. Add some of the hot white sauce to eggs, whisking constantly. Return this mixture to remaining sauce in pan. Season to taste. Add sour cream.

Preheat oven to 350°. Layer eggplant and meat sauce in a 9x12 baking dish, sprinkling each layer with Monterey Jack and Parmesan cheese. End with a layer of eggplant. Pour custard over all, and sprinkle again with Parmesan cheese. Bake uncovered 40 minutes, until golden brown. Cool slightly, then slice and serve. Can be made ahead. Freezes.   Serves 6–8

VEAL CHOPS WITH MUSHROOMS

excellent with Turmeric Rice

½ lb. mushrooms
6 Tbsp. butter, divided
6 veal chops, approximately
   ¾ " thick
¼ cup brandy
3 Tbsp. lemon juice
1 cup whipping cream
1 Tbsp. glacé de viande
Salt and pepper to taste
1 Tbsp. chopped chives

In a large skillet, sauté mushrooms in 4 Tbsp. butter. Set aside. Add 2 Tbsp. butter to pan and sauté veal chops 4 minutes on each side. Remove chops to heated platter. Top with mushrooms and keep warm.

Add brandy to skillet and deglaze pan over high heat. Add lemon juice, cream and glacé de viande. Reduce sauce until thick. Adjust seasonings to taste. Pour sauce over chops and top with chopped chives.

Serves 4

Variation: Marinate veal chops for an hour in lime juice and crushed garlic.

VEAL SCALLOPINI WITH MUSHROOMS

Approximately ½ cup butter,
   divided
1 lb. mushrooms, sliced
Salt and pepper to taste
2 lbs. veal cutlets, pounded
   very thin
Flour
1 cup Madeira
¼ cup sherry

Melt 3 Tbsp. butter in a large sauté pan. Add mushrooms, salt and pepper and cook until mushrooms are tender. Set aside, covered, to keep warm. Coat veal slices lightly with flour. Add more butter to pan and sauté veal quickly on both sides. Return mushrooms to pan with veal. Add Madeira and sherry. Cover and cook for 5–10 minutes.

Serves 6–8

Variation: Use Marsala instead of Madeira.

VEAL SCALLOPINI WITH NOODLES AND PEAS

1½ lbs. veal cutlets, pounded very thin
Paprika
½ cup butter
1 cup consomme or water
¼ cup sherry, or to taste
Salt and pepper to taste
1 pkg. (8 oz.) noodles, cooked according to directions
1 pkg. (10 oz.) frozen peas, cooked and buttered
½ cup grated Parmesan cheese

Preheat oven to 325°. Sprinkle veal slices with paprika, then brown in butter, a few pieces at a time. Set cooked veal aside and keep warm. Deglaze skillet with consomme or water. Add sherry to taste. Season as necessary.

Arrange cooked noodles on ovenproof platter or in casserole. Make a well in the noodles and pour in buttered peas. Arrange meat around edges. Pour sauce over meat and sprinkle Parmesan cheese over all. Heat covered for about 15 minutes, until heated through. Can be assembled ahead. Serves 6

 To heat through, arrange noodles, peas and scallopini on microwave-proof dish (no metal) and cover with wax paper. Cook on High 3–5 minutes until heated through.

Timely Tip:
Darken the color of gravy by adding a small amount of instant coffee.

VEAL PARMESAN

4 veal cutlets, pounded very
  thin
Flour
1 egg, beaten
¾ cup bread crumbs
4 Tbsp. olive oil, divided
1 cup tomato sauce
1 clove garlic, sliced
Salt to taste
4 slices mozzarella cheese
6 Tbsp. grated Parmesan
  cheese

Preheat oven to 300°. Dust veal cutlets with flour. Dip in beaten egg and then in bread crumbs. Sauté in 3 Tbsp. olive oil until golden brown. Make a marinara sauce by combining 1 Tbsp. olive oil, tomato sauce, garlic and salt. Pour a layer of sauce in a 7x11 casserole. Place cutlets on top of sauce.

Bake uncovered for 1 hour. Add more sauce and slices of mozzarella cheese. Top with remaining sauce, and sprinkle Parmesan cheese over all. Return to oven and bake until cheese melts.   Serves 4

Variation: Instead of sautéing, cutlets may be baked at 400° for 20 minutes on each side.

VEAL OSCAR
last minute cooking

4 veal cutlets, pounded very
  thin
2 Tbsp. fresh lemon juice
Salt and pepper to taste
Flour
Butter
16 spears fresh asparagus,
  cooked
4 crab legs, cooked and
  removed from shells
1 cup hollandaise sauce

Sprinkle veal on both sides with lemon juice, then salt and pepper. Dust lightly with flour. Heat butter in a large skillet and sauté cutlets over moderately high heat for 4 minutes on each side, until lightly browned. Remove to a warm platter. On each cutlet place 4 spears of asparagus and one crab leg. Top with hollandaise sauce. Serve immediately.
                    Serves 4

VEAL SCALLOPINI CROCKPOT

2½ lbs. veal stew meat, trimmed
Flour
2-4 Tbsp. butter
Salt and pepper to taste
¾ cup sauterne
¾ cup water
¼ cup lemon juice (the juice of 1 lemon)
2 cloves garlic, pressed
1½ tsp. marjoram
1-1½ lbs. fresh mushrooms, sliced

Coat stew meat with flour. Brown meat on all sides in butter in skillet. Transfer to crockpot and sprinkle with salt and pepper. Add sauterne, water and lemon juice to skillet. Simmer and scrape the brownings, then add to crockpot. Add garlic, marjoram and mushrooms to crockpot. Cover and cook on low for 6-8 hours. Serve over buttered noodles or rice.

Can also be prepared in Dutch oven. Reduce garlic to 1 clove and marjoram to ½ tsp. After browning meat, simmer with liquids, seasonings and mushrooms for 1-1½ hours, depending on tenderness desired.

Serves 4-6

 # BREADING FOR VEAL OR CHICKEN

2-3 lbs. chicken or veal
½ cup butter, melted
½ cup instant potato flakes
½ cup seasoned bread crumbs
1 tsp. parsley flakes
Salt and pepper to taste
½ tsp. paprika

Combine all breading ingredients. Dip chicken in butter and then into breading. Microwave uncovered on High 8-10 minutes, rotating dish several times.

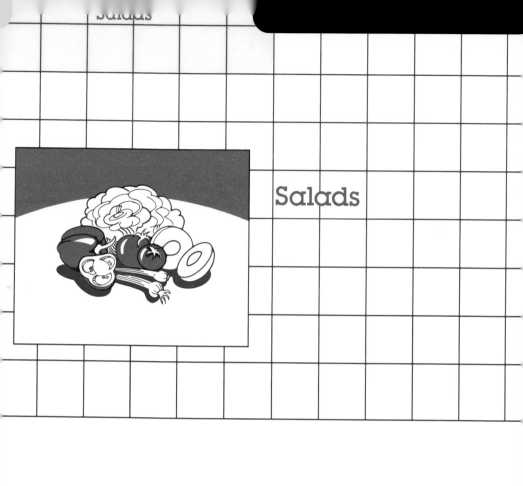

Salads

ALTA'S CHICKEN SALAD

4 cups chopped cooked
   chicken breasts
1 cup green grapes, halved
½ cup slivered almonds
¼ cup sliced green olives
1 cup sliced celery

Dressing
½ cup cider vinegar
½ cup water
1 scant cup sugar
2 Tbsp. butter
2 eggs, beaten
2 heaping tsp. flour
1 tsp. dry mustard
Dash salt

Combine chicken, grapes, almonds, olives and celery. Add enough of the dressing to moisten the salad ingredients. Mix well. Chill and serve on lettuce leaves.

Dressing
Heat the vinegar, water, sugar and butter until sugar melts. Do not boil. Make a paste of the flour, mustard and salt by adding a little water. Mix until smooth and then add to the eggs. Slowly stir the egg-flour mixture into the vinegar mixture. Heat, stirring constantly, until it reaches the bubbling point. Remove from heat and cool.   Serves 6

Variation: Salad can be served in the center of a cantaloupe ring.
Helpful Hints: Refrigerate any remaining dressing for future use. Can mix the dressing with ½ cup mayonnaise.

NUTTY CHICKEN SALAD

1 cup chopped pecans
4 Tbsp. butter
4 cups cooked chicken
   breasts cut in bite-sized
   pieces
½ cup mayonnaise
½ cup Miracle Whip
2 cups seedless grapes,
   halved
Salt and pepper to taste
Lettuce

Saute´ pecans in butter until slightly browned. Mix remaining ingredients in a bowl. Add pecans and toss well. Chill and serve on a bed of lettuce.
    Serves 4

RAINBOW CHICKEN SALAD

2 cups cooked chicken, cut
   in large chunks
3 green onions, finely sliced
   (tops included)
1 cup red seedless grapes
1 cup green seedless grapes
1 cup diced celery
1 cup chopped red apple
⅓ cup chopped pecans
Red lettuce
8 curved cantaloupe slices

Dressing
½ cup Hellmann's
   mayonnaise
¼ cup sour cream
1 tsp. lemon juice
3 Tbsp. chopped chutney
1 tsp. curry powder
¾ tsp. salt (optional)

Combine chicken, onions, red
and green grapes, celery and
apple. Gently mix dressing with
all the salad ingredients. Can be
put together for flavors to mingle
as much as 24 hours ahead.
When ready to serve, put on
large crisp red lettuce leaves
with a slice of cantaloupe on
either side.

Dressing
Mix together mayonnaise, sour
cream, lemon juice, chutney,
curry powder and salt, if desired. Can be made ahead.
Serves 4

Helpful Hint: Dressing may be made in food processor with a few
on and off turns.

CHICKEN RICE CONFETTI

3-4 whole chicken breasts,
   cooked, diced
1 cup cooked rice
2-3 lg. carrots, shredded
3 lg. green onions, diced
1 cup Italian dressing
2 lg. tomatoes, sliced
Lettuce

Combine chicken, rice, carrots,
onions and dressing. Refrigerate, covered, 2 to 4 hours or
overnight. Line a glass bowl or
platter with lettuce and place
salad on lettuce. Garnish with
tomatoes. Must be made ahead.
Serves 8-10

Variations: Frozen peas, green pepper, olives or any combination of vegetables may be used but colorful ones
look best.
Helpful Hint: This salad also molds well.

STEAK AND MUSHROOM SALAD

12 sm. fresh mushrooms
1-1½ lbs. cooked roast or
    steak, thinly sliced
12 cherry tomatoes, halved
1 can (14 oz.) artichoke
    hearts, drained
Leaf lettuce
2 Tbsp. chopped parsley
3 Tbsp. bleu cheese,
    crumbled (optional)

Dressing
½ cup olive oil
2 tsp. Dijon mustard
1 tsp. salt
¼ cup red wine vinegar
1 garlic clove, crushed
½ tsp. sugar
Freshly ground pepper

Wash, dry and slice mushrooms. Combine in a bowl with beef and tomatoes. Cut artichokes in half or fourths and add to beef. Add dressing. Marinate several hours or overnight. Line salad bowl with chilled lettuce and arrange beef on top. Sprinkle with parsley and bleu cheese.

Dressing
Combine all ingredients in a jar. Shake well.   Serves 8-10

CURRIED RICE SALAD
great for tailgate parties

1 pkg. Chicken Rice-a-Roni
1 Tbsp. butter
4 green onions, thinly sliced
12 pimento olives, thinly
    sliced
½ cup chopped green
    pepper
1 jar (3½ oz.) marinated
    artichoke hearts
⅓ cup mayonnaise
½ tsp. curry powder or to
    taste

Cook Chicken Rice-a-Roni as package directs, adding 1 extra Tbsp. butter. Cook until dry. Cool in skillet. Drain artichoke hearts, reserving marinade. Quarter artichoke hearts. Add green onions, pimento olives; green pepper and artichoke hearts to cooled rice. Mix marinade with mayonnaise and curry powder. Add to rice. Toss rice, vegetables and marinade mixture together and chill. Better if made the day ahead.
    Serves 6-8

SHRIMP SALAD

Dressing
1 cup Hellmann's
mayonnaise
2 tsp. olive oil
2 tsp. Dijon mustard
2 tsp. brandy
3 oz. drained capers, to taste

Salad
1 Tbsp. Old Bay Seafood
Seasoning (available at
fish markets)
2½ lbs. cleaned, raw shrimp
3 cups thin, diagonally
sliced celery
Bibb or leaf lettuce
Hard-boiled eggs, quartered
Ripe olives
Watermelon rind pickles
Tomato wedges
Avocado slices (optional)

Dressing
Combine mayonnaise, olive oil, mustard, brandy and capers. Mix after each ingredient is added. Refrigerate 5 hours or overnight.

Salad
Slowly boil water with seafood seasoning, 10 minutes before adding shrimp. Boil shrimp 3-4 minutes. Drain and rinse shrimp in cold water. Place in bowl with ice to refresh. When ready to serve, drain shrimp on paper towels and toss with celery. Add dressing somewhat gradually to thoroughly coat salad, using approximately 1 cup dressing. Do not drown salad. Place salad on bed of bibb or leaf lettuce. Garnish each plate with hard-boiled egg, olives, watermelon rind pickles, tomato wedges and avocado, if desired. May be prepared up to 1 day ahead.
Serves 6-8

Helpful Hint: Dressing is delicious spread on fish filet before
broiling.

Timely Tip:
When making salad dressings, mix herbs and seasonings with vinegar before adding any oil. Oil will coat the herbs and trap the flavor.

SHRIMP AND AVOCADO SALAD

6 cups torn lettuce
1 lb. shrimp, cooked and
     cleaned
18 cherry tomatoes, halved
6 slices bacon, crisply
     cooked, drained and
     crumbled
4 oz. natural cheddar or
     Havarti cheese, cut in
     strips
Freshly ground pepper

Dressing
½ cup buttermilk
1 pkg. (3 oz.) cream cheese,
     softened
1 sm. avocado, pitted,
     peeled and cubed
2 Tbsp. lemon juice
1 sm. clove garlic, chopped
½ tsp. salt
¼ tsp. bottled hot pepper
     sauce (optional)

Place lettuce in 6 individual salad bowls. Arrange shrimp, cherry tomatoes, bacon and cheese strips over each serving. Sprinkle with pepper. Spoon dressing over each serving.

Dressing
In a blender, combine all ingredients. Cover and blend until smooth. Can be made ahead.

Serves 6

ENDIVE SALAD

light and pretty

¼ cup white wine vinegar
2 Tbsp. dry white wine
1 Tbsp. Italian seasoning
Salt to taste
⅔ cup light oil
⅓ cup thinly sliced ripe
     pitted olives
¼ cup diced pimentos
1 Tbsp. chopped chives
1½ lbs. endive spears,
     cleaned and separated

Combine and refrigerate first 8 ingredients at least 2 hours before serving. Artistically arrange endive spears in star or parallel formation, and spoon dressing to taste over all.   Serves 8

SHRIMP AND PASTA SALAD

48 shrimp, cooked and
  cleaned
1 lb. "cut" tubular pasta,
  such as ziti or penne,
  cooked, drained and
  cooled
2 cups fresh or frozen peas
2¼ cups Hellmann's
  mayonnaise
¾ cup finely chopped
  scallions
2-3 Tbsp. tarragon wine
  vinegar
¼ cup capers, drained
Salt and freshly ground
  pepper to taste
½ cup finely chopped herbs
  such as basil, dill and
  parsley

Cut shrimp in half crosswise. If frozen peas are used, pour into a sieve and pour boiling water over them; further cooking is not needed. Combine shrimp and pasta in a mixing bowl. Add remaining ingredients except parsley. Blend well and refrigerate for an hour or so. Sprinkle with chopped parsley. Must be made ahead.   Serves 10-12

Variations: Instead of mayonnaise, add 1 can cream of mushroom soup and 1 can milk. Add chopped celery, black olives, and lemon juice, if desired. Put in 1½-2 quart casserole and bake at 325° for 20 minutes.

Helpful Hint: To keep pasta from sticking together when making a cold salad, mix a small amount of equal parts water and vinegar, toss with drained cooled pasta. Drain excess moisture.

Timely Tip:
Moisten rim of bowl or pan, and plastic wrap will cling better when covering it.

TEA ROOM PASTA SALAD

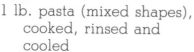

served at the 1984 Showhouse

1 lb. pasta (mixed shapes), cooked, rinsed and cooled
½ cup chopped red onion
1 bunch scallions, chopped
¾ cup frozen peas, thawed, drained
1 green or red pepper, sliced into thin strips
1 cup bite-sized pcs. of ham
½ cup bite-sized pcs. of Provolone cheese
½ pt. cherry tomatoes, halved

Gently combine all ingredients. Toss with dressing.

Dressing
Blend ingredients in a food processor, blender or jar.

Can be made ahead.

Serves 6–8

Dressing
½ cup olive oil
3 cloves garlic, minced
1¼ Tbsp. red wine vinegar
Juice of ½ lemon
½ tsp. salt
Freshly ground pepper
1 tsp. honey
1 Tbsp. chopped fresh dill
1 Tbsp. chopped fresh basil
1 Tbsp. chopped fresh parsley
1 Tbsp. Dijon mustard

> *Variations:* Use any combination of the following: scallops, crab, shrimp, broccoli, cauliflower, water chestnuts, pine nuts, cashews, julienned carrots, pea pods, mushrooms.

To obtain additional juice from a lemon, heat it on High for 30–45 seconds before squeezing.

PASTA SALAD WITH VEGETABLE SAUCE

excellent hot or cold

2-3 cloves garlic, minced
¼ cup sliced or slivered
  almonds
3 Tbsp. olive oil
1½ cups broccoli flowerettes
1½ cups fresh or frozen
  snow peas
1 cup sliced zucchini
10 lg. mushrooms, sliced
6 fresh or frozen asparagus
  spears, cut in 1″ pcs.
¼ cup freshly chopped
  parsley
2 tsp. dried basil
½ tsp. salt
¼ tsp. pepper
12 cherry tomatoes, halved
1 pkg. (12 oz.) spaghetti,
  cooked, rinsed and
  drained, but still hot
⅓ cup butter
1 cup whipping cream
½ cup grated Parmesan
  cheese

Sauté garlic and almonds in oil in Dutch oven until lightly browned, stirring frequently. Add broccoli, peas, zucchini, mushrooms, asparagus, parsley, basil, salt and pepper. Cook until tender-crisp, about 5 minutes. Stir in tomatoes. Melt butter over low heat. Add whipping cream and Parmesan cheese. Add hot spaghetti and toss to coat.

To serve cold, chill both mixtures separately at least one hour. Spoon vegetable mixture over spaghetti.   Serves 6

PEA AND PEANUT SALAD

2 pkgs. (10 oz. each) frozen
  green peas, thawed,
  drained well
1 cup sour cream
2 green onions, chopped
½ tsp. salt
½ tsp. pepper
1 cup dry roasted peanuts
6 slices bacon, cooked and
  crumbled

Combine all ingredients, except bacon, and mix well. Chill. Sprinkle with bacon before serving. Can be made the day ahead.   Serves 6-8

CUCUMBER NOODLES

great for a large crowd

1 lb. Kluski Polish noodles
2 cucumbers, seeded and
  chopped but not peeled
4 green onions, chopped
¾ tsp. salt
¾ tsp. pepper
½ tsp. celery salt
1 tsp. sugar
1 tsp. oregano

Dressing
1½ cups mayonnaise
⅓ cup sour cream
½ cup milk
1 tsp. Dijon mustard
Cherry tomatoes to garnish

Cook noodles according to package directions. Drain. Add cucumbers, green onions, salt, pepper, celery salt, sugar and oregano. Mix mayonnaise, sour cream, milk and mustard for the dressing. Add to the noodles. Toss well. Cover and refrigerate overnight. Garnish with cherry tomato halves. Best 24 hours later, but no longer.

Serves 10–12 salad servings

GREEK SALAD

2 heads lettuce, torn into
  bite-sized pieces
6–8 fresh mushrooms, thinly
  sliced
6 slices bacon, cooked and
  crumbled
1 cup onion croutons
½ cup finely crumbled Feta
  cheese
1 med. onion, chopped

Dressing
¾ cup salad oil
¼ cup wine vinegar
⅓ cup cider vinegar
½ cup sugar
4 tsp. salt
1 tsp. oregano
1 tsp. pepper

Mix all salad ingredients in bowl. Combine all dressing ingredients and blend well. Top salad with dressing and toss. Dressing may be stored several weeks in the refrigerator.

Serves 12

CAESAR SALAD

Dressing
¼ cup olive oil, good
   quality
¾ cup salad oil, or use all
   olive oil
1 clove garlic, mashed
½ tsp. dry mustard
½ tsp. freshly cracked
   pepper
4 anchovies, finely chopped,
   or anchovy paste, to taste
¼ tsp. Tabasco
1 Tbsp. Worcestershire sauce

Salad
3 cups French bread, cubed
Olive oil
2 cloves garlic
2 lg. heads Romaine lettuce
2 eggs, beaten
1 lemon
½ cup freshly grated
   Parmesan cheese

Dressing
In a jar, mix olive and salad oils, garlic, mustard, pepper, anchovies, Worcestershire and Tabasco. Refrigerate overnight, if possible.

Salad
Prepare croutons by frying bread cubes over low heat in olive oil flavored with split garlic clove. Drain on paper towels. Rub salad bowl with another clove of garlic. Wash, spin dry and tear the Romaine into bite-sized pieces. Chill. Place Romaine in salad bowl, pour dressing over and toss. (If dressing has congealed, let stand until room temperature, then shake.) Add raw egg to greens and toss gently. Add juice of one lemon (more, if desired) and grated Parmesan cheese. Toss adding croutons at last minute so they won't get soggy. Serve at once.
Serves 8–10

Timely Tips:
To crisp wilted lettuce or celery, place it in a pan of cold water with a slice of raw potato. Let stand for several hours.

Place a dry sponge in the vegetable drawer of the refrigerator to absorb moisture.

ROMAINE SALAD

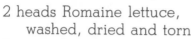

requires a huge container

2 heads Romaine lettuce, washed, dried and torn
2 cups cherry tomatoes, cut in half
1 cup grated Swiss cheese
⅔ cup slivered almonds, toasted
⅓ cup grated fresh Parmesan cheese
¼ lb. bacon, cooked and crumbled
1 cup croutons

Combine all salad ingredients except croutons. Combine dressing ingredients and toss with salad ingredients. Add croutons.

Good croutons can be made by dicing and sautéing 1½ English muffins in 2 Tbsp. butter and dash garlic salt.

Seves 12

Dressing
Juice of 1 lemon
¾ cup salad oil
3 cloves garlic, crushed
Salt and pepper to taste

SPINACH SALAD WITH STRAWBERRIES

1 bag (10 oz.) fresh spinach
1 pt. strawberries

Dressing
½ cup sugar
2 Tbsp. sesame seeds
1 Tbsp. poppy seeds
1½ tsp. minced onion
¼ tsp. Worcestershire sauce
¼ tsp. paprika
½ cup oil
¼ cup cider vinegar

Wash spinach and tear into bite-sized pieces. Wash and hull strawberries, and cut into halves if desired. Arrange on individual salad plates. Make dressing ahead in blender. Don't beat too long, or it will become too thick. A few drops of water can be added if necessary. Just before serving, mix dressing again, drizzle over salad, and toss gently. Serves 4–5

Variations: May add to salad: fresh sliced mushrooms or onions, grapefruit or orange sections, bean sprouts, cauliflower, mandarin oranges, bacon, almonds or cashews.

JACKSON SALAD

1½ heads Romaine lettuce
1 can (14 oz.) artichoke
   hearts, drained and
   chopped
¼ cup finely chopped green
   onion
¼ lb. bleu cheese, crumbled
¼ cup crisp bacon,
   crumbled
1 can (14 oz.) hearts of
   palm, drained and cut
   into bite-sized pieces
   (optional)

Dressing
3 oz. olive oil or salad oil
2 Tbsp. finely chopped
   parsley
2 cloves garlic, pressed —
   juice only.
1 oz. fresh lemon juice

Wash and dry lettuce. Tear into
bite-sized pieces. Add artichoke
hearts, green onion, bleu cheese
and bacon. Toss well. Just before
serving, pour on dressing and
toss.

Dressing
Combine all ingredients. Mix
well. May prepare up to 4 hrs.
ahead.   Serves 8

SUMMER SALAD

4 navel oranges
4 tomatoes
2 bunches watercress,
   cleaned

Mustard Vinaigrette
9 Tbsp. olive oil or salad oil
3 Tbsp. vinegar
2 Tbsp. Dijon mustard
Salt and pepper to taste
¼ tsp. paprika to taste
Garlic powder to taste
Onion powder to taste

Peel oranges so there is no white
pith left on orange. Section
oranges and cut each section in
half. Stem tomato, remove seeds
and chop. Remove stems from
watercress. Toss oranges,
tomatoes and watercress. Chill.
Before serving, toss with dressing. Serve on chilled plates.

Dressing
Combine all ingredients. Mix
well.   Serves 6–8

ORANGE AND WATERCRESS SALAD

1 med. head lettuce
2 bunches watercress
6 oranges
2 Tbsp. chopped mint
1 Tbsp. grated orange rind

Lemon Dressing
4 Tbsp. lemon juice
½ tsp. sugar
¼ tsp. salt
Pinch of pepper
4 Tbsp. olive oil or salad oil

Wash and drain lettuce and watercress. Tear into bite-sized pieces. Peel and slice oranges into rounds. Combine watercress, oranges, mint and grated orange rind. Mix well. Place lettuce in bowl and cover with the watercress and orange mixture. Pour lemon dressing over and serve immediately.

Dressing
Dissolve sugar in lemon juice. Add salt, pepper and oil. Mix thoroughly. Can be made ahead.   Serves 6–8

WATERCRESS SALAD

3–4 bunches watercress (4, if
  they are small)
½ cup (scant) slivered
  almonds, toasted
6 lg. or 12 med. mushrooms,
  sliced

Dressing
6 Tbsp. Bertolli's **light** olive
  oil, divided
2 Tbsp. fresh lemon juice,
  divided
¼ tsp. dry mustard
¼ tsp. salt
¼ tsp. pepper

Clean watercress, remove long stems, and break into bite-sized pieces. Clean, peel and slice mushrooms. Add almonds to watercress and mushrooms. Toss with enough dressing to lightly coat. Serve immediately. Salad may be assembled 2–4 hours ahead of serving if covered and refrigerated. Add dressing at serving time.

Dressing
Whisk together 1 Tbsp. olive oil, 1 Tbsp. lemon juice, dry mustard, salt and pepper. Add 2 Tbsp. olive oil and whisk again. Add 1 Tbsp. lemon juice and 3 Tbsp. olive oil and whisk again. May be made 3 days ahead, but shake before using.   Serves 4

MIXED BEAN SALAD

1 can (15 oz.) chick peas
1 can (15 oz.) red kidney
 beans
1 can (15 oz.) string beans
1 cold, boiled potato, thinly
 sliced
½ cup thinly sliced red
 onion
1 clove garlic, minced
2 radishes, thinly sliced
½ cup oil
½ cup wine vinegar
¼ cup sugar
Lg. pinch of oregano or
 sweet basil
Salt and pepper to taste

Drain and rinse the beans thoroughly. Combine all ingredients gently, but well. Season to taste. Chill well before serving, mixing occasionally. May be stored in the refrigerator and used as desired. Best made several days ahead. Serves 6

BROCCOLI SALAD

2 bunches broccoli
2 med. tomatoes
1 sm. red onion, sliced, or
 chopped scallions, to
 taste

Dressing
Mayonnaise to taste
Lemon juice to taste
Salt and pepper to taste

Variations:
Add mushrooms or chicken.

Prepare broccoli by cutting off large leaves and the bottom of the stalk. Wash well. Cut into bite-sized pieces. Blanch slightly by dropping broccoli into boiling water for about 30 seconds only. It should still be very crisp and bright green. Rinse under cold water and be sure to drain very well. Add chopped tomatoes and sliced red onion or scallions. Mix with dressing and chill.

Dressing
Combine all ingredients.

Can be made ahead several hours. Serves 6–8

BLEU CHEESE COLE SLAW

1 med. head cabbage,
   shredded
½ cup crushed pineapple,
   drained, reserve juice
3–4 oz. bleu cheese

Dressing
⅔ cup mayonnaise
¼ cup sugar
2 Tbsp. pineapple juice
2 Tbsp. vinegar
¼ tsp. salt
Dash ginger

Combine cabbage and pine-apple. Crumble and add bleu cheese. Mix with dressing.

Dressing
Combine all ingredients. May prepare 1 day in advance.
Serves 6–8

Helpful Hint: May use food processor to shred cabbage.

FRENCH VEGETABLE SALAD
unusual — also good warm

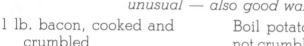

1 lb. bacon, cooked and
   crumbled
3 lbs. sm. red new potatoes,
   unpeeled
1 lb. green beans

Dressing
½ cup light olive oil
¼ cup tarragon vinegar
¼ cup canned beef
  · consomme, undiluted
½ cup chopped green
   onions
¼ cup minced parsley
1 clove garlic, crushed
1 tsp. salt
1 tsp. dry mustard
½ tsp. crushed sweet basil
½ tsp. crushed tarragon
Freshly ground pepper

Boil potatoes until tender, but not crumbly. Slice ¼-inch thick and set aside. Cook green beans until crispy-tender. Drain and set aside.

Combine all dressing ingredients and stir well.

To serve, combine potatoes and beans in a large bowl, add dressing and toss, sprinkle with bacon. Serve at room temperature.
Serves 8–10

MARINATED CARROTS

easy and keeps a long time

5 cups carrots, thinly sliced
1 lg. onion, thinly sliced
1 lg. red bell pepper, thinly sliced (optional)
1 lg. green pepper, thinly sliced
1 can tomato soup, undiluted
¾ cup vinegar
1 tsp. salt
½ cup salad oil
1 tsp. dry mustard (optional)
1 tsp. Worcestershire sauce (optional)
1 cup sugar
1 tsp. pepper

Cook carrots until slightly tender, less than 10 minutes. Drain carrots; combine with sliced onions and peppers. Bring remaining ingredients to a boil to make a marinade. Pour over vegetables. Refrigerate overnight. Drain before serving. Must be made ahead. Keeps 2 months.   Serves 8

CAULIFLOWER SALAD

1 head cauliflower
½ red onion, very thinly sliced
½ cup pitted olives, any kind, very thinly sliced
¼ cup red wine vinegar
⅔ cup salad oil
Salt and pepper to taste
Leaf lettuce
¼ cup bleu cheese, crumbled

Core, section and very thinly slice cauliflower. Combine with onions and olives. Add vinegar, oil, salt and pepper. Toss and chill for at least one hour. When ready to serve, arrange lettuce in salad bowl. Pour mixture into bowl and sprinkle with bleu cheese. Can be made ahead 1 day.   Serves 6

PEA SALAD

an easy microwave dish served hot or cold

2 pkgs. (10 oz. each) frozen green peas
1 can (8 oz.) water chestnuts, chopped
12 slices bacon, cooked and crumbled
1 cup finely chopped green onions, including tops
½ cup Hellmann's mayonnaise
Salt and pepper to taste

Cut bacon into 1-inch pieces and cook between paper toweling 5-6 minutes or until bacon is crisp. Remove from toweling immediately as it will stick. Crumble well. Puncture waxed paper pea boxes (no foil) in several places. Place both boxes in microwave and cook on High power 3-4 minutes. If serving hot, shake packages and cook an additional 3-4 minutes. Toss peas, water chestnuts and bacon. Fold in mayonnaise and add salt and pepper to taste.

If serving hot, microwave 30 seconds, stir, cook 30 seconds more. If serving cold, microwave peas only once for 4 minutes and re-chill peas before tossing with other ingredients.
Serves 8-10

COUSIN BOO'S POTATO SALAD

1 cup finely chopped green onions (including tops)
1 cup finely chopped parsley leaves
6 cups cooked, cooled and diced potatoes (6-8 med. potatoes)
1½ cups Hellmann's mayonnaise
1 cup sour cream
1½ tsp. horseradish
1 tsp. celery seed
½ tsp. salt

Toss onions and parsley. Fold into potatoes. Mix together mayonnaise, sour cream, horseradish, celery seed and salt. Add dressing to salad and toss gently until all is coated. Refrigerate 24 hrs. before serving. May be prepared up to 5 days ahead. Serves 8-10

GLAMOROUS LAYERED SALAD

great summertime salad, good for picnics

1½ lbs. med. potatoes
Salt to taste
2 med. green peppers
1 cucumber, peeled and
 thinly sliced
1 sm. red onion, thinly
 sliced
2 med. tomatoes, peeled and
 thinly sliced
2 Tbsp. finely chopped
 parsley

Vinaigrette Dressing
¼ cup white vinegar
1 tsp. salt
¼ tsp. freshly ground
 pepper
2 Tbsp. sugar
1 tsp. dry mustard
½ clove garlic, crushed
⅔ cup olive or salad oil

Boil potatoes until tender in enough salted water to cover (about 20 minutes). Cool, peel and slice thinly. Layer potato slices in a bowl, preferably glass, and sprinkle with a little salt. Cut green peppers in half lengthwise, core, slice into thin half rings and arrange on top of potatoes. Add, in layers, cucumber slices, onion rings and tomato slices. Sprinkle with chopped parsley.

Dressing
Combine all ingredients in a jar. Shake well and pour over salad.

Cover bowl and refrigerate for several hours or overnight. Baste a couple of times by tilting bowl and using a bulb baster or spoon. Can be made up to 24 hrs. ahead.   Serves 6–8

CRANBERRY WALDORF SALAD

tastes great with turkey dinner

2 cups fresh cranberries
3 cups miniature
 marshmallows
¾ cup sugar
2 cups apples, unpeeled,
 cored and diced
½ cup seedless green grapes
½ cup chopped walnuts
¼ tsp. salt
1 cup whipping cream,
 whipped

Grind cranberries and combine with marshmallows and sugar. Cover and chill overnight. Add apples, grapes, walnuts and salt. Fold in whipped cream and chill at least 3 hours before serving. Can be made 1 to 2 days ahead.
Serves 8–10

BERRY RING

perfect for Thanksgiving or Christmas

2 Pkgs. (3 oz. each) Jell-o, cherry, blackberry, dark cherry, etc.
2 cups boiling water
2 cans (16 oz. each) dark pitted cherries, juice drained and reserved
1 can (16 oz.) orange-cranberry relish
1 can (16 oz.) whole cranberries, drained
1 can (8 oz.) chunk pineapple, drained
1 cup chopped walnuts
Watercress to garnish

Dressing
½ cup sour cream
1 cup mayonnaise
2 Tbsp. powdered sugar

Dissolve Jell-o in boiling water; add reserved juice from cherries for other two cups of liquid. Pour into a 10–11-cup mold and chill until soft set. Add cherries, orange-cranberry relish, whole cranberries, pineapple and walnuts. Mix gently and chill until firm.

Dressing
Mix sour cream, mayonnaise and powdered sugar and serve in the middle of a ring mold or in a side dish. Garnish with watercress.

Must be made ahead.
Serves 12–14

24 HOUR FRUIT SALAD

2 cups iceberg lettuce, shredded
2 Golden Delicious apples
2 Tbsp. orange juice
2 lg. navel oranges
2 cups seedless green grapes
⅓ cup mayonnaise
⅓ cup sour cream
1 cup grated sharp cheese

Spread lettuce on bottom of 2-quart serving dish. Core and peel apples. Slice thinly and layer over lettuce. Sprinkle orange juice over apple slices. Peel and section oranges and lay on top of apple slices. Layer grapes on top. Combine mayonnaise and sour cream. Spread over grapes. Sprinkle cheese over all. Cover dish tightly with plastic wrap and refrigerate overnight. Must make ahead 24 hours.
Serves 6

CHERRIES PORTOFINO

can also be a dessert

2 cans (16 oz. each) pitted
dark, sweet cherries
1 pkg. (6 oz.) black cherry
Jell-o
2 cups boiling water
¾ cup cold water
⅔ cup reserved cherry juice
⅓ cup dark port wine **plus**
enough to cover cherries,
about one cup

Drain cherries, reserving ⅔ cup juice. Cover cherries with port and soak overnight. Dissolve Jell-o in boiling water. Add cold water, ⅔ cup reserved cherry juice and ⅓ cup port. Pour into 8-cup mold or other dish and cool until slightly thickened. Add **drained** cherries. Refrigerate.

Dressing
¾ cup Hellmann's
mayonnaise
1¼ cups sour cream
2⅔ Tbsp. unsweetened
pineapple juice
3 tsp. coriander
5 Tbsp. powdered sugar

Dressing
Combine all ingredients. Yields 1 pint, and stores well, refrigerated. Must be made ahead.

Serve salad on a bed of lettuce.
Serves 10–12

Variation: For milder flavor, use 1 cup cold water, ½ cup
cherry juice, ¼ cup port and 2 cups boiling water.
Helpful Hints: Port wine can be reused for the same dish. Dressing good on many fruit salads.

CRANBERRY MOLD

easy recipe for kids

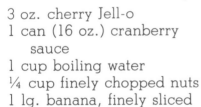

3 oz. cherry Jell-o
1 can (16 oz.) cranberry
sauce
1 cup boiling water
¼ cup finely chopped nuts
1 lg. banana, finely sliced

Dissolve Jell-o in water. Mix in cranberry sauce using electric beater. Fold in nuts and banana. Pour into 5-cup mold and chill. Should be made ahead.

Serves 6

LIGHT BLENDER MAYONNAISE

1 tsp. hot dry mustard
⅓ cup strained fresh lemon
   juice
2 eggs
1 tsp. salt
Dash cayenne
1 pt. Wesson oil

Remove center of top of blender. Dissolve mustard in small amount of lemon juice. Put all ingredients, except oil, in blender, and blend 15 seconds. **On blend,** pour oil into mix in a slow, steady stream. If oil starts to float, stop blender and stir briefly. Blend until thick, about 1–1½ minutes after all oil has been added. Store covered in the refrigerator. Yields 1 pint

Helpful Hint: If it curdles, add an extra egg.
Serve With: Aspic, fresh tomato slices, in chicken salad, etc.

Mayonnaise can be used in the following ways:

Russian Dressing: Add 1 Tbsp. (or more to taste) chili sauce to 1-cup mayonnaise and serve with fresh salad greens.

Tartar Sauce: Mix mayonnaise with finely chopped gherkins or dill pickles, onions and parsley to taste.

Remoulade Sauce: Blend mayonnaise with minced gherkins, capers, parsley, tarragon, chervil and a small amount of anchovy paste.

Lemon Sauce: Mix fresh lemon juice and a little grated lemon rind with mayonnaise. Great with asparagus, broccoli or fish.

VILLAGE MANOR FRENCH DRESSING

1⅛ cups ketchup
¾ cup sugar
1½ cups salad oil
¾ cup cider vinegar
3 Tbsp. lemon juice
¼ cup chopped onion
2 tsp. salt
Dash paprika

Combine all ingredients in a large bowl. Mix with electric mixer on lowest speed for 15 minutes. Refrigerate. Can be made ahead. Yields 4½ cups

FROZEN FRUIT SALAD

2 cups sour cream
½ cup mayonnaise
1 cup sugar
1 Tbsp. fresh lemon juice
⅛ tsp. salt
1 can (8 oz.) crushed
　pineapple, drained
1 can (11 oz.) mandarin
　oranges, drained
1 cup canned peaches,
　drained and chopped
½ cup chopped pecans
¼ cup maraschino cherries,
　drained and chopped
1 banana, peeled and sliced
Lettuce leaves

In a large bowl combine sour cream, mayonnaise, sugar, lemon juice and salt. Gently fold in fruits and nuts. Spoon mixture into a 6-cup mold that has been rinsed in cold water. Freeze overnight or for 24 hours. Thaw about 1 hour and invert on serving dish lined with lettuce leaves. Must be made ahead.

Serves 12

APRICOT PINEAPPLE DRESSING

super on any fruit salad

½ cup sugar
3 Tbsp. flour
1 egg
½ cup pineapple juice,
　unsweetened
½ cup apricot nectar
2 Tbsp. butter, melted
½ pt. whipping cream,
　whipped
¾ cup grated cheddar
　cheese (optional)

Combine sugar, flour and egg. Add ¼ cup of each fruit juice and cook over low heat stirring constantly. Add second ¼ cup of each juice; continue to heat and stir until thick. Add butter and combine thoroughly. Cool until firm. Fold in whipped cream. Spread on any fruit salad, and top with grated cheese.　Serves 8–10

Variation: Add more fruit juice for a thinner dressing.

CHART HOUSE BLEU CHEESE DRESSING

¾ cup sour cream
½ tsp. dry mustard
½ tsp. black pepper
½ tsp. salt
⅓ tsp. garlic powder
1 tsp. Worcestershire sauce
1⅓ cup mayonnaise
4 + oz. imported Danish bleu
    cheese to taste

Combine sour cream, dry mustard, black pepper, salt, garlic powder and Worcestershire sauce in a mixing bowl. Using an electric beater, blend 2 minutes at low speed. Add mayonnaise. Blend ½ minute at low speed. Then blend 2 minutes at medium speed. Crumble bleu cheese by hand into very small pieces and add. Blend at low speed no longer than 4 minutes. Refrigerate 24 hours. Serve over tossed green salad. Must be made ahead. Yields 2½ cups

SPINACH SALAD DRESSING

½ cup vinegar
½ cup water
1 tsp. salt
1 egg, well-beaten
¾ cup sugar

Mix all ingredients in a 4-cup glass measuring cup or glass bowl. Cook on High in microwave oven 2–3 minutes until mixture boils. Cool and serve over fresh spinach, crumbled bacon, hard-boiled eggs and croutons. Can be made ahead up to 2 weeks. Yields 2 cups

Helpful Hint: Can also be cooked conventionally in saucepan on range top.

SOUR CREAM DRESSING FOR CUCUMBERS

easy, delicious and different topping for cucumbers

Sauce

1 cup sour cream
Dash cayenne pepper
¼ cup cider vinegar
1 heaping Tbsp. grated
  onion
1 tsp. salt
2 Tbsp. sugar, or to taste

Combine all ingredients and store in a relatively air-tight container in the refrigerator. Sauce will last 2-3 weeks, but will separate and need stirring. It will cover several cucumbers.

Preparation of Cucumbers
Peel and thinly slice (about ⅛ in. thick or less) the amount of cucumbers that will be served. In a mixing bowl, layer ice and cucumbers, ice and cucumbers, etc., ending with ice. Cover and refrigerate at least 1 hour and no more than 5. When ready to serve, drain cucumbers on paper towels and serve immediately on lettuce leaves. Top with a spoonful of sauce; use 1 tsp. sauce per 5-8 slices of cucumbers.   Yields 1¼ cups

Variation: Also delicious on tomatoes.

LEMON CELERY SEED DRESSING

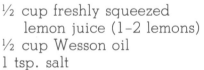

lovely on a fruit salad

½ cup freshly squeezed
  lemon juice (1-2 lemons)
½ cup Wesson oil
1 tsp. salt
1 tsp. paprika
1 Tbsp. sugar
½ tsp. celery seed
Dash of dry mustard
Dash of fresh ground pepper

Combine all ingredients in a jar. Cover and shake well. Can be made ahead.   Yields 1 cup

Desserts

RUTH'S ANGEL FLUFF

1 angel cake (loaf or round)
½ cup butter, softened
1½ cups powdered sugar
Pinch salt
3 egg yolks
3 Tbsp. lemon juice
3 egg whites, stiffly beaten
1 pt. whipping cream,
    whipped
1 can (3½ oz.) flaked
    coconut

Cream butter, sugar and salt. Add egg yolks one at a time and beat well. Add lemon juice. Fold in beaten egg whites and half of the whipped cream.

Remove crusts from cake and slice lengthwise very thinly. Line a 9x13 pan with half of the cake. Pour half of the filling over the cake. Layer remaining half of cake on top, and cover with remaining filling. Top with remaining whipped cream. Sprinkle with coconut and refrigerate overnight. Cut into squares.   Serves 12–14

CRANBERRY CAKE WITH VANILLA SAUCE

Cake
1 cup sugar
½ cup butter, softened
1 cup milk
2 cups flour
2½ tsp. baking powder
½ tsp. salt
2 cups raw whole
    cranberries

Sauce
1 cup hot water
1 cup sugar
½ cup butter
1–2 Tbsp. flour
2 tsp. vanilla

Cake
Preheat oven to 350°. Cream sugar and butter. Mix in milk, flour, baking powder and salt. Add cranberries. Bake in 2 greased 9-inch pie pans at 350° for 25 minutes.

Sauce
Boil all sauce ingredients until thickened. Cut cake in pie shaped pieces and top with a spoonful of warm sauce.
                Yields 12 pieces

HOT FUDGE BUTTERCREAM CAKE

Chocolate Cake
2¼ cups flour
1½ cups sugar
4½ Tbsp. cocoa
1 tsp. salt (scant)
1½ tsp. vinegar
1½ tsp. vanilla
2 tsp. baking soda
½ cup plus 1 tsp. Wesson
    Oil or melted shortening
1½ cups cold water

Quick Buttercream
¾ cup evaporated milk
½ cup butter
½ cup solid shortening
1 cup sugar
1½ tsp. vanilla

Never Fail Fudge Frosting
2 cups sugar
¼ cup light corn syrup
½ cup milk
½ cup butter
6 Tbsp. cocoa
Dash salt
1 tsp. vanilla

Cake
Preheat oven to 350°. Place all ingredients in large mixing bowl and mix with electric mixer until smooth. Bake in two 9-inch cake pans greased and lined with wax paper at 350° for 20-25 minutes. (Or, a 9x13 pan at 350° for 30-35 minutes.) Test for doneness; top will spring back when done.

Buttercream
Scald milk; cool to just slightly warm. Mix butter, solid shortening and sugar and beat until fluffy. Add vanilla. Continue beating while adding scalded milk slowly. Beat on high an additional 15 minutes. (Cannot beat too much; just makes it creamier.)

Frosting
Mix all ingredients except vanilla in heavy saucepan. Stir over medium heat until butter and chocolate are melted. Bring to boil and boil for **1 minute** only. Remove from heat; stir in vanilla. Beat until thick enough to pour over cake (about 15 minutes by hand with wooden spoon). It has to be stiff enough to stay on cake but still pourable. Best made next day — see assembly.

HOT FUDGE BUTTERCREAM CAKE
(continued)

Assembly
Frost first layer with buttercream on top only; cover with second layer. With buttercream, make 5 ribbons (about ½ inch wide and 1 inch high) with pastry tube across top of cake and continue down sides. (Make first ribbon in center and 2 ribbons on each side.) Freeze until buttercream is solid. Pour fudge over top and allow to drip down sides. It is best to frost cake with buttercream the night before and freeze, putting fudge frosting on the following day.   Serves 12

GREEK WALNUT CAKE

Cake
2 cups Bisquick
1 cup finely chopped walnuts
1 cup sugar
1 cup milk
1 cup oil
4 eggs
1½ tsp. baking powder
½ tsp. baking soda
1 tsp. cinnamon
½ tsp. ground cloves
1 tsp. nutmeg
1 tsp. grated orange peel

Topping
1 cup sugar
1 cup water
1 tsp. grated orange peel

Cake
Preheat oven to 350°. Grease a 9 × 13 pan. Mix together all ingredients by hand until smooth. Bake at 350° for about 30 minutes.

Topping
Boil sugar, water and orange peel in small pan. Pour over cake as it comes out of oven.

When cake is cool, cut into diamond shaped pieces. Best served the same day.   Serves 16

S.M.U. SHEET CAKE

Cake
2 cups flour
2 cups sugar
1 tsp. baking soda
½ tsp. salt
1 cup butter
4 Tbsp. Hershey's cocoa
1 cup water
½ cup buttermilk
2 eggs, slightly beaten
1 tsp. vanilla

Icing
½ cup butter
4 Tbsp. Hershey's cocoa
6 Tbsp. buttermilk
1 lb. box powdered sugar
1 tsp. vanilla

Cake
Preheat oven to 350°. Sift flour, sugar, baking soda and salt into large bowl. Melt butter in saucepan; add cocoa and water and bring to a boil. Pour over dry ingredients. Add buttermilk, eggs, vanilla and stir well. Mixture is thin. Pour into greased and floured 16 × 10 × 1 jelly roll pan. Bake at 350° for 15-20 minutes.

Icing
While cake bakes, melt butter; add cocoa and buttermilk and bring to a boil. Remove from heat and add powdered sugar and vanilla. Beat until very smooth. Pour over hot cake. Cool before cutting. Freezes.
Yields 15-18 pieces

JUNE KLEEB LEMON CAKE

won a blue ribbon at the 1983 Michigan State Fair

Cake
1 pkg. (3 oz.) lemon Jell-o
¾ cup boiling water
⅔ cup vegetable oil
1 pkg. Duncan Hines Lemon Supreme cake mix
4 eggs

Topping
2 cups powdered sugar
Juice of 2 lemons

Preheat oven to 350°. Grease a tube pan. Dissolve Jell-o in boiling water. Let cool. Stir oil and cooled Jell-o into cake mix. Beat in eggs, one at a time. Continue to beat 4 minutes after all eggs are added. Pour in tube pan. Bake at 350° for 55 minutes. Heat topping ingredients and pour over hot cake. Remove from pan when cake cools.
Yields 8-10 pieces

D.A.'S GRAND MARNIER CAKE

very elegant

Cake
1 cup butter, softened
1 cup sugar
3 eggs, separated
2 cups flour
1 tsp. baking powder
1 tsp. baking soda
1 cup sour cream
Grated rind of one orange
½ cup chopped almonds

Topping
½ cup sugar
¼ cup orange juice
⅓ cup Grand Marnier

Preheat oven to 350°. Cream butter and sugar until light and fluffy. Add 3 egg yolks and beat. Sift together flour, baking powder and baking soda and add to egg mixture alternately with sour cream. Beat until smooth. Stir in orange rind and nuts. Fold in 3 stiffly beaten egg whites. Pour into 9-inch greased tube pan and bake at 350° for about 50 minutes or until done.

Topping
Mix topping ingredients together. Spoon over hot cake in pan. Cool thoroughly in pan, at least 3 hours. Freezes beautifully, or keeps a long time in refrigerator. Yields 8 pieces

Variations: Decorate with slivered or whole almonds.

DATE NUT DESSERT

½ cup sugar
2 eggs
1 cup chopped dates
½ cup chopped nuts
1 heaping Tbsp. flour
1 tsp. baking powder
Whipped cream to garnish

Preheat oven to 350°. Grease a 10-inch pie plate. Beat sugar and eggs together. Add remaining ingredients. Pour into pie plate. Bake at 350° for 25 minutes. Cool. Serve with whipped cream. Can be made ahead up to 3 days. Freezes. Serves 8

Timely Tips:
You may substitute honey for sugar (1 cup honey = 1 cup sugar), but you must reduce the total liquid in the recipe by ¼ cup. Use a lower oven temperature when baking with honey.

GATEAU HÉLÈNE

Cake
2 eggs
1 cup sugar
¼ tsp. salt
1 tsp. rum flavoring
½ cup milk
1 Tbsp. butter
1 cup flour
1 tsp. baking powder

Marinade
1 cup strong coffee
1 cup sugar
¼ cup rum

Cream Layer
⅓ cup sugar
2 Tbsp. cornstarch
Dash salt
1 cup coffee cream
1 egg, slightly beaten
1 tsp. rum flavoring

Apricot Topping
1 cup apricot preserves

Whipped Cream Topping
½ cup whipping cream
1 Tbsp. sugar
1 tsp. rum flavoring

Cake
Preheat oven to 350°. Grease and flour one 9-inch cake pan. Beat eggs until thick and light. Add sugar, salt and rum flavoring and continue to beat until very thick and light cream in color. Heat milk and butter together until scalding.

In separate bowl, sift flour and baking powder together. Beat hot milk mixture into egg mixture. Add dry ingredients. Pour into pan. Bake at 350° for 30–40 minutes. Cool in pan on cake rack 10 minutes. Remove cake from pan. Place on rack with pan under rack to catch extra marinade.

Marinade
While cake is cooling, combine sugar and coffee together in saucepan and boil for 3 minutes. Cool. Stir in rum. Spoon coffee mixture over cake as it cools on rack. Spoon any sauce which drips through cake rack onto top of cake. Let stand at least 1 hour.

GATEAU HÉLÈNE (continued)

Cream Layer

Combine sugar, cornstarch and salt thoroughly in saucepan. Add coffee cream, stirring until smooth. Cook, stirring, over low heat, until thickened. Stir a little of hot mixture into egg. Blend this into remaining hot mixture and cook 1–2 minutes. Remove from heat. Chill. Stir in rum flavoring.

Assembly

Split cake carefully, horizontally, into two layers. Fill with the cream filling. Cover top of cake generously with apricot preserves. Beat together whipping cream, sugar and rum flavoring until stiff. Frost top of cake in decorative pattern. Refrigerate. Make ahead, up to 2 days.   Serves 10–12

CHOCOLATE ECLAIR CAKE

Cake

1 box (1 lb.) graham
    crackers
2 pkgs. (3⅝ oz. each) instant
    vanilla pudding
3 cups milk
1 pkg. (8 oz.) Cool Whip

Frosting

2 squares unsweetened
    chocolate, melted
3 Tbsp. milk
2 tsp. vanilla
2 Tbsp. light corn syrup
1½ cups powdered sugar

Cake

Grease bottom and sides of a 9x13 pan. Line bottom of pan with whole graham crackers. Beat pudding and milk together. Let stand at room temperature until thickened. Fold in Cool Whip.

Pour half of the pudding mixture over crackers. Add a layer of graham crackers. Pour the rest of pudding mixture over this. Top with another layer of graham crackers.

Frosting

Mix together chocolate, milk, vanilla, corn syrup and sugar until smooth. Pour over cake. Refrigerate overnight.

Serves 10–12

HUNGARIAN NUT TORTE
from the Golden Mushroom

7½ oz. filberts, finely
   ground, cold
4 oz. unsalted butter, finely
   diced, cold
¼ cup granulated sugar,
   cold
⅓ cup flour, cold
1½ cups shredded coconut
4 whole eggs
1 egg yolk
10 oz. brown sugar
1 tsp. baking powder
¾ lbs. walnuts, chopped
⅔ cup flour
½ cup dark Jamaican rum
Pure raspberry preserves
Whipped cream
Walnut halves
Powdered sugar

Preheat oven to 375°. Butter and dust with flour, the bottom and sides of two 10-inch spring form pans. Mix cold filberts, cold flour, cold sugar and coconut. Crumble in the cold butter. Divide this mixture between the two pans and pack down flat.

Beat eggs, brown sugar and baking powder at high speed until foamy. Remove from mixer and fold in chopped walnuts and flour. Pour over the packed down base and spread flat. Bake about 20 minutes or until center is just barely set. Remove from oven and cool 15 minutes.

Sprinkle rum over both cakes. Remove rings. Spread raspberry preserves ¼ inch thick on one layer, cover with the other layer, so that both bottoms are on outside. Cover well and refrigerate overnight.

Next day, before serving, dust with powdered sugar and decorate with whipped cream and walnut halves.   Serves 8–12

Variation: Frost with Buttercream Frosting instead of whipped cream.

Timely Tip:
When you are short on eggs for a cake mix, substitute 2 Tbsp. Hellmann's mayonnaise for each egg you are missing.

QUEEN ELIZABETH CAKE

also good for breakfast

Cake
1 cup boiling water
1 cup chopped dates
1 tsp. baking soda
1 cup sugar
¼ cup butter
1 egg
½ tsp. salt
1½ cups four
1 tsp. vanilla
½ cup chopped nuts
   (optional)

Icing
5 Tbsp. brown sugar
5 Tbsp. whipping cream
2 Tbsp. butter
Chopped nuts

Cake
Preheat oven to 350°. Grease a 9 × 12 pan. Pour 1 cup boiling water over chopped dates and baking soda. Set aside. Beat together sugar and butter. Add egg, salt, flour and vanilla. Blend date mixture into this batter. Add nuts if desired. Bake at 350° for 35 minutes.

Icing
Boil together brown sugar, cream and butter for 3 minutes. Spread on cake while hot. Sprinkle with chopped nuts.

Serves 12

NANTUCKET CRANBERRIES

2 cups raw cranberries
1½ cups sugar, divided
½ cup chopped walnuts
¾ cup butter, melted
2 eggs, beaten
1 cup flour
1 tsp. almond extract
Whipped cream or vanilla
   ice cream for topping

Preheat oven to 325°. Grease 10-inch pie pan. Wash and dry cranberries. Place in pie plate. Sprinkle ½ cup sugar and nuts over cranberries. Cream butter and 1 cup sugar. Add beaten eggs, flour and almond extract. Mix until blended and pour batter over berries. Bake at 325° for 40 minutes. Top with ice cream or whipped cream.

Serves 8–10

Helpful Hint: Buy cranberries during holidays and freeze for future use.

STRAWBERRY TORTE

1 cup sifted flour
1 tsp. baking soda
¼ tsp. salt
½ cup butter, softened
1½ cups sugar, divided
5 eggs, separated
1 tsp. vanilla
3 Tbsp. milk
¾ tsp. almond extract,
    divided
½ cup slivered almonds
2 cups whipping cream
3 pts. strawberries, cleaned,
    hulled and halved

Preheat oven to 350°. Grease and flour two 9-inch cake pans. Sift flour, baking soda and salt together. Cream butter with ½ cup sugar. Beat in egg yolks. Add vanilla and milk. Fold in flour mixture. Spread evenly in pans.

Beat egg whites with ¼ tsp. almond extract until foamy and doubled in volume. Sprinkle ¾ cup sugar over egg whites, a little at a time. Beat until firm peaks are formed. Spread evenly over batter in pans. Sprinkle with almonds. Bake at 350° for 30 minutes until meringue is lightly browned. Cool for 5 minutes. Remove from pans and cool on wire racks.

Beat whipping cream with ¼ cup sugar and ½ tsp. almond extract until stiff. Top one meringue with half of the whipped cream mixture and half of the strawberries. Add the second meringue, then the remaining cream and top with the remaining strawberries.   Serves 8

Timely Tip:
Vegetables and fruits ripen faster when placed in a paper bag and stored in a drawer or cupboard.

ALMOND CHEESECAKE

1982 Showhouse Tea Room recipe

Crust
1 cup graham cracker
   crumbs
1 Tbsp. sugar
1 tsp. flour
¼ cup butter, melted

Filling
4 pkgs. (8 oz. each) cream
   cheese, softened
1 cup sugar
2 eggs
1 tsp. almond extract
1 tsp. vanilla

Topping
2 cups sour cream
¾ cup sugar
¾ tsp. almond extract
Chocolate shavings

Preheat oven to 350°. Grease a 9-inch spring form pan. Combine all crust ingredients. Press crumbs on the bottom of the spring form pan. Bake at 350° for 5 minutes. Remove from oven and cool. TURN OFF OVEN AND OPEN DOOR TO COOL THE OVEN.

Filling
Mix all filling ingredients with electric mixer at medium speed. Pour filling into cooled crust. Place in COLD oven, turn to 350° and bake 30 minutes.

Topping
Combine sour cream, sugar and almond extract. Pour over baked cheesecake. Return to oven for 8 minutes longer.

Refrigerate overnight. Sprinkle top with chocolate shavings. Make ahead, up to 2 days. Freezes.

Yields one 9-inch cheesecake

STRAWBERRIES ELEGANTE

1½ cups sour cream
½ cup brown sugar
¼ cup Grand Marnier
1 qt. fresh strawberries,
   washed and hulled
Mint sprigs, if desired

Mix sour cream with brown sugar and press out lumps. Add liqueur. Pour sauce over strawberries in parfait glasses, and garnish with mint sprig. Sauce can be made 2–3 days ahead, but will need stirring before serving.
Serves 6

CHERRIES GRAND MARNIER

1 can (16 oz.) pitted dark
    sweet cherries, drained
6 Tbsp. Grand Marnier
1 Tbsp. grated orange peel
3 tsp. lemon juice
1 cup whipping cream
¼ cup sugar

Drain cherries and marinate overnight in mixture of Grand Marnier, orange peel and lemon juice. Before serving, drain cherries, reserving marinade. Place cherries in individual serving dishes. Whip cream with sugar until stiff. Top cherries with whipped cream and drizzle 1 Tbsp. of marinade over each serving. Serves 4

Variations: Substitute dark rum or kirsch for Grand Marnier.

BAVARIAN APPLE TORTE

Sweet Crust
½ cup butter, softened
⅓ cup sugar
¼ tsp. vanilla
1 cup flour

Cheese Filling
1 pkg. (8 oz.) cream cheese,
    softened
¼ cup sugar
1 egg
½ tsp. vanilla

Topping
⅓ cup sugar
½ tsp. cinnamon
4 cups apples, peeled, cored
    and sliced
¼ cup slivered almonds

Crust
Preheat oven to 450°. Cream butter and sugar. Beat in vanilla. Blend in flour. Mixture will be crumbly. Pat into greased 9-inch spring form pan on bottom and 1½ inches up sides.

Filling
Beat cream cheese and sugar. Add egg and vanilla. Blend well and pour into pastry crust; spread to edges.

Topping
Combine sugar and cinnamon. Toss apples with sugar mixture. Place on filling. Top with nuts. Bake 10 minutes at 450°. Reduce oven to 400° and bake 25 minutes. Loosen edges from pan with sharp knife. Remove when cool. Freezes Serves 6-8

BLUEBERRY CHEESECAKE

Crust
1½ cups zwieback crumbs
2 Tbsp. butter, softened
2 Tbsp. sugar

Cheesecake
2 pkgs. (8 oz. each) cream
    cheese, softened
1 cup sugar
5 eggs, separated
2 cups sour cream
1 tsp. vanilla
1 tsp. lemon juice

Topping
2 Tbsp. cornstarch
½ cup sugar
½ cup water
1½ cups blueberries
1 tsp. lemon juice

Crust
Preheat oven to 300°. Mix zwieback crumbs, butter and sugar together. Press into 9-inch spring form pan.

Cheesecake
Cream together cream cheese and sugar. Add egg yolks, sour cream, vanilla and lemon juice. Stir until smooth. Beat egg whites until stiff. Very carefully fold egg whites into cream cheese mixture. Pour into spring form pan. Bake at 300° for 1 hour. Turn off oven. Leave cake in the oven with door closed for 1 hour. Open oven door and leave cake in oven ½ hour more.

Topping
Mix cornstarch and sugar. Add ½ cup water. Stir until smooth. Add blueberries and lemon juice. Cook over low heat until clear. Chill.

Remove spring form from pan. Spread blueberry topping over cheesecake. Make ahead, up to 2 days.

Best to store cheesecake in spring form pan if preparing ahead. Store topping separately. Unmold and top when ready to serve.

Yields one 9-inch cheesecake

CHEESECAKE SQUARES

a great Christmas gift

Crust
3 cups flour
1 cup brown sugar
1 cup butter, melted
1½ cups chopped walnuts

Cheesecake
1 cup sugar
3 pkgs. (8 oz. each) cream
 cheese
3 eggs
6 Tbsp. milk
1 Tbsp. lemon juice
1 tsp. vanilla
½ cup sour cream
¼ cup flour

Crust
Preheat oven to 350°. Mix flour, brown sugar, butter and nuts to make a crumb mixture. Set 3 cups aside for topping. Press remaining mixture into 15½ × 10½ × 1 jelly roll pan. Bake at 350° for 10 minutes.

Cheesecake
Beat together sugar, cream cheese, eggs, milk, lemon juice and vanilla. Fold in sour cream and flour. Pour over baked crust. Sprinkle with reserved crumb mixture. Bake at 350° for 25 minutes.

Cool and cut into 2-inch squares. Freezes.

Yields 3 doz. squares

STRAWBERRY SCRUMPTIOUS

1½ cups crushed vanilla
 wafers
½ cup plus 2 Tbsp. sugar,
 divided
4 Tbsp. butter, melted
4 egg whites
1 cup whipping cream
1 qt. strawberries, sliced and
 sugared or 2 pkgs. (8 oz.
 each) of frozen berries

Preheat oven to 350°. Combine crushed wafers, 2 Tbsp. sugar and melted butter. Press into 8x8x2 baking dish. In a large bowl, beat egg whites until soft peaks form. Gradually add ½ cup sugar, beating until stiff peaks form. Spread meringue over crumbs. Bake in 350° oven for 15–17 minutes. Cool. Whip cream and sweeten slightly. Spread over meringue and chill. When ready to serve, top with strawberries. Can be made ahead up to 1 day. Serves 8

FROZEN CHOCOLATE CHEESECAKE

everyone will want the recipe

Crust
1½ cups chocolate wafer
　　cookie crumbs
⅓ cup butter, melted

Cheesecake
1 pkg. (8 oz.) cream cheese
1 tsp. vanilla
½ cup sugar, divided
1 pkg. (6 oz.) semi-sweet
　　chocolate chips
2 eggs, separated
1 cup whipping cream,
　　whipped
¾ cup chopped nuts
　　(optional)

Crust
Preheat oven to 325°. Mix cookie crumbs and melted butter together. Press into an 8 or 9-inch spring form pan. Bake at 325° for 10 minutes. Cool about 1 hour.

Cheesecake
Beat together cream cheese, vanilla and ¼ cup sugar until well blended. Melt chocolate chips over low heat in heavy saucepan. Stir 2 beaten egg yolks and chocolate into the cream cheese mixture. Mix until well blended.

Beat 2 egg whites until stiff peaks form. Gradually add ¼ cup sugar. Beat until stiff. Fold into cream cheese mixture. Fold in whipped cream. Add nuts if desired. Pour into crust and freeze.

May top with whipped cream before serving. Can be made ahead up to 3 days.
　　Yields one 9-inch cheesecake

DEVON CREAM

1 pkg. (3 oz.) cream cheese
1 + Tbsp. granulated sugar
　　to taste
Pinch salt
1 cup whipping cream

Cream cheese with salt and sugar. Stir until smooth. Stir in cream. Beat all ingredients until stiff. Make ahead.
　　　　　　　　Serves 4

A DIFFERENT CHEESECAKE

unique and incredibly light

Crust

1½ cups honey graham
  cracker crumbs
½ cup finely crushed All
  Bran cereal
¼ cup finely chopped
  walnuts
1 tsp. cinnamon
⅓ cup butter, softened
⅓ cup sugar

Filling

3 pkgs. (8 oz. each) cream
  cheese
1 cup sugar
4 eggs, separated
1 Tbsp. vanilla

Topping

1½ cups sour cream
2 Tbsp. sugar
1 tsp. vanilla

Crust

Preheat oven to 350°. With steel blade in work bowl of food processor, pulse each of dry ingredients separately until finely crushed. Measure into mixing bowl. Toss with cinnamon. With steel blade in work bowl, process softened butter. Gradually add sugar through feed tube. Scrape sides. Add dry ingredients to work bowl. Process until thoroughly blended.

Reserve small amount for topping. Press remainder into bottom and up sides of 10-inch spring form pan. Bake 10 min. at 350°.

Filling

With steel blade in work bowl, process cream cheese with sugar, egg yolks and vanilla, stopping to scrape sides and bottom 2–3 times until smooth and well blended. In large bowl, beat egg whites until stiff. Fold in cream cheese mixture. Pour into baked crust. Bake at 350° until top cracks at edges and toothpick removes cleanly from center, approximately 45 min.

A DIFFERENT CHEESECAKE
(continued)

Topping
Raise oven temperature to 400°.
With steel blade in work bowl,
process all ingredients until
smooth and well-blended.
Spread sour cream mixture on
top of cheesecake. Bake 10 min.
Sprinkle with reserved crust topping while warm.

Refrigerate at least 6 hours before serving. Make up to 1 day
ahead. Freezes.
Yields one 10-inch cheesecake

Variation: You may eliminate crumbled topping and use
sliced fresh fruit instead.
Helpful Hint: Can be prepared without food processor.

PECAN CREAM CHEESE PIE
quick and very rich

1 9" pie shell, unbaked

Filling
1 pkg. (8 oz.) cream cheese,
   softened
2 tsp. vanilla, divided
6 Tbsp. sugar, divided
4 eggs, divided
¾ cup light corn syrup
3 to 4 oz. crushed pecans

Preheat oven to 375°. Beat together cream cheese, 1 tsp.
vanilla, 4 Tbsp. sugar and 1 egg
until sugar is dissolved. In separate bowl, beat together 3 eggs,
corn syrup, 2 Tbsp. sugar and 1
tsp. vanilla. Pour cream cheese
mixture into pie shell. Sprinkle
pecans on top. Carefully pour
syrup mixture on top of pecans.
Bake at 375° for 35 minutes.
Serve warm or chilled. Store in
the refrigerator.
Yields one 9-inch pie

DAIQUIRI FLUFF

tastes like a frozen daiquiri

Crust

1¼ cups graham cracker
  crumbs
¼ cup sugar
6 Tbsp. butter, melted

Filling

1 env. unflavored gelatin
1 cup sugar, divided
½ cup white rum
2 tsp. grated lime peel
1 tsp. grated lemon peel
½ cup lime juice
4 egg yolks, beaten
2 pkgs. (8 oz. each) cream
  cheese, cubed and
  softened
4 egg whites
1 cup whipping cream

Crust

Combine graham cracker crumbs, sugar and melted butter. Set aside 2 Tbsp. crumb mixture for garnishing. Press remaining crumbs in bottom and one inch up sides of a 10-inch spring form pan. Chill 45 minutes.

Filling

In medium saucepan, combine gelatin and ½ cup sugar. Stir in rum, citrus peels, lime juice, and beaten egg yolks. Cook over medium heat, stirring until thickened, about 10 minutes. Remove from heat. Beat in cream cheese until smooth.

Beat egg whites until soft peaks form. Gradually add ½ cup sugar, beating until stiff peaks form. Fold egg whites into mixture. Whip cream and fold into mixture. Pour into crumb lined pan. Sprinkle reserved crumbs around edge. Cover. Chill until firm, several hours or overnight. Make ahead up to 2 days. Freezes.

Yields one 10-inch cheesecake

To soften cream cheese, remove foil wrapper and place cream cheese on glass plate in microwave. Cook on Medium-High for 45 seconds-1 minute.

MARBLE CHEESECAKE

improves with age

Crust

1½ cups graham cracker
   crumbs
¼ cup sugar
6 Tbsp. butter, melted

Cheesecake

4 pkgs. (8 oz. each) cream
   cheese, softened
2 tsp. vanilla
1¾ cups sugar
6 eggs
2 cups coffee cream
2 squares unsweetened
   chocolate, melted and
   cooled slightly

Crust

Combine graham cracker crumbs, sugar and butter. Press into bottom and 2 inches up side of 10-inch spring form pan.

Cheesecake

Preheat oven to 450°. Beat cream cheese and vanilla until fluffy. Gradually stir in sugar. Add eggs, one at a time, beating until just blended. Stir in cream. Combine about 3 cups batter with cooled chocolate. Pour plain cheese mixture into crust. Gradually add chocolate mixture using zigzag motion. Bake at 450° for 15 minutes. Reduce heat to 300° and bake 1 hour 10 minutes. Cool 1 hour before removing sides of pan. Refrigerate 12–24 hours.
Yields one 10-inch cheesecake

BANANAS FOSTER

4 Tbsp. butter
½ cup brown sugar
4 ripe bananas, peeled and
   sliced lengthwise
¼ tsp. cinnamon
2 oz. banana liqueur
4 oz. white rum

Melt butter in chafing dish. Add brown sugar and blend well. Add bananas and sauté. Sprinkle with cinnamon. Pour banana liqueur and rum over mixture. Ignite, baste bananas with flaming liquid. Serve when flame dies out.   Serves 4

Serve With: Ice cream.

PUMPKIN CHEESECAKE

Crust
2 Tbsp. butter, softened
⅓ cup gingersnap crumbs

Cheesecake
4 pkgs. (8 oz. each) cream
  cheese, softened
1½ cups firmly packed dark
  brown sugar
5 eggs
¼ cup flour
1 tsp. cinnamon
1 tsp. allspice
¼ tsp. ginger
¼ tsp. salt
2 cups (one 16 oz. can)
  pumpkin pureé
Maple syrup and walnut
  halves (optional)
Whipped cream to top
  (optional)

Crust
Generously grease a 9-inch spring form pan with the softened butter. Sprinkle gingersnap crumbs into the pan and shake to coat bottom and sides evenly.

Cheesecake
Preheat oven to 325°. In large bowl, cream the cream cheese with a wooden spoon until fluffy. Gradually beat in the brown sugar. Add the eggs, one at a time, beating well after each addition. Sift the flour, cinnamon, allspice, ginger and salt together. Blend flour mixture into batter. Beat in pumpkin pureé. Pour batter into prepared pan.

Bake in the center of oven at 325° for 1½–1¾ hours or until cake pulls away from side of pan and toothpick inserted in center comes out clean. Cool in the pan 1 hour. Remove spring form from pan and finish cooling. Refrigerate. Brush top of cake with syrup and garnish with walnuts if desired. Top with whipped cream.

Yields one 9-inch cheesecake

Timely Tip:
Keep a new powder puff in your flour canister for dusting greased cake and loaf pans.

APPLE BAKE WITH HOT BUTTER SAUCE

¼ cup butter, softened
1 cup sugar
3 med. tart cooking apples,
    peeled and grated
2 eggs, well-beaten
1 cup flour
1 tsp. baking soda
1 tsp. nutmeg
1 tsp. cinnamon
¼ tsp. salt

Hot Butter Sauce
1 cup sugar
½ cup coffee cream
½ cup butter
1½ tsp. vanilla

Preheat oven to 350°. Cream butter and sugar. Add grated apples and beaten eggs; mix well. Stir in remaining ingredients. Pour into ungreased 9-inch glass pie plate. Bake 45–50 minutes or until top springs back. Serve warm with Hot Butter Sauce.

Hot Butter Sauce
Combine all ingredients in top of double boiler. Heat over hot water until butter is melted and sugar is dissolved. Keep hot until ready to serve, or may be prepared ahead and reheated.

Serves 6–8

BLUEBERRY CREAM TART

1 9" pie shell, baked

Cream Mixture
1 pkg. (3 oz.) cream cheese,
    softened
½ cup sugar
1 tsp. vanilla
1 cup whipping cream,
    whipped

Blueberry Mixture
1 pt. blueberries, washed
    and drained
5 oz. currant jelly
2 Tbsp. dark rum

Cream Mixture
Cream together the cream cheese and sugar. Add vanilla. Fold whipped cream into cheese mixture. Spread evenly over pie shell.

Blueberry Mixture
Spread washed blueberries on towel to remove as much water as possible. Whip currant jelly with rum until smooth. Add blueberries and stir gently. Do not mash the berries. Spread over cream mixture. Chill several hours.

Yields one 9-inch pie

VANILLA LACE APPLES

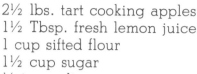

lovely delicate dessert

2½ lbs. tart cooking apples
1½ Tbsp. fresh lemon juice
1 cup sifted flour
1½ cup sugar
¼ tsp. salt
¼ tsp. cinnamon
⅔ cup finely chopped,
   blanched almonds
½ cup unsalted butter,
   melted
1 Tbsp. vanilla extract
1½ cups whipping cream,
   softly whipped

Preheat oven to 375°. Peel, core and thinly slice apples. Toss apples with lemon juice to coat. Butter a 1½-quart baking dish and spread apples over the bottom.

Sift together flour, sugar, salt and cinnamon. Stir in almonds. Mix the melted butter with 1 Tbsp. vanilla extract. Add almond-flour mixture and toss with a fork until mixed and crumbly. Sprinkle evenly over apples.

Bake at 375° until topping is richly browned about 35–40 minutes. Partially cool on rack. Serve with softly whipped cream. Can be made ahead.

Serves 6

PEAR PIE

1 9" pie shell, unbaked

Filling
6 medium pears, peeled,
   cored and sliced
¾ cup sugar, divided
3 Tbsp. lemon juice
½ cup flour
½ tsp. ginger
¼ tsp. mace
½ tsp. cinnamon
⅓ cup butter, firm

Preheat oven to 400°. Toss pears with half of the sugar and the lemon juice. Arrange in shell. Combine flour and remaining sugar and spices. Cut in butter until crumbly. Sprinkle over pears. Bake at 400° for 45 minutes. Can be frozen after baking, but best served same day.

Yields one 9-inch pie

ORANGE FILLED CUPS

holiday dessert

8 navel oranges
Additional fresh orange juice
   to make 3 cups
1⅓ cups sugar
2 oz. rum or to taste
2 env. unflavored gelatin
½ cup cold water
1½ cups whipping cream

Cut off top ¼ of each orange and carefully scoop out insides, leaving peeling intact; flute the edges of each orange. Mash the pulp and strain it. If necessary, add fresh strained orange juice to reach 3 cups juice. Add sugar and rum to juice and stir until sugar is dissolved.

Combine gelatin and cold water in top of a double boiler over hot water to dissolve. In a mixing bowl, slowly add gelatin to juice. Slowly add unwhipped cream. Spoon into orange cups. Refrigerate. Garnish as you like — fresh mint sprigs are lovely. Can be made ahead 1 day if kept covered.
Serves 8

DERBY PIE

1 10" pie shell, unbaked

Filling
2 eggs
½ cup unsifted flour
½ cup sugar
½ cup firmly packed brown
   sugar
1 cup butter, melted and
   cooled
1 pkg. (6 oz.) semi-sweet
   chocolate chips
1 cup chopped walnuts
Whipped cream or vanilla
   ice cream to top

Preheat oven to 325°. In large bowl, beat eggs until foamy. Beat in flour and sugars until well blended. Add butter. Stir in chocolate chips and chopped walnuts. Pour into pie shell. Bake at 325° for 1 hour. Serve warm with whipped cream or vanilla ice cream.
Yields one 10-inch pie

STRAWBERRY MERINGUE TORTE

Meringue

4 egg whites, room
    temperature
Pinch salt
¼ tsp. cream of tartar
1 tsp. cider vinegar
1 tsp. vanilla
1 cup sugar

Meringue

Preheat oven to 275°. Beat egg whites, salt, cream of tartar, vinegar and vanilla until soft peaks form. Gradually beat in sugar, 1 Tbsp. at a time, until stiff and glossy. Separate egg whites carefully, as even a trace of yolk will prevent beaten whites from reaching full volume.

Line cookie sheets with parchment, or wax paper. Trace three 8-inch circles. Spread the meringue evenly over the circles. Bake for 1 hour until meringues are light brown. Turn off oven and open door for 15 minutes more. Remove from oven and peel meringues from paper. Put on racks to dry.

Variation:
Extra strawberries may be sliced and sugared to top each slice when served.
Helpful Hint:
Brown paper bags can be used instead of parchment or wax paper.

Filling

1 pkg. (6 oz.) semi-sweet
    chocolate chips
3 Tbsp. water
4 cups whipping cream
4 Tbsp. powdered sugar
1 Tbsp. vanilla
2 qts. fresh strawberries,
    washed and sliced
    (reserve several whole
    berries for garnish)

Filling

Melt chocolate chips and water in double boiler over hot water. When smooth, remove from heat and stir occasionally to keep it soft. Whip cream until very stiff, gradually adding powdered sugar and vanilla. Slice strawberries lengthwise and drain on paper towels.

Assembly

Place a meringue layer on serving platter, flat side down. Spread a thin layer of chocolate over meringue. Top with a layer of whipped cream and a layer of strawberries. Place second layer of meringue over strawberries and repeat layers. Top with third layer of meringue. Cover entire torte (top and sides) with remaining whipped cream. Refrigerate at least 6 hours or overnight. May decorate the top with whole strawberries. Must be made ahead up to one day.

Serves 10

BETTY ANNE'S STRAWBERRY SUPREME

3 egg whites
1 cup sugar
1 tsp. vanilla
12 soda crackers, crushed
   very fine
½ cup chopped pecans
1 pt. fresh strawberries,
   sliced (reserve 1 or 2
   large whole berries for
   garnish)
1 cup whipping cream
2 Tbsp. powdered sugar
1½ Tbsp. Curacao or other
   orange flavored liqueur

Preheat oven to 325°. Beat egg whites until they form soft peaks. Add sugar and vanilla gradually, beating continuously until it forms stiff peaks and retains shine. Fold in crushed soda crackers and pecans. Pour into one well-greased 8-inch round cake pan. Bake for 35 minutes. Cool. Remove from pan.

Top meringue with strawberries. Whip the cream, gradually adding powdered sugar and Curacao until stiff. Spread on top of strawberries. Garnish with reserved berries. Chill for 4 hours before serving.

Serves 6–8

Variation: Use a graham cracker crust.

FRENCH SILK CHOCOLATE PIE

1 9″ deep dish pie crust,
   baked

Filling
4 oz. unsweetened chocolate
1 cup butter, softened
1½ cups sugar
2 tsp. vanilla
4 eggs

Melt chocolate in double boiler over hot water. Cool slightly. Cream butter. Gradually add sugar and cream well. Blend in chocolate and vanilla. Add eggs one at a time, beating 5 minutes after each addition. Pour into pie shell. Chill several hours.

Yields one 9-inch pie

Serve With: Whipped cream and walnuts

Timely Tip:
Eggs that have been refrigerated for up to 2 weeks produce a better meringue than fresh eggs.

SUMMER PUDDING

1 pt. raspberries
1 qt. strawberries
1 pt. blueberries
1 cup + 2 Tbsp. sugar
1 loaf firm white bread
1 cup whipping cream

Wash and drain fruit. Mix fruit and sugar in saucepan and cook over low heat for 10 to 15 minutes. Stir gently a couple of times to allow fruit juices to run and all of the fruit to become tender. Remove from heat and cool.

Remove crust from bread slices. Line a glass 6–8 cup mixing bowl with bread slices. **Cut to fit exactly** and press firmly. Add part of cooled fruit mixture to lined bowl, put in a layer of bread, add remaining fruit. Top with another slice of bread. Fill bowl with any leftover juice.

Top pudding with a 2 lb. weight on a plate that fits inside the mixing bowl (an item on your canned goods shelf may be the proper weight). Refrigerate 24 hours.

Just before serving, top with cream (unwhipped or whipped as you desire). Must be made ahead; up to 36 hours is fine.

Serves 8

Variations: Without the bread, fruit sauce can be used as a sauce for pound cake or angel food cake.
Helpful Hint: Put a plate under pudding in refrigerator as it may drip over edge of bowl.

BLUEBERRY CUSTARD PIE

1 9" deep dish pie shell,
   baked.

Custard
2 cups milk
3 Tbsp. flour
1½ Tbsp. cornstarch
½ cup sugar
¼ tsp. salt
2 egg yolks, beaten
1 tsp. vanilla

Blueberry Topping
1 pt. blueberries, washed
   and drained
⅓ cup sugar
¼ cup firmly packed brown
   sugar
⅛ tsp. salt
1 Tbsp. vinegar or lemon
   juice
Mixture of 2-3 Tbsp.
   cornstarch with 1-2 tsp.
   water
½ pt. whipping cream,
   whipped

Custard
Scald milk in top of double boiler. Combine flour, cornstarch, sugar and salt. Add to scalded milk and cook until thick and smooth, stirring constantly. After mixture thickens, continue to cook 15 minutes longer, stirring constantly.

Stir small amount of custard mixture into egg yolks. Add egg mixture to custard in double boiler. Cook a few minutes longer. Cool. Add vanilla. Pour into baked pie crust. Chill.

Blueberry Topping
Mix blueberries, sugars, salt, lemon juice or vinegar and 2 tsp. water. Cook over low heat, stirring constantly and gently. When fully cooked, add cornstarch and water mixture very slowly. Cook a few minutes longer until it is very thick. Refrigerate. When fully cooled, pour over custard. Top with whipped cream. Make ahead, up to 1 day.

Yields one 9-inch pie

Helpful Hint: Don't leave custard cooking; must stir constantly to avoid burning.

Timely Tip:
A fresh pineapple is ripe when a leaf from the center comes out easily.

MARY'S BLUEBERRY NECTAR PIE

Pastry for double crust pie

Filling
1 qt. fresh blueberries or 2
  pkgs. (8 oz. ea.) frozen
  berries
⅔ cup sugar
2½ Tbsp. quick cooking
  tapioca
Dash salt
1 Tbsp. lemon juice
½ cup brown sugar
1 Tbsp. butter

Preheat oven to 425°. Wash and dry blueberries. Place in large bowl. In small bowl, mix together sugar, tapioca and salt. Add to blueberries and mix, stirring gently. Add lemon juice. Let stand about 10 minutes. Pour filling into a 9-inch pastry shell. Sprinkle with brown sugar and dot with butter. Cover with top crust or lattice top. Bake at 425° for 30–40 minutes. Serve warm with vanilla ice cream.

Yields one 9-inch pie

Timely Tip:
Before baking any filled pie, place the rack in lower third of oven.

PEANUT BUTTER ICE CREAM PIE

kids love it, but grown-ups sneak back for more!

1 8" graham cracker or
  vanilla wafer pie crust

Filling
¾ cup peanut butter
2 cups vanilla ice cream,
  softened
1 cup Cool Whip

Mix peanut butter and ice cream with electric mixer. Stir in Cool Whip. Pour into pie crust. Freeze. Garnish with one or more of the following: chocolate curls, chopped peanuts, hot fudge sauce or more Cool Whip.

Yields one 8-inch pie

Helpful Hint: A graham cracker crust will come out of pie plate more easily if baked for 5 minutes at 350°. You may microwave a graham cracker crust in a glass pie plate for 2 minutes on High turning plate once after 1 minute.

MONTANA PEACH PIE

Pastry for a double crust pie

Filling
8–10 fresh ripe peaches,
   peeled, pitted and
   quartered
1 cup sugar
6 Tbsp. flour
½ cup butter, hard
Dash salt

Preheat oven to 450°. Line a 9-inch pie plate with half of pastry. Make a crumbled mixture of sugar, flour, butter and salt with pastry blender or fork. Place about one third of the crumbled mixture in the unbaked pie shell.

Place peaches pit side down over crumbled mixture. Sprinkle remaining crumbled mixture over peaches. Top with a lattice crust using remaining pastry.

Bake at 450° for 15 minutes to brown. Reduce heat to 350° and bake an additional 45 minutes. Can be made the night before, but best served the same day.
Yields one 9-inch pie

Helpful Hint: Partially cook the bottom pie crust for best results.

TURTLES

1 pkg. (12 oz.) Oreo cookes,
   crushed
2 Tbsp. butter, melted
½ gal. vanilla ice cream
1 cup Hershey's fudge
   topping, warm
1 can (8 oz.) salted peanuts

Pam spray or lightly grease 9x12 pan. Mix Oreo cookies with butter. Spread in prepared pan. Slice ice cream and lay on top of cookie mixture as evenly as possible. Pour warm fudge sauce over ice cream. Top with peanuts. Freeze 2–3 hours until firm. Cut into squares. Cover with foil if made ahead.
Serves 12

SINFUL BUT DELICIOUS

1 graham cracker pie crust
1 qt. Baskin and Robbins'
 Pralines and Cream ice
 cream, softened
2 pkgs. (3⅝ oz. each) or 1
 pkg. (5¼ oz.) instant
 vanilla pudding
2 cups milk
8 Heath Bars, crumbled,
 divided
1 carton (8 oz.) Cool Whip
Part of 1 square of
 unsweetened chocolate
 for shavings

Bake crust 8 minutes at 350°.
Cool.

Combine ice cream, dry pudding, milk and ½ of crumbled Heath Bars with beater until thoroughly blended. Pour into pie crust. Refrigerate 4-5 hours until thoroughly set. If serving within 36 hours, cover with plastic wrap and keep refrigerated. Otherwise, cover with tin foil and freeze. If pie is frozen, put in refrigerator 6-8 hours before next step.

Blend remaining crumbled Heath Bars into Cool Whip. Spread on pie and sprinkle with chocolate shavings. Keep refrigerated until ready to serve.
Serves 8-10

CHOCOLATE COFFEE FREEZE

1 cup vanilla wafer crumbs
⅔ cup butter, softened
2 cups powdered sugar
3 egg yolks
2 squares unsweetened
 chocolate, melted
½ cup chopped pecans
3 egg whites
1 tsp. vanilla
½ gal. coffee ice cream
15 Tbsp. dark rum

Line bottom of 9x13 pan with crumbs. Cream butter and powdered sugar. Beat egg yolks into creamed mixture. Add chocolate and pecans. Beat egg whites until stiff and fold into chocolate mixture; add vanilla. Pour over crumbs and freeze 3 hours. Spread with softened ice cream and refreeze. Cut into squares to serve and pour 1 Tbsp. rum over each serving.   Serves 15

BROWNIE BAKED ALASKA

1 qt. vanilla (or other) ice
cream
½ cup butter
2 squares (1 oz. each)
unsweetened chocolate
¾ cup flour
½ tsp. baking powder
½ tsp. salt
2 eggs, beaten
2 cups sugar, divided
1 tsp. vanilla
1 cup chopped pecans
5 egg whites

Ice Cream
Line a 1-quart (7–8 inch in diameter) bowl with wax paper. Pack with ice cream and freeze until very firm.

Brownie Layer
Preheat oven to 350°. Melt butter and chocolate. Mix together flour, baking powder and salt. Add to chocolate. Add beaten eggs; stir in 1 cup sugar and blend. Add vanilla and pecans. Bake in a greased 8-inch round cake pan at 350° for 30 minutes. Cool and remove from pan.

Assembly
Place brownie layer on oven-proof plate. Invert ice cream onto brownie layer. Do not remove wax paper. Return to freezer.

Prepare meringue by beating egg whites until soft peaks form. Gradually add 1 cup sugar, beating until stiff. Remove cake from freezer and remove wax paper. Quickly spread meringue over entire surface, making sure edges are sealed. Bake at 500° for 3–4 minutes or until peaks are browned. Serve immediately.   Serves 10–12

Helpful Hint: After meringue is sealed, dessert can be frozen up to one week and baked just before serving.

OREO MINT DESSERT

20 Oreo cookies, crushed
8 Tbsp. butter, melted and
   divided
1 cup chocolate chips
3 eggs
2 cups powdered sugar
¾ cup chopped nuts
½ gal. vanilla ice cream
3 oz. green Creme de
   Menthe

Mix cookie crumbs with 7 Tbsp. melted butter. Press into bottom of ungreased 9x13 pan. Melt chocolate chips with remaining 1 Tbsp. butter in double boiler or microwave. Beat eggs with an electric mixer. Blend in a little of the chocolate mixture, then add remaining chocolate mixture and beat until thick. Add powdered sugar and beat until smooth. Add nuts. Pour over Oreo layer. Freeze.

Soften vanilla ice cream. Add Creme de Menthe. Mix well. Pour over frozen Oreo layer. Refreeze. Remove from freezer and keep in refrigerator 20 minutes before serving. Must be made ahead.   Serves 12

Variation: Amaretto and almonds.

QUICK ICE CREAM DESSERTS

White Creme de Menthe on coffee ice cream. Sprinkle with a few grains of instant coffee or chocolate shavings.

Triple Sec on raspberry sherbet. Garnish with mint leaves or fresh fruit.

Cherry Heering on peach ice cream. Garnish with peach slices, strawberries or raspberries.

Cointreau on orange sherbet. Garnish with strawberries or grated coconut.

Green Creme de Menthe on lemon sherbet. Garnish with pomegranate seeds.

Vanilla ice cream rolled in coconut. Top with Creme de Menthe or Kahlua.

Curaco on pineapple sherbet. Garnish with shredded coconut.

GRAPEFRUIT ICE WITH CHAMPAGNE

from the Grosse Pointe Yacht Club

Syrup
3 lbs. sugar
1 qt. water
1½ qts. fresh pink grapefruit
    juice
1 cup Asti Spumante
¾ cup fresh lemon juice

Prepare syrup by bringing water and sugar to a boil to dissolve sugar. Let cool. Measure 1 quart of syrup and mix with grapefruit juice, Asti Spumante and lemon juice. Strain mixture through cheese cloth, if necessary. Place ¼ cup of this mixture in freezer to test if it freezes. Too much syrup or alcohol won't freeze. If it doesn't freeze, add more lemon juice.

Place mixture in an ice cream maker surrounded with crushed ice and rock salt. Run until frozen. Store in freezer.

Helpful Hint:
This is basic recipe for all citrus fruit ices.

Can be made without an ice cream maker by partially freezing and then whipping with an electric mixer or blender. Repeat several times until a light consistency. Keeps frozen for months.   Serves 15-20

PEACH MELBA SAUCE

½ cup orange juice
½ cup sugar
2 cups canned peaches,
    diced
1 cup red raspberries

Mix orange juice, sugar and peaches. Add raspberries. For fine texture, blend in blender or food processor. Serve over ice cream. Make ahead.
                    Yields 3 cups

Variation: Can use frozen peaches and raspberries.

ICE CREAM SOUFFLÉ WITH STRAWBERRY SAUCE

1 qt. vanilla ice cream
24 coconut macaroons,
    crumbled
4 Tbsp. orange juice or
    Grand Marnier
1 cup whipping cream,
    whipped
4 tsp. powdered sugar
4 Tbsp. chopped almonds,
    toasted

Strawberry Sauce
1 qt. fresh strawberries or 2
    pkgs. (10 oz. each) frozen
    strawberries
1 cup sugar
4 Tbsp. orange juice or
    Grand Marnier

Soften ice cream slightly. Stir in crumbled macaroons and orange juice or Grand Marnier. Fold in whipped cream and spoon into 6 to 10 serving bowls. Sprinkle with powdered sugar and almonds. Cover with plastic wrap and freeze 4–5 hours.

Strawberry Sauce
Cut strawberries into halves and place in saucepan with one cup sugar. Simmer, stirring gently until soft but not mushy. Remove from heat and add orange juice or Grand Marnier. Pour over ice cream and serve immediately.

Serves 6–10

CHOCOLATE DELIGHT

1 cup flour
½ cup butter, softened
½ cup finely chopped
    pecans
1 pkg. (8 oz.) cream cheese,
    softened
1 cup powdered sugar
1 med. sized Cool Whip,
    divided
2 pkgs. (3⅝ oz. each)
    chocolate instant pudding
    and pie filling
3 cups milk
Chocolate curls

Preheat oven to 350°. Combine flour, butter and pecans. Press into a 9x13 pan, and bake for 15 minutes at 350°. Cool. Mix cream cheese, powdered sugar and 1 cup Cool Whip. Spread over cooled crust. Mix pie filling with milk and beat according to package directions. Spread over cheese mixture. Top with remaining Cool Whip and chocolate curls. Chill, preferably overnight.

Serves 10–12

CHOCOLATE CREAM SQUARES

1 angel food cake (12 oz.)
1 pkg. (6 oz.) semi-sweet
  chocolate bits
2 egg yolks, beaten
1 tsp. vanilla
1 cup chopped walnuts
2 egg whites
1 cup whipping cream,
  whipped

Break cake into 1-inch pieces. In a double boiler over hot water, not boiling, melt chocolate bits. Remove from heat and cool slightly. Stir beaten egg yolks, vanilla and nuts into chocolate.

In a small bowl, beat egg whites until stiff. Fold egg whites into chocolate mixture. Fold in whipped cream.

In an 8-inch square pan, place half of the cake pieces. Cover with half of the chocolate mixture. Repeat layers. Cover with plastic wrap and refrigerate at least 2 hours before serving. Can be made up to 1 day ahead.

Serves 6–9

NO BAKE PEANUT BUTTER BARS

tastes like Reese's Peanut Butter Cups

½ cup butter, melted
1½ cups powdered sugar
1½-1¾ cups graham
  cracker crumbs
1½ cups crunchy peanut
  butter
1 pkg. (12 oz.) semi-sweet
  chocolate chips
1 Tbsp. solid shortening

Melt butter. Mix in powdered sugar, graham cracker crumbs and peanut butter. Press into 9 × 13 pan. Melt chocolate chips and shortening together and spread over top. Refrigerate for 20 minutes only. Cut into 1-inch squares. Store in refrigerator. Freezes.

Yields 30–40 squares

Variation: Add chopped peanuts.
Helpful Hint: Score before refrigerating to prevent breaking.

CHOCOLATE SHELLS

Shells
½ cup semi-sweet chocolate
    bits
1 Tbsp. butter
6 paper cupcake cups

Filling
1 cup whipping cream
3 Tbsp. Droste's cocoa
4 Tbsp. powdered sugar
½ tsp. vanilla
Pinch salt

Shells
Melt chocolate and butter in double boiler over low heat, or in microwave. Using a brush, spread mixture evenly inside paper cupcake cups. Refrigerate until hard, then freeze 15 minutes. Peel off paper. Store in refrigerator, do not keep frozen.

Filling
Mix whipping cream, cocoa, powdered sugar, vanilla and salt together. Chill, then whip until stiff. Fill cups with whipping cream mixture. Can be made ahead.   Serves 6

EGG CUSTARD

3 lg. eggs
⅓ cup sugar
⅛ tsp. salt
1 tsp. vanilla
2 cups whole milk
Ground nutmeg

Variation:
After straining, add ¾ cup cooked rice and ⅓ cup raisins.

Yields 5 custard cups
    or a 1½-quart dish

Preheat oven to 325°. Beat eggs slightly by hand. Add sugar, salt and vanilla. Blend by hand. Gradually add milk to egg mixture.

Pour mixture through a fine sieve into 5 buttered custard cups or a 1½-quart shallow glass baking dish. Sprinkle top with ground nutmeg. Set dish in pan of warm water and bake uncovered at 325° for 30 minutes to an hour.

Test with knife blade for doneness. Do not overcook or custard will become watery. Refrigerate immediately, uncovered.

TIPSY TRIFLE

2-3 doz. lady fingers
1 jar (12 oz.) cherry or
  strawberry preserves
½ cup sherry
1 lg. pkg. (5¼ oz.) instant
  vanilla pudding
1½ cups milk
½ cup rum
3-4 bananas, sliced
1 can (11 oz.) mandarin
  orange slices, drained
12 coconut macaroons
1 pt. whipping cream
2 heaping Tbsp. powdered
  sugar
8 Tbsp. Grand Marnier,
  divided
¼ lb. sliced almonds,
  toasted

Line large glass bowl with lady fingers, and lavishly spread with preserves. Top with second layer of lady fingers and sprinkle with the sherry. Mix vanilla pudding with milk and rum. Let stand until thick. Spread over lady fingers. Arrange fruit over pudding.

Crumble macaroons and soak with 6 Tbsp. Grand Marnier. Spread over fruit. Whip cream with sugar and 2 Tbsp. Grand Marnier until peaks form. Spread over macaroons. Top with toasted almonds and chill thoroughly. Must be made ahead at least 4 hours. Can be made 12 hours ahead.

GENEVE'S ENGLISH TOFFEE

1 cup sugar
1 cup butter
1 Tbsp. light corn syrup
3 Tbsp. water
Pinch salt
1 cup very finely chopped
  pecans
2 plain Hershey chocolate
  bars, grated
Softened butter (to coat
  cookie sheet)

Butter a cookie sheet. Combine sugar, butter, corn syrup, water, and salt. Cook and stir until it reaches 290° on a candy thermometer (hard crack stage).

Sprinkle 80% of the pecans and chocolate on buttered cookie sheet. Pour cooked candy mixture over nuts and chocolate. Sprinkle with remaining pecans and chocolate. Put in cool place (**not** refrigerator). When perfectly hard and cold, break into pieces. Keeps for several weeks if stored in tin can.

WIGGLEY WINE

wonderful after a heavy meal

2 env. unflavored gelatin
1 cup cold water
3 cups boiling water
½–1 cup sugar
Juice of 2 lemons, strained
1 cup dry sherry, claret,
    white wine or rosé

Mix gelatin with cold water. Add boiling water and sugar and stir until dissolved. Cool slightly, then stir in lemon juice and sherry. Pour into pretty crystal serving bowl. Refrigerate overnight. It will have a ·"shakey" consistency. May be garnished with cream and/or fresh berries. Make ahead up to 3–4 days, and cover with plastic wrap.

Yields 5 cups

CARAMEL CORN

1 cup popcorn
1 can (1 lb.) cocktail peanuts
1 cup pecans
2 cups brown sugar
1 cup butter
1 tsp. salt
½ cup light corn syrup
½ tsp. baking soda
1 tsp. vanilla

Preheat oven to 250°. Pop corn and put in large roaster. Add cocktail peanuts and pecans. In a saucepan, mix together brown sugar, butter, salt and light corn syrup. Bring to full rolling boil, stirring constantly. Boil five minutes. Remove from heat and stir well. Add baking soda and vanilla. Stir together in saucepan and beat until light in color and baking soda stops fizzing. Pour over popped corn. Bake at 250° for one hour, stirring every fifteen minutes. When corn has cooled enough to handle, place in an airtight container.

Yields 5 quarts

Timely Tip:
Refrigerate unpopped popcorn in a tightly covered jar to keep fresh and achieve more fully popped corn.

O'HENRY BARS

⅔ cup butter, softened
1 cup brown sugar
½ cup corn syrup
1 Tbsp. vanilla
4 cups quick oats
1 pkg. (6 oz.) semi-sweet
   chocolate chips
⅔ cup peanut butter

Preheat oven to 350°. Grease a 9x13 pan well. Cream together the butter and sugar. Stir in syrup, vanilla and oats. Spread this mixture on the bottom of the pan evenly. Bake for 15 minutes at 350°. Remove from oven and cool. (The mixture will not appear to be thoroughly cooked, but it is. Do not leave in oven longer).

In heavy saucepan, melt chocolate chips and peanut butter over low heat. Spread over cooled oat mixture. Refrigerate until firm. Cut in small pieces and serve. Yields 2 dozen

INSTANT FUDGE BROWNIES

½ cup butter
2 squares unsweetened
   chocolate, melted
1 cup sugar
2 eggs
⅔ cup flour
1 tsp. vanilla
¼ tsp. salt
½ cup chopped walnuts
   (optional)

Preheat oven to 350°. Melt butter in 8×8 pan. Remove from heat. Add all remaining ingredients. Blend with fork until smooth, at least one minute, especially in corners of pan. Bake at 350° for 30–35 minutes. Can be made ahead up to 1 day. Freezes.
Yields 16–20 squares

Variations: May be dusted with sifted confectioners sugar or frosted with a chocolate frosting topped with slivered almonds.

GRAPEFRUIT RIND CANDY

this makes a lovely Christmas gift

4 lg. thick-skinned grapefruit
Granulated sugar,
   approximately 5 lbs.
Water

Scrub and dry grapefruit. Peel grapefruit deeply, to the actual fruit. Leave all the white meat attached to the peel. Peel on a slant in a circular spiral making a strip ¾ to 1 inch wide. Gently scrape any fruit pulp from the peel. Reserve fruit for other uses. Cut rind strip into 3-inch lengths. Cut each 3-inch strip lengthwise so that pieces are now 3 inches long by ¼ to ½ inch wide.

Fill 1½–2-quart saucepans ⅓ full of the rinds. Add ½ cup sugar to each pan and cover rinds with hot water. Bring to a boil and boil 20 minutes. Drain. Add another ½ cup sugar, hot water to cover, bring to a boil and boil for 20 minutes. Repeat this process until rind has boiled 6 times in fresh sugar and water or until the rind is translucent. Sometimes this can take 8 boilings before the rind is translucent.

Drain and place rinds as close as possible on wire racks which have been placed on cookie sheets covered with wax paper (for portability). Let cool and dry for several hours. Sprinkle liberally with sugar and let stand 5 or more hours (overnight when necessary). Turn strips, sprinkle liberally with sugar, and let dry as before. Repeat the sprinkling/drying procedure several times until rinds are dry to the touch and well-coated with sugar. The number of times this procedure is repeated will vary, depending on the temperature and the humidity of the room.

Store in single layers separated by wax paper in airtight tins in a cool place (the refrigerator is okay). These may be frozen.

If for some reason the candy gets near heat and becomes mushy, start over at the point where you sprinkle with sugar and dry on racks.

Helpful Hint: Do not make this candy before mid-October.

CARROT CAKE

Cake
2 cups flour
2 tsp. salt
2 tsp. baking soda
2 tsp. cinnamon
¼ tsp. nutmeg
¼ tsp. cloves
¼ tsp. ginger
1¼ cups vegetable oil
4 eggs
2 cups sugar
3½ cups grated carrots

Frosting
1 lb. box powdered sugar
½ cup butter, softened
1 pkg. (8 oz.) cream cheese,
    softened
1 tsp. vanilla

Cake
Preheat oven to 350°. Sift together first 7 dry ingredients. Combine oil, eggs, sugar and carrots. Add dry ingredients. Mix well. Pour into ungreased tube or bundt pan. Bake at 350° for 50–60 minutes.

Frosting
Mix frosting ingredients together. Frost cake when cool.

Make ahead.

Serves 8–10

Variations: May add ½ cup chopped nuts to cake batter or 1 8 oz. can crushed pineapple (drained).

FRENCH CREAM CAKE

2 cups vanilla wafer crumbs,
    divided
½ cup butter, softened
1 cup powdered sugar
2 eggs, well beaten
1 cup whipping cream
½ cup chopped nuts
1 cup canned crushed
    pineapple, drained

Place 1½ cups vanilla wafer crumbs in bottom of ungreased 8-inch square pan. Cream butter and sugar together. Add eggs and beat well. Spread carefully over crumbs. Combine whipping cream, nuts and pineapple. Spread over creamed mixture. Sprinkle remaining ½ cup vanilla wafer crumbs on top. Refrigerate for 18–24 hours. Cut into squares.   Serves 8–12

PRALINE TOURNE

2 cups brown sugar
2 cups pecan halves
½ cup hot water
2 Tbsp. grated orange rind
(approx. 2 oranges)

Boil sugar and water until the syrup spins a 3-inch thread when dropped from spoon (238°). Add pecans and orange rind and remove from heat. Stir quickly until pecans are well coated, as mixture hardens rapidly. Place glazed, separated nuts on wax paper to cool. Store in an airtight tin.

Yields 1½ lbs.

MACAROON CAKE

6 eggs, room temperature, separated
1 cup vegetable shortening
½ cup butter
3 cups sugar
1 tsp. almond extract
3 cups flour
1 cup milk
2 cans (3½ oz. each) flaked coconut

Preheat oven to 300° Grease 10-inch tube pan. Beat egg yolks at high speed of electric mixer. Add shortening and butter. Beat until well blended. Gradually add sugar, beating until light and fluffy. Add almond extract. At low speed of electric mixer, beat in flour in fourths, alternating with milk in thirds. Begin with flour and end with flour. Add coconut and blend well.

Beat egg whites just until stiff peaks form. Gently fold into batter. Pour into pan. Bake at 300° for 2 hours or until a toothpick inserted in center comes out clean. Cool in pan.

Yields 12–16 pieces

To freeze, wrap in foil. To serve, heat at 300° in foil until thawed and warm, about 1 hour and 15 minutes. Make 1 day ahead.

Special Sections

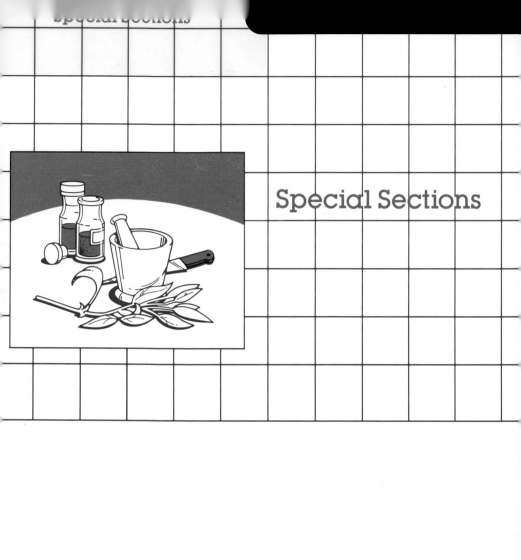

Special Sections

HERBS AND SPICES

The greatest speed tools available to a cook are a well-stocked spice shelf and a bit of adventurous spirit. Herbs and spices enhance common foods and can make their taste on **your** table very special. The only caution to bear in mind is that one can use too much flavoring — so start with a light touch and progress until the taste pleases you. A good basic rule is generally to use no more than three herbs to flavor any one dish. Also, remember —

1/4 tsp. dried, finely crushed = 3/4 - 1 tsp. dried, loosely crushed

= 1½ - 2 tsp. fresh, chopped

A little experimentation will reap rewards you never imagined. Evolving a "personal cuisine" can be an enormous satisfaction.

Rice is an easy dish with which to begin. It completely changes character with a little spice added to the cooking water or sprinkled through it. Try rice cooked in bouillon and saffron one day, buttered and sprinkled with pine nuts another, and then rice cooked in broth with finely chopped green pepper and a little oregano or basil.

What follows is a two-fold guide. First, a list of various foods with the herbs and spices which best complement them. Next, herbs and spices are listed by the ethnic cuisine in which they are used most frequently. We will then provide the same menu (sauteed chicken breasts, rice, carrots, and a green salad), with seasoning suggestions to transform it into a Greek, a Chinese, and then a French meal.

Finally, we offer a few ideas for the home gardener.

HERBS AND SPICES TO ACCENT FOODS

BEEF

bay leaf	horseradish	peppercorns
caraway	juniper berries	savory
curry	marjoram	tarragon
garlic	oregano	thyme
ginger	paprika	

Using any of the green-leafed herbs, make a sauce with Madeira or red wine.

A little cinnamon or clove perks up the flavor of beef stew.

GROUND BEEF

allspice	fennel	oregano
bay leaf	garlic	parsley
caraway	ginger	sage
chervil	horseradish	savory
coriander	juniper berries (crushed)	tarragon
curry	marjoram	
dill	mustard seed (ground)	

HERBS AND SPICES TO ACCENT FOODS

CHICKEN

basil	ginger	rosemary
bay leaf	lemon balm	saffron
cayenne	marjoram	sage
coriander	mint	savory
curry	oregano	tarragon
dill	paprika	thyme
garlic	parsley	turmeric

Make a sauce with any of the above in butter or heavy cream with port, sherry, white wine, or Madeira.

FISH - White Meated - including bass, catfish, cod, flounder, halibut, perch, pickerel, pompano, red snapper, sole, trout, etc.

Bake on a bed of:

bay leaves	dill	marjoram
chervil	fennel	tarragon
cumin	lemon balm	

Make a butter sauce for plain baked fish with:

bay leaf	ginger	tarragon
chervil	lemon balm	
dill	marjoram	

Make a cream sauce with:

basil	dill	tarragon
cumin	fennel	thyme
curry	saffron	turmeric

FISH - Heavy and/or Oily Meated - including bluefish, grouper, mackerel, sea bass, swordfish, etc.

To lighten the flavor, bake with:

chervil	marjoram	rosemary
lemon balm	parsley	

To retain the full flavor, bake with:

curry	juniper berries	tarragon
dill	peppercorns	thyme

Make a butter sauce for plain baked fish with:

chervil	garlic	tarragon
dill	marjoram	

Make a cream sauce with:

curry	saffron
dill	tarragon

HERBS AND SPICES TO ACCENT FOODS

GAME
For sweetness, make a sauce with port, Marsala or Madeira, flavored with allspice **plus** one or more of the following:

bay leaf	marjoram	oregano
lemon balm	mint	

For a tarter flavor, make a sauce with red wine, dry sherry, or vermouth, seasoned with juniper berries **plus** one or more among:

garlic	oregano	savory
mustard seed (ground)	sage	

LAMB

allspice	dill	mustard seed (ground)
basil	garlic	parsley
chervil	ginger	rosemary
coriander	marjoram	savory
cumin	mint	thyme
curry	mustard (Dijon style)	

A sauce of butter and Madeira or white wine with any of the above is delightful. Try adding a little whipping cream.

LIVER

basil	mustard (Dijon style)	sage
marjoram		

Try Dijon mustard with whipping cream.

PORK

anise	ginger	rosemary
caraway	juniper berries	sage
coriander	marjoram	savory
cumin	nutmeg	thyme
curry	oregano	turmeric
garlic	parsley	

Make a sauce using any of the above with butter and Marsala, Madeira or sherry.

VEAL

basil	lemon balm	saffron
bay leaf	nutmeg	savory
coriander	parsley	thyme
curry	rosemary	

Make a sauce seasoned with any of the above and dry white wine or Marsala plus butter; add a little cream.

SHELLFISH

basil	garlic	parsley
bay leaf	mustard seed (ground)	tarragon
chervil	oregano	thyme
curry		

Make a sauce with any of the above and white wine, or try whipping cream added to the cooking juices with a touch of Pernod.

HERBS AND SPICES TO ACCENT FOODS

ASPARAGUS
curry
dill
garlic
lemon balm
marjoram
nutmeg
oregano

BEETS
allspice
bay leaf
cinnamon
clove
dill
ginger
mint

BROCCOLI
cumin
curry
garlic
mustard seed (ground)
oregano
savory

BRUSSELS SPROUTS
caraway
chervil
curry
dill
mint

CABBAGE
caraway
celery seed
oregano
savory

CARROTS
cinnamon
clove
coriander
curry
dill
ginger
mint
nutmeg
oregano

CORN
chives
coriander
paprika
parsley

EGGPLANT
allspice
basil
cumin
dill
garlic
marjoram
oregano
sage

GREEN BEANS
basil
curry
dill
garlic
lemon balm
marjoram
nutmeg
oregano
savory

GREEN PEAS
basil
marjoram
mint
savory

MUSHROOMS
dill
garlic
ginger
marjoram
oregano
rosemary
tarragon
thyme
turmeric

ONIONS
basil
dill
nutmeg
oregano
sage

POTATOES
caraway
chives
cumin
dill
horseradish
nutmeg
paprika
parsley
sesame seed

SPINACH
basil
mace
nutmeg
rosemary

TOMATOES
basil
burnet
dill
garlic
lemon balm
marjoram
mint
oregano

ZUCCHINI
bay leaf
coriander
curry
dill
marjoram
nutmeg
oregano
tarragon

HERBS AND SPICES TO ACCENT FOODS

Where They Fit by Taste

NON-SWEET		SWEET
basil	mustard (prepared)	allspice
bay leaf	mustard seed	anise & star anise
calendula	nasturtium	basil
caraway	oregano	cardamon
chervil	paprika	cinnamon
chives	parsley	clove
coriander	peppercorns	coriander
cumin	rosemary	fennel
dill	saffron	ginger
fennel	sage	mace
garlic	savory	mint
horseradish	shallots	nutmeg
juniper berries	tarragon	rosemary
lemon balm	thyme	saffron
marjoram	violets (true wild, not "African")	
mint		

WINES & ESSENCES FOR FLAVORING

Brandies and Cognacs

Citrus juices and peels

Fruit liqueurs

Marsala, Madeira, Sherry, and Port wines

Olive, seed, and nut oils

Red wines

Vermouth

Vinegars

White wines

HERBS AND SPICES TO ACCENT FOODS
Common Combinations

BASIC BOUQUETS GARNI
Tie **fresh** herbs with a string. Tie **dried** herbs in a bag made from a 4-inch square of cheese cloth.

FRESH HERBS	DRIED HERBS
½ bay leaf	½ tsp. bay leaf (crushed)
1 sprig marjoram	½ tsp. marjoram
2 sprigs parsley	1 tsp. parsley flakes
2 sprigs thyme	1 tsp. thyme
1 bay leaf	1 tsp. bay leaf (crushed)
5-6 sprigs parsley	1 Tbsp. parsley flakes
2 sprigs rosemary	1 tsp. rosemary
5-6 sprigs tarragon	1 Tbsp. tarragon
2-3 sprigs thyme	1 tsp. thyme

BASIC FINE HERBS
Combine equal proportions of:

chervil	basil	burnet	chervil
chives	chives	parsley	chives
parsley	parsley	thyme	parsley
			tarragon

SPICE PARISIENNE or QUATRE SPICES
1 Tbsp. ground cinnamon
1 tsp. ground cloves
1 tsp. ground ginger
1 tsp. ground nutmeg

Have fun making your own Special Blend, such as the imaginative one given below. They have many applications.

DASH OF HERBS
great gift idea

1 Tbsp. sesame seeds
1 Tbsp sugar
2 tsp. dried oregano
1½ tsp. basil
1 tsp. rosemary
1 tsp. thyme
½ tsp. seasoned salt (Lawry's)
¼ tsp. garlic powder
¼ tsp. seasoned pepper (Lawry's)

Combine all ingredients; place in a dry covered jar and shake well. Store in a cool dry place. May be used:
— As a dip with yogurt or sour cream.
— To enhance the flavor of eggs.
— As a coating for chicken or fish when mixed with flour.
— To season baked potatoes.
— To mix with hamburger before broiling.
Keeps for months.   Yields ¼ cup

HERBS AND SPICES IN ETHNIC CUISINES

(The flavorings of highest frequency use are starred)

Caribbean
*rosemary
*oregano
*thyme
coriander
allspice
bay leaf

Indian
*curry powder
*turmeric
*cumin
*chili pepper & cayenne
cloves
mint
cardamon

Middle Eastern
*cumin
*turmeric
*mint
*bay leaf
marjoram
cardamon
rosemary
coriander

French
*tarragon or rosemary
*marjoram
*sage
*thyme
parsley
dill
chervil
celery seed & leaves

Italian
*oregano
*basil
*garlic
fennel
rosemary
thyme
sage
pignolas (pine nuts)
bay leaf

Oriental
*ginger
*garlic
*soy sauce
*rice wine or sherry
sesame seed, sesame oil
star anise
mint
cinnamon

German
*caraway
*dill
*clove
*ginger
paprika
bay leaf
ground dry &
prepared mustards

Latin American
*oregano
*coriander
*cumin
*garlic
chili powder
saffron
bay leaf

Spanish
*garlic
*saffron
*cilantro or parsley
*bay leaf
mint
cumin
thyme

Greek
*oregano
*allspice
*rosemary
*nutmeg
marjoram
thyme
garlic
pignolas (pine nuts)
basil

Mexican
*chili powder
*garlic
*cilantro or parsley
*oregano
*cinnamon
bay leaf
coriander

VARIABLE ETHNIC MENUS

GREEK MONDAY
Chicken Breasts Sautéed in Butter
with Garlic and Rosemary
Buttered Rice with Pine Nuts
Buttered Carrots with Allspice or Cloves
Green Salad with Vinegar & Oil Dressing
Seasoned with Marjoram, Garlic & Basil
California Chardonnay White Wine
Baklava or Honey Vanilla Ice Cream

CHINESE WEDNESDAY
Chicken Breasts Sautéed with Thinly Sliced
Onions, Green Pepper, Water Chestnuts, Mushrooms & Chinese Cabbage,
Spiced with Garlic, Ginger, Sherry & Soy Sauce
Rice with Butter and Chopped Scallion Tops
Buttered Carrots Sprinkled with Cinnamon
Boston Lettuce with Vinegar & Oil Dressing,
Liberally Sprinkled with Sesame Seeds
Italian Pinot Grigio White Wine
Vanilla Ice Cream Sprinkled with Almond Liqueur
or Citrus Sherbet

FRENCH FRIDAY
Sautéed Chicken Breasts Sprinkled with Tarragon
in a Sauce of White Wine and Chopped Tomatoes
Rice Cooked in Broth Diluted with Water
and Sprinkled with Snipped Parlsey
Buttered Carrots Steamed with Bay Leaf or a Little Mint
Green Salad with Vinegar & Oil Dressing
Spiced with Dill, Garlic and Mustard
French or California Chablis
Fresh Apple Slices and Camembert or Brie

IDEAS FOR THE HOME GARDENER

HERB FLAVORED VINEGARS

In a tightly covered jar, place 2-4 ounces of fresh, cleaned and well-drained herbs with 1 quart of room temperature vinegar. Let stand at room temperature 5-6 weeks, occasionally turning container over, to develop flavor. Strain into clean bottles. Insert a fresh sprig of the herb, both for appearance and identification. Cap tightly and store.

Suggestions include:

Burnet (4 ounces) with white wine vinegar — particularly good in salads or for pickling beets

Basil (3-4 ounces) in either red or white wine vinegar — wonderful with tomatoes or in salad.

Dill heads (3-4 ounces) plus 4 large cloves garlic in red wine vinegar — multiple uses, especially with an Italian meal.

Tarragon (2 ounces, picked just before it blooms) in white wine vinegar — multiple uses.

Variations:
Tarragon (2 ounces), 3 whole cloves and 2 cloves garlic halved in white wine vinegar. Remove garlic after first week.

Tarragon (2 ounces), 4 strips lemon rind and 2 whole cloves in white wine vinegar.

Oregano (2-3 ounces) in red wine vinegar — multiple uses, particularly in an Italian meal.

Rosemary (1½ ounces) plus thyme (1½ ounces) **or** 3 ounces of rosemary in white wine vinegar — excellent with pork roasts.

Celery seeds (4 ounces pounded) with white wine vinegar. In this instance, shake the bottle every day, and strain through cheese cloth after 5-6 weeks — multiple uses.

Oils can be seasoned in the same fashion, but beware of your oils. Use only the best, preferably virgin oils. They may be expensive, but you will be repaid many times over by their quality.

HERB GARNISHES
With the wealth in your garden, why rely on parsley. Try:

Burnet sprigs — with tomatoes, potato salad, pickled beets, cold sliced roast beef, shrimp or lobster salad — anywhere you might enjoy a slight suggestion of cucumber.

Basil leaves — superb with fresh sliced tomatoes.

Mint leaves or sprigs — with lamb dishes, green peas, orange or grapefruit salads, and innumerable fruit drinks and desserts, to mention only a few uses.

Use your imagination!

IDEAS FOR THE HOME GARDENER
Preserving Herbs

DRYING IN THE MICROWAVE

Herbs such as celery leaves, chives, marjoram, mint, oregano, parsley, rosemary, sage, savory, tarragon and thyme can all be successfully dried in the microwave. To dry them, wash and pat dry 1 cup of leaves. Place on a piece of cardboard between paper toweling. Microwave on High 2-4 minutes, stirring once or twice while drying. Increase time to 5-6 minutes if drying 2 cups of leaves at once. If the herbs are dry enough, they will be brittle. If more time is needed, repeat process. Cool leaves and crumble. To store, place in an air-tight container.

FREEZING

Finely chop each herb, removing stems whenever possible (use scissors for basil, chives and dill). **Pack** into ice cube trays, fill with water, and freeze. When frozen, spray with soda water to keep cubes from sticking to each other, and store in freezer in plastic bags. Don't forget to label them.

Or, wrap small cleaned and drained dry bunches of any herb in foil, pressing out as much air as possible. Label and freeze. As needed, crumble **frozen** herbs directly into foods.

Do not store frozen herbs for more than 6-8 months.

Finally, if you ever have a surfeit of parsley in your garden, try:

FRENCH FRIED PARSLEY

Fresh parsley
1/2 pt. half & half or cream

Flour to coat parsley
salt

Do NOT attempt this recipe with bought parsley. Harvest full-leafed parsley, wash and drain dry. Removing all stems, separate into bite-sized flowerets. Refrigerate in plastic bag 1-2 hours to crisp, but no longer.

In deep fat fryer, heat vegetable oil to maximum heat. Place half & half in a bowl. Place about ¾-1 cup flour in a plastic bag. You will need to add more flour several times. Remove parsley from refrigerator, checking to make sure it is dry. Working with one large handful of parsley at a time, dip in half & half, shake off excess, toss in flour to coat. Drop into HOT grease and fry about 1 minute. When you remove parsley from oil, it should look creamy frosted, **not** slightly browned. Drain on paper grocery bags, lightly salting immediately. Making sure grease has returned to HOT, repeat process until all parsley is fried. Store at room temperature on paper towels in aluminum foil up to 3 days. Reheat in foil, if desired, in warm oven.

EQUIVALENTS AND SUBSTITUTIONS

WEIGHTS AND MEASURES

A pinch	=	less than ⅛ teaspoon
20 drops	=	¼ teaspoon
2 tablespoons	=	1 fluid ounce
1 jigger	=	1½ fluid ounce (3 tablespoons)
3 teaspoons	=	1 tablespoon
4 tablespoons	=	¼ cup
5⅓ tablespoons	=	⅓ cup
8 tablespoons	=	½ cup
16 tablespoons	=	1 cup (8 fluid ounces)
2 cups	=	1 pint
4 cups	=	1 quart
2 pints	=	1 quart
16 cups	=	1 gallon
4 quarts	=	1 gallon
16 ounces	=	1 pound

PASTA AND RICE

Macaroni (uncooked)	1 pound	=	4 cups (uncooked)
Macaroni (uncooked)	1 cup	=	2¼ cups (cooked)
Noodles (uncooked)	1 cup	=	1½ cups (cooked)
Rice (converted)	1 cup	=	3-4 cups (cooked)
Rice (pre-cooked)	1 cup	=	2 cups (cooked)
Rice (long-grain, wild or brown)	1 cup	=	4 cups (cooked)
Spaghetti (uncooked)	1 pound	=	4¾ cups (uncooked)
Spaghetti (uncooked)	1 cup	=	2 cups (cooked)

Allow ⅔ cup cooked rice per person
Allow 1 cup cooked pasta per person

CRUMBS

Bread, fresh	1½ slices	=	1 cup soft crumbs
Bread, dry	1 slice	=	¼ cup fine dry crumbs
Potato chips	4 ounces	=	2 cups coarse crumbs
Saltine crackers	28 crackers	=	1 cup fine crumbs
Bread crumbs, dry	1 cup	=	¾ cup cracker crumbs

NUTS

Nuts (unshelled)	¼ pound	=	± 1 cup (chopped)

EQUIVALENTS AND SUBSTITUTIONS

BAKING

Sugar (brown)	1 pound (1 box)	=	2¼ cups (packed)
Sugar (granulated)	1 pound	=	2¼ cups
Sugar (powdered)	1 pound (1 box)	=	3½ cups
Chocolate	1 square (1 ounce)	=	3 tablespoons (grated)
Flour (all-purpose)	1 pound	=	3 cups (unsifted)
			4 cups (sifted)
Flour (cake)	1 pound	=	4¾ cups (sifted)
Yeast (dry active)	1 tablespoon	=	1⅗ oz. cake yeast
Chocolate	1 square	=	3 Tbsp. cocoa plus 1 Tbsp. butter
Flour (all-purpose)	1 cup	=	1 cup plus 2 Tbsp. sifted cake flour
Flour (cake)	1 cup	=	1 cup minus 2 Tbsp. sifted all-purpose flour
Sugar	1 cup	=	1 cup honey plus ½ tsp. soda (reduce liquid in recipe ¼ cup)
		=	1 cup maple syrup plus ¼ tsp. soda (reduce liquid in recipe ¼ cup)
		=	1 cup molasses plus ½ tsp. soda (reduce liquid in recipe ¼ cup)
		=	½ cup maple syrup plus ¼ cup corn syrup (reduce liquid in recipe ¼ cup)

DAIRY

Cheese	4 ounces	=	1 cup (grated or crumbled)
Cream cheese	3 ounces	=	6 tablespoons
Cottage cheese	1 pound	=	2 cups
Cream, whipping	1 cup	=	2 cups (whipped)
Evaporated milk	13 oz. can	=	1⅔ cups
Ice cream	1 gallon	=	30 scoops
Cream	1 cup	=	⅞ cup buttermilk or yogurt plus 3 Tbsp. butter
Sour milk or buttermilk	1 cup	=	1½ Tbsp. lemon juice or vinegar plus sweet milk to equal 1 cup
Cream, whipping (whipped)	½ pint	=	½ pint coffee cream plus 1 egg white

FRUIT

Apples (whole)	1 pound (3 medium)	=	2¾ cups (sliced)
Bananas (whole)	1 pound (3-4)	=	1⅓ cups (mashed)
Cherries	1 pound	=	2 cups (pitted)
Cranberries	1 pound	=	2 cups
Candied fruits	1 pound	=	3 cups
Dates (pitted)	1 pound	=	2½ cups
Dates (unpitted)	1 pound	=	1¾ cups (chopped)
Lemon	1 medium	=	3 tablespoons juice
		=	± 1 teaspoon grated peel
Orange	1 medium	=	⅓ cup juice
Peaches and pears	1 pound (3 medium)	=	2 cups (sliced)
Raisins (seedless)	1 pound	=	2¾ cups
Strawberries	1 quart	=	4 cups (sliced)

EQUIVALENTS AND SUBSTITUTIONS

VEGETABLES

Beans (green)	1 pound (3 cups)	=	2½ cups (cooked)
Cabbage	1 pound (1 head)	=	4½ cups (shredded)
			2½ cups (cooked)
Carrots (without tops)	1 pound	=	3 cups (shredded or grated)
		=	2½ cups (diced)
Corn	12 medium ears	=	2½ cups (cooked kernels)
Green pepper	6 ounces (1 large)	=	1 cup (diced)
Mushrooms	¼ pound (sliced)	=	¼–½ cup (cooked)
Onions	1 medium	=	½ cup chopped
Peas or limas (in shells)	1 pound	=	1 cup (shelled)
Potatoes, tomatoes, beets, turnips, etc.	1 pound (3 medium)	=	2 cups (cubed, cooked)
		=	1¾ cups (mashed)
		=	2½ cups (sliced)
Onion	1 fresh	=	1 tablespoon instant minced onion
Tomato sauce	1¾ cups	=	¾ cup tomato paste plus 1 cup water

MEATS

Chicken breast	1 whole	=	± 1 cup (cooked, diced)
Crab meat	1 pound	=	2 cups
Ham (boneless)	12 pounds	=	20 servings
Turkey (whole)	20 pounds	=	20 servings

OTHER

Coffee	1 pound	=	40–50 cups of coffee
Gelatin	1 oz. envelope	=	3 tablespoons
Honey, molasses or syrup	1 pound	=	1⅓ cups
Marshmallows	1 large	=	10 miniature
Marshmallows	8 large	=	1 cup (chopped)
Marshmallows	16 large	=	¼ pound
Punch	1 quart	=	6 punch glasses
Bay leaf	1 whole	=	¼ teaspoon crushed
Herbs, fresh	1 tablespoon	=	1½ teaspoons dried herbs
Flour	1 tablespoon	=	½ tablespoon cornstarch,
		=	¾ tablespoon quick-cooking tapioca, or
		=	1½ teaspoons arrowroot (for thickening)
Honey	1 cup	=	1¼ cups sugar plus ¼ cup liquid
Mustard (dry)	1 teaspoon	=	1 tablespoon mustard (prepared)
Fat	2 tablespoons	=	1 ounce

EQUIVALENTS AND SUBSTITUTIONS

TEMPERATURE DEFINITIONS

220°	=	Jelling point for jams and jellies
234°–240°	=	Soft ball stage for syrups
255°	=	Hard crack stage for syrups
320°	=	Caramel stage for syrups

OVEN TEMPERATURES

175°–200°	=	Warm	350°	=	Moderate
250°	=	Very slow	375°	=	Moderately hot
300°	=	Slow	400°	=	Hot
325°	=	Moderately slow	450°–500°	=	Very hot

PAN SIZE EQUIVALENTS

4-Cup Dishes:
- 7⅜ × 3⅝ × 2¼ loaf pan
- 8 × 1¼ layer-cake pan
- 9-inch pie plate

4½-Cup Dish:
- 8½ × 2¼ ring mold or tube pan

6-Cup Dishes:
- 8½ × 3⅝ × 2⅝ loaf pan
- 8 or 9 × 1½ layer-cake pan
- 10-inch pie plate
- 7½ × 3 ring mold, tube or bundt pan
- 7 × 5½ × 4 oval mold

8-Cup Dishes:
- 9 × 5 × 3 loaf pan
- 8 × 8 × 2 square pan
- 11 × 7 × 1½ rectangular pan
- 9¼ × 2¾ ring mold, tube or bundt pan
- 9½ × 3½ brioche pan

8¾-Cup dish:
- 9 × 9 × 1¾ square pan

9-Cup Dish:
- 9 × 3½ ring mold, tube or bundt pan

10-Cup Dishes:
- 9 × 9 × 2 square pan
- 11¾ × 7½ × 1¾ rectangular pan
- 15 × 10 × 1 jelly-roll pan

12-Cup Dishes:
- 13½ × 8½ × 2 rectangular pan
- 8 × 3 spring form pan
- 9 × 3½ angel-food cake pan
- 9 × 3½ ring mold or tube pan
- 10 × 3¾ bundt pan

15-Cup Dish:
- 13 × 9 × 2 rectangular pan

16-Cup Dishes:
- 10 × 4 ring mold or tube pan
- 9 × 3 spring form pan

18-Cup Dish:
- 10 × 4 angel-food cake pan

19-Cup Dish:
- 14 × 10½ × 2½ rectangular pan

MICROWAVE COOKING

A microwave oven can be a tremendous asset to the cook in search of Clock Wise Cuisine. It can speed up individual steps in a recipe, or it can be used to cook an entire dish in a fraction of the time conventional cooking would require.

While it is not our intention in this section of our cookbook to write the complete and all-encompassing guide to microwave cooking (several excellent books on ·this topic are already available), we do want to include here a few pages of basic ideas and instructions for the cook who wants to make the most of a microwave oven in the interest of saving time in the kitchen.

The following are basic suggestions to help you use your microwave effectively:
- Use round pans, dishes, and platters whenever possible for more even cooking.
- Stir during cooking to ensure even cooking.
- The quantity of food to be cooked determines the amount of time required for cooking. To increase or decrease a recipe, decide how many minutes it takes to cook one cup and adjust the time accordingly.
- It takes approximately 2 minutes to heat food directly from the refrigerator and 1½ minutes to heat food that is at room temperature.
- Unless a recipe indicates a particular power setting, assume that it is to be cooked on High or 100% power.
- Recipes with cooking times on lower settings require less constant attention.

The following suggestions offer assistance in cooking specific types of foods:

Meats
- To add color, you may use a browning dish, dried gravy mixes, or paprika.
- You may use a little tenderizer if you feel it would be desirable.
- Do not salt meat until after it has been cooked.
- Make a wax paper tent over roasts; this prevents splattering and helps to retain moisture while cooking.
- To brown ground beef in a microwave, place the beef in a heavy duty plastic colander and place the colander on a glass pie plate in the microwave. Cover with wax paper. Cook on High for 4½–5 minutes per pound, stirring once. All of the fat from the meat will drain onto the pie plate as the meat cooks.
- To cook bacon for a garnish, cut bacon into 1-inch pieces and place pieces between layers of paper towels. Cook 6–8 minutes on High, or until crisp. Remove from paper toweling to cool. Crumble.

Vegetables
- Cover most vegetables with wax paper to retain moisture and prevent splattering while cooking. This is not necessary with potatoes. Do not use plastic wrap, as this has the effect of steaming the vegetables.
- To cook fibrous vegetables (carrots, green beans, etc.) begin cooking on High and then turn down the power so as not to lose moisture.
- Cook baked potatoes until you can squeeze them. Then remove them from the oven, wrap them in foil and let sit for at least 10 minutes.
- Frozen vegetables may be defrosted in the microwave. If vegetables are wrapped in foil, remove the foil and place vegetables in glass dish in microwave. If vegetables are packaged in a paper box, pierce box and place it in microwave. Cook 10-ounce package on High for 3–5 minutes.

MICROWAVE COOKING

Desserts
- Rotate the pan during cooking time for even baking of cakes, brownies, etc. This is particularly important during the last half of the cooking time. Pan should be rotated in ¼ or ½ turns. Rotation is not necessary if your oven has a turntable, but it is desirable to place the dish to one side on the turntable so as to enhance the rotation.
- To melt chocolate chips or caramels, place them in a shallow glass dish and cook on Medium for 2½–3 minutes, stirring once or twice.
- To make ice cream easier to scoop, place half gallon of ice cream in microwave and cook on High for 1– minutes.
- To soften cream cheese, remove foil wrapper and place cream cheese on glass plate. Cook on Medium-High for 45 seconds to 1 minute.
- To dissolve gelatin, combine gelatin and water in a 2-cup glass measuring cup. Cook on High for 2–3 minutes. Stir.

Fruit
- To obtain additional juice from a lemon, heat it on High for 30–45 seconds before squeezing.

Miscellaneous
- To scald milk or cream in microwave, place it in a glass measuring cup and cook on Medium for 3–5 minutes.
- To melt butter or margarine, place it in a glass dish and cook on High for 45 seconds to 1 minute.
- If your microwave has a temperature control or probe, you may heat liquids for breadmaking to the exact temperature required.

Many recipes, whether from this cookbook or from your own personal collection, can easily be converted from conventional to microwave cooking. The following guidelines will be of use to you in making conversions.
- Select recipes with which you are familiar at first, so that you can tell what the finished product should look like.
- Try to find a similar recipe which is written for microwave cooking to serve as a guide. If you cannot locate a similar recipe, remember that a microwave oven cooks food in ¼ the amount of time that a conventional oven would require.
- Noodles, rice and most pasta may be cooked in the microwave, but they actually cook more quickly using conventional means.
- A few recipes may require a change in the amount of liquid. If you need to reduce a liquid, you may add a tablespoon of cornstarch or flour to help thicken the liquid.
- Certain foods do not cook well in a microwave oven. These include puff pastries, pastry-wrapped foods, pies with double crusts, hard-boiled eggs, and any food which is to have a crisp crust.
- Most microwave recipes in this book have been tested in ovens with wattage of 600–700. If your oven is 500–600 watts, add 15 seconds to each minute of cooking time; if your oven is 400–500 watts, add 30 seconds to each minute of cooking time.
- Check food during the cooking process; stir and rotate when necessary. If additional cooking time appears to be necessary, add the time in 30-second increments.
- Be sure to make notations on your recipe about cooking times for future reference.

INDEX

To enable a cook to locate a recipe quickly and easily, recipes are listed in this Index under recipe title, type of dish (appetizer, dessert, etc.), major ingredients and flavors.

A

INDEX

INDEX

INDEX

INDEX

INDEX

INDEX

INDEX

INDEX

INDEX

INDEX

INDEX

INDEX

INDEX

INDEX

INDEX

INDEX

INDEX

INDEX

INDEX

INDEX

INDEX

Cookbook Committee

1983-1984

Co-Chairmen

Nan Tull McDaniel
Mary Ann Tindall

Steering Committee

Lorrie Catherine Ball
Deanna R. Brickman
Katherine Cavanaugh
Nadine Adams Cusack
Ann Blair Dalby
Libby Danaher
Betsy M. Farner
Alis Lovering Fern
Martha Smith Fordon
Marilyn Georgi Galsterer
Patricia Leidlein Gast
Tina Hughes Griffin
Nicky Grimshaw
Deborah Worzniak Grob
Kathleen Burke Harness
Danielle Harris
Pamela J. Hartmann
Wendy Clark Jennings
Karen Glenny Joslyn

Victoria E. Kling
Lynne Byrne Krieg
Carol Crain Lytle
Mary Jo Ready Mack
Diane V. McCormack
Valerie Slear Moran
Cynthia Wilson Ottaway
Eileen A. Reynolds
Marnie Weyhing Reynolds
Anne Wells Roberts
Cookie Roehm
Anne Blackwell Ryan
Shannon Mulrooney Scanlon
Karen L. Schaupeter
Jacquelyn Pollak Scott
Sally Clarke Spain
Martha Johnson Speer
Linda E. Sullivan
Karyn Weir Walsh

Financial Contributors

Patrons

Anonymous
Mr. and Mrs. Ronald K. Dalby
Mrs. William L. Drennen
Miss Ethel W. Flinn
Mrs. Harvey C. Fruehauf, Jr.
Mrs. Robert G. Hartwick
Mrs. Charles Vincent Hicks

Mr. and Mrs. Danforth Holley
Mr. and Mrs. Charles P. Huebner
Mrs. Peters Oppermann
Mrs. Joseph G. Standart, Jr.
Mrs. John W. Stroh
Mrs. William C. Tost
Mrs. Robert E. Valk

Contributors

Anonymous
Mrs. H. Bradford Aarons
Mr. and Mrs. David W. Bianchi
Mr. and Mrs. Wilber M. Brucker, Jr.
Mrs. J. Lawrence Buell, Jr.
Mr. and Mrs. Thomas J. Burke
Mrs. Theodore R. Buttrick
Mr. and Mrs. John E. Danaher
Mrs. Stanley R. Day
Mrs. Nancy M. Edwards
Mrs. Henry T. Ewald, Jr.
Mrs. George R. Fink
Mrs. Donald R. Flintermann
Mrs. Gordon T. Ford
Mrs. Douglas D. Freeth
Mr. and Mrs. John H. French, Jr.
Mrs. H. Richard Fruehauf, Jr.
Mrs. Edgar B. Galloway
Mrs. William Y. Gard
Rick and Joan Goodrich
Mrs. H. James Gram, Jr.
Mr. and Mrs. Noel B. Haberek
Mr. and Mrs. Richard T. Heglin
Dr. and Mrs. C. Paul Hodgkinson
Mrs. J. Stewart Hudson
Barbara B. Jewett
Mrs. Daniel L. Johnson

Dr. and Mrs. E. Michael Krieg
Mrs. Henry M. Kuhlman
Mr. and Mrs. Richard B. Marsh
Mrs. J.F. McClelland, Jr.
Mr. and Mrs. William P. McDaniel
Mrs. Arthur B. McGraw
Mrs. George R. McMullen
Susan and John Mozena
Mr. and Mrs. Frederick Ollison, III
Susan O'Rourke
Mr. and Mrs. John P. Ottaway, Jr.
Dr. and Mrs. Francisco J. Rodriguez
Carole and Jim Selmo
Sally S. Shelden
Judith L. Sieber
Mrs. Howard F. Smith, Jr.
Mrs. Stanton K. Smith, Jr.
Mrs. Quinn D. Thomas
Marana Webber Tost
Mr. and Mrs. Paul H. Townsend, Jr.
Karyn Weir Walsh
Dr. and Mrs. B.T. Weyhing, III
Mrs. Robert B. Wood
Mrs. Stevens Woodruff
Mrs. John P. Worcester
Martha R. Wylie

Cuisine Chez Amis

Mr. and Mrs. Randoph J. Agley
Mr. and Mrs. John S. Albright
Mr. and Mrs. Robert J. Bagno
Mr. and Mrs. David W. Bianchi
Mr. and Mrs. Bruce D. Carey
Mr. and Mrs. Ronald K. Dalby
Mr. and Mrs. Stanley R. Day
Mr. and Mrs. Gordon Tanner Ford
Mr. and Mrs. James W. Goss
Dr. and Mrs. Benjamin F. Haddad
Mr. and Mrs. Hugh G. Harness
Mr. and Mrs. Jeffrey M. Harness
Danielle Harris
Mr. and Mrs. F. Charles Kaess, III
Mr. and Mrs. James G. Kordas

Dr. and Mrs. John M. Lesesne
Dr. and Mrs. Miguel Lorenzini
Mr. and Mrs. John A. McCormick
Mr. and Mrs. Manuel J. Moroun
Mr. and Mrs. Patrick A. Moran
Mr. and Mrs. Frederick Ollison, III
Mr. and Mrs. Roger K. Powers
Dr. and Mrs. John H. Roberts
Dr. and Mrs. Francisco Rodriguez
Anne Blackwell Ryan
Mr. and Mrs. Thomas A. Sullivan
Mary Ann Tindall
Mr. and Mrs. G. Howard Willett, III
Mr. and Mrs. Donald S. Young, II

Recipe & Creative Contributors

The Junior League of Detroit, Inc., owes particular thanks to those listed below for their invaluable donation of inspiration and professional services.

John D. Mabley
Bill McCormack
Gene Ryan
Louis E. Sigler, III
Alex Suczek
Karen Tarapata
Mary Anne & Royal A. Wilson
Cato Johnson Detroit
Campbell-Ewald Co.
Hill, Lewis, Adams, Goodrich & Tait
Harriet Sorge Personnel Agency, Inc.
D.J. Kennedy Design Studio

The Junior League of Detroit, Inc., would like to thank its members and their families and friends who contributed their recipes, time and creative ideas.

Martha Greenhalgh Adams
Judy A. Agley
Mickey Allardice
Eileen Boscarelli Andrepont
Jan Arndt
Gayle Arnold
Elizabeth C. Bachmann
Patty Bachus
Peggy Baer
*Sherry Bagno
*Suzanne Helzer Barbour
Betty Barrows
Susanne Kemp Bartlett
*Marilyn Trent Bartley
Bayview Yacht Club
Mary S. Benfer
Ann Berschback
Terri Young Berschback
Jean Restrick Bethea
Dorothy Chace Beyer
Cherry C. Bianchi
Tracy Jackson Blatt
Kathy McNiece Boccaccio
Barbara Puckett Bockstanz
Andy Bogart
Patricia Balcerzak Bologna
*Carolyn Dobbs Bonanni
Lynn Bolding Bossler
Julie Boyd
Martha Ross Braun
Betty Anne Brennen
Deanna R. Brinkman
Babs Brock
Barbara Longyear Broderick
Sally Brook
Terry Brooks
Arlene Brow
Liz Thompson Brown
Doris Shover Brucker
Dotti Bryant
Lois Bryant
Cherry Buhl
Becky Kelser Burton
Cheryl Busbey
Mrs. George E. Bushnell, Jr.
Carla Butterly
Gayle S. Camden
Martha Cavanagh Cameron
Kitty Carey

Elsie Caulkins
Mildred Cavanagh
Katherine B. Cavanaugh
Carol Cobane
Sara Elliott Colley
Dorothy B. Combs
Gerry Conway
Ellen Erikson Cooper
Louise Crain
Mary Kay Stahl Crain
Mimi Crawford
Nancy Denomme Criger
Janet N. Crone
Sharon Cure
Beverly Curtiss
Nadine Adams Cusack
Jan Dahl
Ann Blair Dalby
Libby Danaher
Missy Danaher
Grace C. Dansbury
Marcella Raffa Davies
Gretchen Wells Davis
Diane Mehling Dawson
Lina Dean
Joanne Schneider DeFour
Peggy Delozier
Kim Schwartz DeMeulemeester
Charlotte S. Dey
Sarah Fisher Dingeman
Ann E. Disser
Jean Martin Doelle
Cheryl Z. Dorman
Terese O'Sullivan Dow
Mary Kathryn DuCharme
Janice Gerard Ducsay
Connie Zimmerman Dunlap
Candy Bartlett Dunn
Janet N. Dunn
Trudy Dunwell
Susan E. Durant
Eleanor Hawkins Durno
Linda Duval
Theresa Hakim Fiedler
Flaming Embers Restaurant
Linda Knickerbocker Ford
Colby Culbertson Fox
*Jane Fox
Sandy Frame

Susanne McMaster Fruehauf
Shirley Gagne
Marilyn Georgi Galsterer
May Anne Frenzel Gargaro
Carol F. Gaskin
Mary Dugan Gast
Pat Leidlein Gast
Freda P. Giblin
Peggy Gibson
Carole Paler Gilleran
Clara Lou Glenny
Mamie Glenny
Patricia M. Gmeiner
Golden Mushroom Restaurant
Joan Biddison Goodrich
Martha Gorey
Rita M. Goss
Carol Rodgers Gove
*Joan Grant
Diana Maiullo Greenwood
Barb Gregory
Mary Lou Deck Grieve
Tina Hughes Griffin
Grosse Pointe Hunt Club
Grosse Pointe Yacht Club
Chef Jeff Gabriel
Marilyn Flynn Gushee
Beth Ramsey Gustafson
Marcella Panlillo Haberek
Rosalie Hammond
Stephanie Hall Hampton
Sally Bolton Hanley
Mary Jean Sloniker Harland
Kathleen Burke Harness
Patricia D. Harper
Amy Duke Harris
Danielle Harris
Ruth Harris
Elaine Hartmann
Patricia S. Hayes
Christine Gillespie Hea
Barbara Z. Heck
Mary Shenefield Heglin
Susan E. Heinen
Janice Hendrie
Mary Lou Henry
Peggy Thill Hermann
Lois Ann Hernquist
*Mrs. Charles V. Hicks

Diana May Hicks
Ann H. Hoag
Susan B. Howbert
Adele L. Huebner
Cynthia Keydel Huebner
Martha Brown Hutting
Mary Beth Bowlen Jagger
Wendy Clark Jennings
Anne Johnstone
Karen Glenny Joslyn
Gail White Kaess
Margaret Carnahan Keeler
Linda Garner Kelly
Andree D. Keneau
Sharon Johnston Kenny
Sybil Rewers Kickham
Christine Kirchner
C. Suzanne Klein
Patricia Eldredge Kolojeski
Coleen Kordas
Nancy Kornmeier
Stephanie S. Kost
Ellen Eichenlaub Krease
Eleanor Zorn Kressbach
Lynne Byrne Krieg
Mrs. Henry M. Kuhlman
Karen F. Kurrie
Diane S. Kurtz
Susan Brady LaBarge
LaCosta Spa
Harriett Bradshaw Lafer
Mary Ann Large
Gary Leddick
Kathy McBride Lenz
Josephine Bowen Lewis
Erica Lindow
Emigh E. Litch
Lochmoor Club
Cynthia Loker
Drew Page Louisell
Peg Loveland
Pat Bostic Lowry
Jean Lucas
Carol Crain Lytle
*Maureen Crowley McCabe
Elise White McCartney
Ann duMais McCormick
Kathleen Helm McCormick
Nan Tull McDaniel
Diane McFeely
Ellie McFeely
Jane Wood McFeely
Gayle McGarvah
Patricia Turner McKenna
Susan Hunt McKim
Gioconda Cinelli McMillan
Hadley Mack
Mary Jo Ready Mack
Elsie Hopton MacKethan
Nancy J. MacLean
Betsy Chesbrough Maitland
Diane Davison Marston
Marty White Martin
Leslie Martin
Har Massart

Judith Hassel Mathews
Andrea Graham Mattei
Sharon Georgi Mertz
Anne Sewell Mertz
Joan Micou
Diane Wickham Miller
Judy Miller Miller
Marie Miller
Alexandra Georgeson Moisides
Catherine Brennan Molloy
Valerie Slear Moran
Nora Berquist Moroun
Betsy Ann Prentice Morris
Margaret Fitzgerald Morrison
Dinah Wentling Murphy
Michaele Murphy
Shirley Bird Murphy
Catherine Clark Murray
Mary Meier Murray
Suzanne Phillips Nicholson
Scottie Odell
Margie Vibbert Ogden
Lynne Hacala Olds
Mary Galloway Ollison
Anna May Olmsted
Susan Gehrke O'Rourke
Nancy Powell Orr
Marv Alice Wall O'Toole
Anne Galvin Ottaway
Cynthia Wilson Ottaway
Patricia Dennis Palm
Margaret Mahony Peabody
Carol Pease
*Keith Ann McIntosh Pechonick
Margaret Sessions Penirian
Wendy Penkszik
Bonnie Willingham Perkins
Clair Wilcoxon Perry
Hope Henney Peslar
Pam Gooding Petersen
Mary Anne Mancourt Petz
Pontchartrain Wine Cellars
Lornie Rickel Porter
Sarah Stroud Rainey
Patricia Valach Ramge
Andrea Smart Rasmussen
Sally Jo Cornelius Redding
Lynn Becker Reed
Peachy Rentenbach
Dona DeSantis Reynolds
Marnie Weyhing Reynolds
Trudy Aichholz Rhoades
Ann Haney Rice
Anne Wells Roberts
Annette Lovorn Robson
Christina Villanyi Roehl
Nancy Saviano Roney
Phyllis Ross
Susan Griffith Royer
Robin Harris Russell
Marian Doepken Sanford
Mickey Hoffmann Schaefer
Karen Szabo Schaefer
Karen L. Schaupeter
Priscilla Webb Schaupeter

Jane Schmidt
Chef David T. Schneider
Milo Schulte
Alice Gage Schultes
Sally Haizlip Schweikert
Susan Schweitzer
Carole Magyari Selmo
Pearl Sergison
Sara Sessions
Connie McKnight Sfire
Sally S. Shelden
Ginna Ives Short
Judith Rome Sieber
Beth Lucas Simpson
Beatrice Moekle Skinner
Joan Smith
Kay Beissel Smith
Myrna Moxley Smith
Sharon Sweeny Snyder
Pam Kornmeier Stanton
Marilyn J. Stocker
Julie Childress Stroh
Mary Jane Jennings Stutz
Charity Suczek
Linda E. Sullivan
Dody Cuttle Swenson
Anne Watkins Taliaferro
Cheryl L. Teetaert
Grace Cracchiolo Tindall
Mary Ann Tindall
Mary Meyerholtz Tipp
Sheila Tomkoviak
Betsy Wheat Townsend
Marlene Tulas
Helen Pfister Tull
Karol DeWulf Tyler
Sally Novak VanDusen
Priscilla Kruse vanHorne
Cynthia Matthews Van Pelt
*Carroll Goodheart Velie
Jane Johnson Vieweg
Cynthia A. Vogt
Karyn Weir Walsh
Kay C. Wasinger
Lois L. Waterman
Donna Hockaday Waterston
Ann Krieger Watkins
Susan Weakley
Barbara Nash Weiss
Lisa Liffers Wenzler
Patricia West
Andi Egan Weyhing
Pamela Marshall Wheeler
Carol W. Whitehead
Bethine S. Whitney
Denise Whitney
Ellanore Brown Wiener
Barbara Morris Willett
Ann Robinson Willett
Ilze Willison
Sherrill Dickeson Wolford
Susan Wood
Joan N. Woodhouse
Kim Woodhouse
Elaine Hight Yates
Mary Jo Youngblood

*Former Steering Committee member

Clock Wise Cuisine
Junior League of Detroit

PLEASE SEND _____ COPIES @ $13.95 each $_____
MICHIGAN RESIDENTS ADD 4% @ $ .56 each $_____
POSTAGE AND HANDLING @ $ 2.00 each $_____
GIFT WRAP DESIRED @ $ 1.00 each $_____
TOTAL ENCLOSED $_____
PLEASE MAKE CHECKS PAYABLE TO JLD Clock Wise Cuisine
US FUNDS ONLY

32 Lakeshore Road, Grosse Pointe Farms, MI 48236 (313) 881-0040

NAME

ADDRESS

CITY   STATE   ZIP

Clock Wise Cuisine
Junior League of Detroit

PLEASE SEND _____ COPIES @ $13.95 each $_____
MICHIGAN RESIDENTS ADD 4% @ $ .56 each $_____
POSTAGE AND HANDLING @ $ 2.00 each $_____
GIFT WRAP DESIRED @ $ 1.00 each $_____
TOTAL ENCLOSED $_____
PLEASE MAKE CHECKS PAYABLE TO JLD Clock Wise Cuisine
US FUNDS ONLY

32 Lakeshore Road, Grosse Pointe Farms, MI 48236 (313) 881-0040

NAME

ADDRESS

CITY   STATE   ZIP

Clock Wise Cuisine
Junior League of Detroit

PLEASE SEND _____ COPIES @ $13.95 each $_____
MICHIGAN RESIDENTS ADD 4% @ $ .56 each $_____
POSTAGE AND HANDLING @ $ 2.00 each $_____
GIFT WRAP DESIRED @ $ 1.00 each $_____
TOTAL ENCLOSED $_____
PLEASE MAKE CHECKS PAYABLE TO JLD Clock Wise Cuisine
US FUNDS ONLY

32 Lakeshore Road, Grosse Pointe Farms, MI 48236 (313) 881-0040

NAME

ADDRESS

CITY   STATE   ZIP

Please list any store in your area that might like to handle
CLOCK WISE CUISINE (name and address)

_____

_____

_____

_____

All copies will be sent to same address unless otherwise specified. If you wish one or any number of books sent as gifts, furnish a list of names and addresses of recipients. If you wish to enclose your own gift card with each book, please write name of recipient on outside of the envelope, enclose with order, and we will include it with your gift.

Please list any store in your area that might like to handle
CLOCK WISE CUISINE (name and address)

_____

_____

_____

_____

All copies will be sent to same address unless otherwise specified. If you wish one or any number of books sent as gifts, furnish a list of names and addresses of recipients. If you wish to enclose your own gift card with each book, please write name of recipient on outside of the envelope, enclose with order, and we will include it with your gift.

Please list any store in your area that might like to handle
CLOCK WISE CUISINE (name and address)

_____

_____

_____

_____

All copies will be sent to same address unless otherwise specified. If you wish one or any number of books sent as gifts, furnish a list of names and addresses of recipients. If you wish to enclose your own gift card with each book, please write name of recipient on outside of the envelope, enclose with order, and we will include it with your gift.

Clock Wise Cuisine
Junior League of Detroit

PLEASE SEND _____ COPIES @ $13.95 each $_____

MICHIGAN RESIDENTS ADD 4% @ $ .56 each $_____

POSTAGE AND HANDLING @ $ 2.00 each $_____

GIFT WRAP DESIRED @ $ 1.00 each $_____

TOTAL ENCLOSED $_____

PLEASE MAKE CHECKS PAYABLE TO JLD Clock Wise Cuisine
US FUNDS ONLY

32 Lakeshore Road, Grosse Pointe Farms, MI 48236 (313) 881-0040

NAME

ADDRESS

CITY   STATE   ZIP

Clock Wise Cuisine
Junior League of Detroit

PLEASE SEND _____ COPIES @ $13.95 each $_____

MICHIGAN RESIDENTS ADD 4% @ $ .56 each $_____

POSTAGE AND HANDLING @ $ 2.00 each $_____

GIFT WRAP DESIRED @ $ 1.00 each $_____

TOTAL ENCLOSED $

PLEASE MAKE CHECKS PAYABLE TO JLD Clock Wise Cuisine
US FUNDS ONLY

32 Lakeshore Road, Grosse Pointe Farms, MI 48236 (313) 881-0040

NAME

ADDRESS

CITY   STATE   ZIP

Clock Wise Cuisine
Junior League of Detroit

PLEASE SEND _____ COPIES @ $13.95 each $_____

MICHIGAN RESIDENTS ADD 4% @ $ .56 each $_____

POSTAGE AND HANDLING @ $ 2.00 each $_____

GIFT WRAP DESIRED @ $ 1.00 each $_____

TOTAL ENCLOSED $_____

PLEASE MAKE CHECKS PAYABLE TO JLD Clock Wise Cuisine
US FUNDS ONLY

32 Lakeshore Road, Grosse Pointe Farms, MI 48236 (313) 881-0040

NAME

ADDRESS

CITY   STATE   ZIP

Please list any store in your area that might like to handle
CLOCK WISE CUISINE (name and address)

_____

_____

_____

_____

All copies will be sent to same address unless otherwise specified. If you wish one or any number of books sent as gifts, furnish a list of names and addresses of recipients. If you wish to enclose your own gift card with each book, please write name of recipient on outside of the envelope, enclose with order, and we will include it with your gift.

Please list any store in your area that might like to handle
CLOCK WISE CUISINE (name and address)

_____

_____

_____

_____

All copies will be sent to same address unless otherwise specified. If you wish one or any number of books sent as gifts, furnish a list of names and addresses of recipients. If you wish to enclose your own gift card with each book, please write name of recipient on outside of the envelope, enclose with order, and we will include it with your gift.

Please list any store in your area that might like to handle
CLOCK WISE CUISINE (name and address)

_____

_____

_____

_____

All copies will be sent to same address unless otherwise specified. If you wish one or any number of books sent as gifts, furnish a list of names and addresses of recipients. If you wish to enclose your own gift card with each book, please write name of recipient on outside of the envelope, enclose with order, and we will include it with your gift.

Clock Wise Cuisine
Junior League of Detroit

PLEASE SEND _____ COPIES @ $13.95 each $_____
MICHIGAN RESIDENTS ADD 4% @ $ .56 each $_____
POSTAGE AND HANDLING @ $ 2.00 each $_____
GIFT WRAP DESIRED @ $ 1.00 each $_____
TOTAL ENCLOSED $_____
PLEASE MAKE CHECKS PAYABLE TO JLD Clock Wise Cuisine
US FUNDS ONLY

32 Lakeshore Road, Grosse Pointe Farms, MI 48236 (313) 881-0040

NAME

ADDRESS

CITY   STATE   ZIP

Clock Wise Cuisine
Junior League of Detroit

PLEASE SEND _____ COPIES @ $13.95 each $_____
MICHIGAN RESIDENTS ADD 4% @ $ .56 each $_____
POSTAGE AND HANDLING @ $ 2.00 each $_____
GIFT WRAP DESIRED @ $ 1.00 each $_____
TOTAL ENCLOSED $_____
PLEASE MAKE CHECKS PAYABLE TO JLD Clock Wise Cuisine
US FUNDS ONLY

32 Lakeshore Road, Grosse Pointe Farms, MI 48236 (313) 881-0040

NAME

ADDRESS

CITY   STATE   ZIP

Clock Wise Cuisine
Junior League of Detroit

PLEASE SEND _____ COPIES @ $13.95 each $_____
MICHIGAN RESIDENTS ADD 4% @ $ .56 each $_____
POSTAGE AND HANDLING @ $ 2.00 each $_____
GIFT WRAP DESIRED @ $ 1.00 each $_____
TOTAL ENCLOSED $_____
PLEASE MAKE CHECKS PAYABLE TO JLD Clock Wise Cuisine
US FUNDS ONLY

32 Lakeshore Road, Grosse Pointe Farms, MI 48236 (313) 881-0040

NAME

ADDRESS

CITY   STATE   ZIP

Please list any store in your area that might like to handle
CLOCK WISE CUISINE (name and address)

_____

_____

_____

_____

All copies will be sent to same address unless otherwise specified. If you wish one or any number
of books sent as gifts, furnish a list of names and addresses of recipients. If you wish to enclose
your own gift card with each book, please write name of recipient on outside of the envelope, enclose
with order, and we will include it with your gift.

_____

Please list any store in your area that might like to handle
CLOCK WISE CUISINE (name and address)

_____

_____

_____

_____

All copies will be sent to same address unless otherwise specified. If you wish one or any number
of books sent as gifts, furnish a list of names and addresses of recipients. If you wish to enclose
your own gift card with each book, please write name of recipient on outside of the envelope, enclose
with order, and we will include it with your gift.

_____

Please list any store in your area that might like to handle
CLOCK WISE CUISINE (name and address)

_____

_____

_____

_____

All copies will be sent to same address unless otherwise specified. If you wish one or any number
of books sent as gifts, furnish a list of names and addresses of recipients. If you wish to enclose
your own gift card with each book, please write name of recipient on outside of the envelope, enclose
with order, and we will include it with your gift.

Clock Wise Cuisine
Junior League of Detroit

PLEASE SEND _____ COPIES	@ $13.95 each	$_____
MICHIGAN RESIDENTS ADD 4%	@ $ .56 each	$_____
POSTAGE AND HANDLING	@ $ 2.00 each	$_____
GIFT WRAP DESIRED	@ $ 1.00 each	$_____
TOTAL ENCLOSED		$_____

PLEASE MAKE CHECKS PAYABLE TO JLD Clock Wise Cuisine
US FUNDS ONLY

32 Lakeshore Road, Grosse Pointe Farms, MI 48236 (313) 881-0040

NAME

ADDRESS

CITY   STATE   ZIP

Clock Wise Cuisine
Junior League of Detroit

PLEASE SEND _____ COPIES	@ $13.95 each	$_____
MICHIGAN RESIDENTS ADD 4%	@ $ .56 each	$_____
POSTAGE AND HANDLING	@ $ 2.00 each	$_____
GIFT WRAP DESIRED	@ $ 1.00 each	$_____
TOTAL ENCLOSED		$_____

PLEASE MAKE CHECKS PAYABLE TO JLD Clock Wise Cuisine
US FUNDS ONLY

32 Lakeshore Road, Grosse Pointe Farms, MI 48236 (313) 881-0040

NAME

ADDRESS

CITY   STATE   ZIP

Clock Wise Cuisine
Junior League of Detroit

PLEASE SEND _____ COPIES	@ $13.95 each	$_____
MICHIGAN RESIDENTS ADD 4%	@ $ .56 each	$_____
POSTAGE AND HANDLING	@ $ 2.00 each	$_____
GIFT WRAP DESIRED	@ $ 1.00 each	$_____
TOTAL ENCLOSED		$_____

PLEASE MAKE CHECKS PAYABLE TO JLD Clock Wise Cuisine
US FUNDS ONLY

32 Lakeshore Road, Grosse Pointe Farms, MI 48236 (313) 881-0040

NAME

ADDRESS

CITY   STATE   ZIP

Please list any store in your area that might like to handle
CLOCK WISE CUISINE (name and address)

_____

_____

_____

_____

All copies will be sent to same address unless otherwise specified. If you wish one or any number of books sent as gifts, furnish a list of names and addresses of recipients. If you wish to enclose your own gift card with each book, please write name of recipient on outside of the envelope, enclose with order, and we will include it with your gift.

— — — — — — — — — — — — — — — — — —

Please list any store in your area that might like to handle
CLOCK WISE CUISINE (name and address)

_____

_____

_____

_____

All copies will be sent to same address unless otherwise specified. If you wish one or any number of books sent as gifts, furnish a list of names and addresses of recipients. If you wish to enclose your own gift card with each book, please write name of recipient on outside of the envelope, enclose with order, and we will include it with your gift.

— — — — — — — — — — — — — — — — — —

Please list any store in your area that might like to handle
CLOCK WISE CUISINE (name and address)

_____

_____

_____

_____

All copies will be sent to same address unless otherwise specified. If you wish one or any number of books sent as gifts, furnish a list of names and addresses of recipients. If you wish to enclose your own gift card with each book, please write name of recipient on outside of the envelope, enclose with order, and we will include it with your gift.